At the Picture Show

AT THE
PICTURE SHOW

SMALL-TOWN AUDIENCES
AND THE CREATION OF
MOVIE FAN CULTURE

Kathryn H. Fuller

SMITHSONIAN INSTITUTION PRESS

Washington and London

Chapter 1 originally appeared, in somewhat different form, as "The Cook and Harris High Class Moving Picture Company: Itinerant Exhibitors and the Small Town Movie Audience, 1900–1910," in *New York History* 75, no. 1 (January 1994), pp. 5–38, and is published herein by permission of the New York State Historical Association, Cooperstown, New York. Chapter 5 originally appeared, in somewhat different form, as "'You Can Have the Strand in Your Own Town': The Marginalization of Small Town Exhibition in the Silent Film Era" and is reprinted by permission from *Film History* (vol. 6, no. 2, 1994), copyright © 1994 John Libbey & Company Ltd. Chapter 7 originally appeared, in somewhat different form, as "*Motion Picture Story Magazine* and the Gendered Construction of the Movie Fan," in Gary Edgerton, ed., *In the Eye of the Beholder* (Bowling Green, Ohio: Bowling Green State University Popular Press, 1996), and is published herein by permission of the Bowling Green State University Popular Press.

Copy Editor: Catherine McKenzie
Production Editor: Duke Johns
Designer: Kathleen Sims

Library of Congress Cataloging-in-Publication Data
Fuller, Kathryn H.
At the picture show : small-town audiences and the creation of
movie fan culture / Kathryn H. Fuller.
p. cm.
Includes bibliographical references and index.
ISBN 1-56098-639-5 (alk. paper)
1. Motion pictures—Social aspects—United States. 2. Motion picture audiences—
Psychology. 3. City and town life—United States—History. I. Title
PN1993.5.U6F77 1996
302.23'43—dc20 95-51344

British Library Cataloguing-in-Publication Data is available

Manufactured in the United States of America
03 02 01 00 99 98 97 96 5 4 3 2 1

∞ The paper used in this publication meets the minimum requirements of the American National Standard for Information Sciences—Permanence of Paper for Printed Library Materials ANSI Z39.48-1984.

To MLH and DNF with love and thanks

Contents

CONTENTS

Preface

When advertising flyers that were scattered along the dusty Main Street of a small Pennsylvania town in 1897 announced the imminent arrival of "a marvelous exhibition of moving pictures at the opera house," the entire community was swept up in anticipation of experiencing the latest entertainment novelty, straight from the big city. As one participant remembered:

> The day of the "show" came. The courts adjourned. Stores closed, the blacksmith dropped his tongs, and school "let out" at noon. The people went in droves, even the ministers and their wives and all the deacons, because the bills said the exhibition was "indorsed [sic] by scientists and the clergy." The opera house was packed, with an eager, expectant and mystified audience. The house was darkened, and suddenly a glimmering light began to play on a canvas dropped like a curtain across the stage. And the first moving scene "thrown" was one of a lazy policeman trying to hurry an old man and a crippled mare across a street. The town wag let out a whoop, everybody caught the spirit—the moving pictures were a go![1]

In the earliest years of film exhibition in the United States, motion pictures seemed largely an urban phenomenon. The films' brief scenes were photographed in New York City (or imported from Paris); they featured urban themes, from the adventures of the corner cop to locomotives chugging into city stations, panoramas of crowds on the street, and snippets of Broadway sights such as dancer Loie Fuller and the celebrated *May Irwin Kiss*. The films were viewed most noticeably by audiences in the larger cities' vaudeville houses and at fairs, expositions, amusement parks, and other places where city people congregated. But despite this supposed predominance of the city in early motion picture production and exhibition, the movies were never solely an urban experience. The ease with which they could be duplicated and projected, and the eagerness with which audiences greeted them, helped the movies spread across the land like wildfire. The movies quickly became as much a small-town phenomenon as an urban one, and viewers from both audience segments became the movie fans who participated in creating a popular culture of film.

The history of the movies' impact on small-town communities in the silent film era is particularly worth exploring because in the early 1900s nonurban settlements still predominated. The United States was not yet a fully urban nation; 70 percent of its citizens resided outside the major cities in rural areas and small towns of ten thousand or fewer in population. Movie performances such as the Pennsylvania show were occurring in farmers' fields, rural churches, villages, and towns of every region of the country. By their sheer numbers, small-town viewers represented a vital component of the American movie audience, and they played an active role in shaping the development of the film industry. In turn, small-town audiences felt the social and cultural transformations wrought by the movies on their communities, from films' very beginnings through the movies' ascendance to the center of poplar culture in the 1920s.

Scholars' interest in the social history of movie audiences has long lagged behind their study of motion pictures themselves and the means and conditions of film production. Surveys of moviegoers in the 1910s and 1920s were undertaken not by historians but by reformers and social scientists who worried about the erosion of standards of public morality. They sought connections between violent or escapist films and the misbehavior of the youngest, most vulnerable members of the movie audience.[2] Although in the 1940s sociologist and communications researcher Mae Huettig warned that "[w]ithout an understanding of the intensity and suddenness of the demand for movies, much of the history of the industry is incomprehensible," historical research into American film audiences remained largely moribund for decades.[3]

In the mid-1970s, however, there was a sudden explosion of interest among several groups in film audiences of the past and the influences that movies had had upon them. Historians of media and culture began to study the movies' impact on shifting class, race, and gender relations in twentieth-century society.[4] Concurrently, film and cultural studies scholars developed historical contexts for audience members' positions as film spectators in hypotheses drawn from film theory, linguistics, psychoanalytic theory, and feminist studies.[5]

Over the past twenty years, scholarship in American film history has seen an exciting, ever expanding stream of studies about film audiences, spectators, and fans in various historical moments. Research in the early era of film exhibition has been particularly rich. Unfortunately this wealth of scholarly activity has been accompanied by sharp methodological disagreements over the appropriate balance between the construction of theory and the application of evidence.[6]

I came to this project while in graduate school; I was interested in the impact of social forces such as class, gender, and race on the evolution of popular culture in America at the turn of the century. Having been a passionate fan of silent films since my adolescence, I was delighted to discover that social historians and media scholars were exploring the place of the nickelodeon theater in a rapidly changing American society, and the role of early movie audience members as cultural actors struggling to express their own voices.[7]

The ongoing debate in the literature about the movies' role in the creation or obfuscation of cultural hierarchy at the turn of the century drew my attention. However, because so much early history of film exhibition and audiences had been dismissed or forgotten, some widely accepted myths emerged that have hampered historians and clouded any complete understanding of who saw films, how the viewers received the movies, and how the movies became incorporated into popular culture. The old standard explanation maintained that at the time of their debut in 1896, motion pictures found great popularity with big-city vaudeville patrons, but about 1902 they suddenly fell out of popular favor and disappeared.[8] Sometime between 1905 and 1907, dingy, disreputable little storefront nickelodeon movie theaters began cropping up in the big cities. These nickelodeons, we were told, flourished only in the tenement districts of New York and Chicago, and attracted hordes of poor immigrant viewers. Nickelodeons also uniformly drew the disapprobation of the middle class and of social reformers. In the mid-1910s, however, at some magic moment (the premiere of director D. W. Griffith's film *The Birth of a Nation*? the emergence of major stars?) the urban middle class and the rest of country did an about-face and embraced the movies en masse. Suddenly, film moved from being treated with disdain to gaining full acceptance at the heart of American popular culture. A lively and rich literature addressing the missing elements of this story has already grown, especially on the evolving role of movies as urban entertainment and on the social and cultural conflicts between urban reformers and nickelodeon audiences.[9]

Nevertheless, I remained especially intrigued by the lack of information on movie audiences and film exhibition practices in areas outside New York City and Chicago. When, where, and how did nonurban audiences gain access to the movies? Did small-town viewers see the same films as their city cousins and in similar types of theaters? How did their film preferences differ? How did the small-town and urban middle classes contribute to the spread of movies into mainstream popular culture? When and how did the idea of the movie fan develop, and what role did the early movie fan magazines play in the fan's evolution? This study, which developed from those questions, is a social history of small-town nickelodeon audiences and movie fans that I hope will contribute historical context and specific evidence to support and enrich our growing understanding of film spectatorship and of mass media's relationship to society.[10]

The book is roughly chronological in organization. The first half charts the flowering of motion picture entertainment in small towns, from itinerant movie shows through the establishment of permanent film theaters. Small-town folk adopted the movies so readily in part because motion pictures combined new technology with the already familiar entertainment forms of the travelogue slide show and the itinerant theatrical troupe. Enterprising nickelodeon exhibitors packaged their programs in redecorated store buildings and opera houses that literally flashed, blazed, and shouted out the wonders within through their evocative names and brilliant illumination.

The small-town nickelodeon movie show offered patrons a combination of educational and uplifting film subjects, from scenic panoramas to depictions of industrial manufacturing processes to informative newsreels. Biblical imagery and historical tableaux were also popular themes with rural viewers. Nevertheless, small-town exhibitors faced opposition in the 1910s from conservative religious groups who objected to inappropriately worldly films and sometimes put on their own sanitized movie shows inside their churches. Lacking sufficient religious movies, they often exhibited promotional films produced by consumer-product manufacturers. The wide diversity of regional, religious, ethnic, and gender ideals among communities across the nation meant that exhibitors faced a host of challenges in pleasing their audiences. Some elements of church shows and small-town film genres were eventually incorporated by the film industry into their standardized product.

Cultural tensions between big-city and small-town values were voiced frequently by film exhibitors in the trade journals as they jealously compared each others' movie theaters, film choices, and audiences. Some members of the small-town middle class felt that their cultural influence was threatened by the growing dominance of urban businesses, entertainments, and codes of behavior. Their prejudice against urban ethnic groups was revealed in exhibitors' and critics' calls for film producers to pay more attention to neglected small-town film preferences and in their prideful boasts about the distinctiveness and respectability of the small-town nickelodeon and its audiences. As the film industry continued to expand toward the end of the nickelodeon era (1912–1915), Mary Pickford and Charlie Chaplin performed their antics simultaneously on screens in Wyoming cow towns, in Maine fishing villages, at dusty Georgia crossroads, and on the Loop in Chicago. However, the rise of luxurious picture palaces in big cities soon hastened the perception of the shrinking of the small-town movie theater from being everything the village could desire to its incorporation into a national framework that made the small-town theater appear quite meager in comparison to the city's really big show.

The second half of the book examines the rise of the movie fan. Fan activity smoothed over the growing differences between big-city and small-town movie theaters in the latter part of the nickelodeon era and helped link the most enthusiastic audience members in a nationwide popular culture of film. Fans played an important role in the creation of the early movie magazines, particularly influencing the evolving purpose and content of *Motion Picture Story Magazine* and *Photoplay*. The movie magazines initially catered to fan interests deemed both "masculine" and "feminine," but by the late 1910s their focus had shifted to material that was geared primarily to young, female moviegoers. In the 1920s, James

Quirk, the editor of *Photoplay*, conducted a crusade to reshape the public perception of movie fans as the widely lamented mobs of giggling, autograph-seeking girls to a view of them as respectable, knowledgeable middle-class film patrons. At the same time, Quirk created a representation of movie fans in the advertising trade press as "perfect consumers"—young women addicted to leisure, frivolous pleasures, and spending, even in hard times. Paradoxically, his messages intensified the movie fan's image as psychologically vulnerable to the hypnotic influence of the movie screen. Quirk's efforts reveal some of the shifting ideas about gender, consumption, and media influence the movies brought to American popular culture.

The final chapter combines the two main themes in a case study of a group of University of Chicago undergraduates (middle-class and wealthy students raised in small-town and suburban settings) who in 1929 were asked by sociologists connected with the Payne Fund Studies to recount their experiences of a lifetime of moviegoing. They described what they perceived to be their film-influenced attitudes, behavior, and self-conceptions as they evolved from children playing cowboy movie games, to starstruck teens looking in their mirrors for resemblances to Garbo and Valentino, to sophisticated young adults who privately admitted they still avidly read fan magazines. Their original, unedited comments reveal that motion pictures had a pervasive impact on this first generation of middle-class children to come of age at the picture show.

My research for the project drew on a wide variety of sources, most of them nonfilmic. The film exhibition industry's trade journals, particularly *Nickelodeon, Exhibitor's Trade Review,* and *Moving Picture World,* helped me to gain a feel for issues, problems, and challenges facing small-town movie theater operators in different sections of the country. Collections of exhibitors' papers located at the Warshaw Collection of Business Americana at the Smithsonian Institution's National Museum of American History in Washington, D.C., and at the New York State Historical Association Library in Cooperstown, New York, offered invaluable insights into the operations of early small-town movie theaters. Other primary source documents that I located in the National Museum of American History's Archive Center and in local history and private collections give a hint that nearly every community has a rich history of moviegoing waiting to be explored. Published histories of small towns enriched my understanding of social life in various regions of the country at the turn of the century; sociological investigations conducted in the era helped to recover some of the voices of poorer white, black, ethnic, female, and younger film viewers.

Movie fan magazines such as *Motion Picture Story Magazine, Photoplay, Classic,* and *Film Fun* offered letters from readers, editorials, articles, and cartoons that revealed the evolution of movie fans' interests and concerns. References to movie fans and theaters in Tin Pan Alley sheet music; in magazine advertisements for consumer products, children's toys and juvenile novels; and in postcard and photo collections—all contributed to a general impression of the place of moviegoing in American culture. Unpublished autobiographical accounts and statistical data on moviegoers originally gathered for the Payne Fund Studies and other social science research projects in the 1920s also provided invaluable contemporary insight into the influence of movies on young people, even though the information was filtered through the questions and imperatives important to researchers of the day.

Acknowledgments

I owe a great debt to the many friends and colleagues who helped me to write this book. First I want to thank Ronald Walters, my graduate advisor at the Johns Hopkins University, who opened many doors to the study of social history and popular culture for me, and who has given me invaluable encouragement and friendship. When this book was in its early stages, a fellowship from the National Museum of American History, Smithsonian Institution, Washington, D.C., allowed me the luxury of a year of full-time research. Louis Galambos, Douglas Gomery, and Garth Jowett merit special thanks for their generous advice, support, and careful readings of the manuscript during many stages of its development.

Other scholars who have read various chapters of the manuscript and provided helpful comments include Henry Jenkins, Frank Couvares, Susan Douglas, Gary Edgerton, members of the Five College Social History Seminar, Richard Koszarski, Jim Moore, Charles Musser, Kathy Peiss, Calvin Pryluck, Wendell Tripp, and Pierre Véronneau. Karan Sheldon of Northeast Historic Film has shared her boundless enthusiasm for regional film and audience history with me, and David Bowers has been extraordinarily generous in lending me his insight, resources, manuscripts from his personal collection, and proofreading skills. Both have enriched this book immensely. Charles McGovern and Barbara Humphreys of the National Museum of American History and Library of Congress, respectively, inspired me to explore links between film and other forms of popular culture. Edward Wagenknecht and Lillian Gish were both very kind to respond at length to my inquiries. And I am very grateful to Sally McCloskey for sharing with me many personal memories of her grandparents, Bert and Fannie Cook.

Thanks go, too, to my dear friends and colleagues who read portions of the manuscript, helped me locate movie fan ephemera, and blessed me with their good humor and moral support, including Ila Burdette, Alice Harra, J. K. Helgesen, Lee Heller, Martha Kearsley, Bonnie Konowitch, Jay Prag, Margaret Rung, and Kelly Schrum, and to my encouraging teachers and mentors at Agnes Scott College, John Gignilliat and Penelope Campbell.

Dedicated staffs at the archives and libraries I consulted made my work much easier. Jim Roan and fellow librarians at the National Museum of American History Library; staff members of the Interlibrary Loan Office at the Milton S. Eisenhower Library at the Johns Hopkins University; Vanessa Broussard Simmons, Stacy Flaherty, and other staff members of the National Museum of American History's Archive Center; staff members of the New York State Historical Association Library in Cooperstown—all were tremendously helpful.

I would also like to thank my acquisitions editor, Mark Hirsch, at the Smithsonian Institution Press and my very talented copy editor, Catherine McKenzie, who expertly uncovered each incomplete endnote and made me track down the missing information.

Finally, I wish to express my special gratitude to Mary Lou Helgesen and Douglas Fuller, whose love, patience, and enthusiasm have sustained me, and this project, from the start.

The Cook and Harris High Class Moving Picture Company

Itinerant Exhibitors and the Construction of the Small-Town Movie Audience

Advertising handbills for the Cook and Harris High Class Moving Picture Company, an itinerant film exhibition troupe operated by Bert and Fannie Cook, enticed small-town upstate New Yorkers to its show in 1904 with the twin lures of novelty and decorum.

> TO-NIGHT! The Cook & Harris High Class Exhibition of Moving Pictures
>
> COME AND SEE   The Highest Grade exhibition of moving pictures in America, Comprising the Most Wonderful Depicture [*sic*] of Living Beings and Objects in Motion Ever Obtained by Mechanical Means.
>
> Important—this Refined and Beautiful Entertainment is Recommended Highly by the Press and Clergy Wherever Presented.
>
> Hear all the Very Latest and Popular Illustrated Songs with Beautiful Colored Slides Taken from Life.
>
> Remember—this is not a Stereopticon or Magic Lantern Exhibition, but the Very Latest Marvel.

When the Cooks presented one of their first exhibitions in Medina, New York, in September 1904, an audience of a thousand people, one-third the village's population, turned out to see it. This flattering review in the Medina newspaper appeared to confirm the Cook and Harris company's promise of "A Meritorious Exhibition! Nothing to Offend! Everything Moral! You Cannot Afford to Miss It!"

> The entertainment at the opera house last evening, under the auspices of St. John's Church, attracted an immense audience, despite the fact that the weather was not all that could be desired. When the doors were closed on the would-be spectators, there was no such thing as standing room left inside. . . . All of the pictures shown were entirely new, especially "The Drama in Mid Air," "Fireworks," "Indians and Cowboys" and "The Lost Child." From first to last the entertainment was well worthy of the crowd which enjoyed it. The illustrated songs by Cook and Harris were especially pleasing.[1]

The Cook and Harris High Class Moving Picture Company, based in Cooperstown, traveled throughout New York State and northern New England between 1904 and 1911 with portable projection equipment, bringing motion picture entertainment to hundreds of small towns. Itinerant movie-show people played an important but largely forgotten role in the creation of substantial audiences for motion pictures outside the largest cities in the formative years of the silent film era. Itinerants attracted a small-town audience of middle-class and working-class families to the movies at a time when it appeared to many urban critics that middle-class vaudeville audiences had completely tired of films and that the movies belonged solely to the immigrant patrons of tenement district nickelodeons. Traveling shows like the Cook and Harris company shaped small-town audiences, and in turn, small-town audiences' film preferences and standards of propriety had a significant impact on the operation of itinerant shows. The Cooks ran a successful and creative show. To remain in business, though, they had to stay abreast of developments in the film exhibition industry and in rapidly changing small-town leisure habits. Examining how entrepreneurial show people fashioned a new kind of commercial amusement that drew on, and then transformed, established patterns of small-town entertainment illustrates in a new way how motion pictures helped to shape twentieth-century American popular culture.

Entertainment and
Turn-of-the-Century Small-Town Life

Upstate New York in 1900 was overwhelmingly rural, but so was much of the country. The 1920 census declared the American population to be 50 percent urban, but census takers set the urban threshold at towns of twenty-five hundred people—settlements that were hardly metropolises and had little in common with New York City or Chicago. In 1920, more than half of Americans lived in small towns and the rural countryside. Seventeen percent of the population lived in towns of twenty-five hundred to ten thousand people, and a further 40 percent resided in unincorporated rural areas. The United States was rapidly becoming a more urban nation; the proportion of Americans living in large cities of one hundred thousand or more people climbed from 20 to 25 percent between 1900 and 1920. Still, in 1920 a full 75 percent of Americans lived in smaller cities, towns, and rural areas.[2]

Small towns at the turn of the century were, nevertheless, faced on all sides with economic, social, and cultural changes brought by industrialization and urban influences. Motion pictures came to small towns along with a steady stream of foreign immigrants and farm families moving into town from outlying areas. Small towns were increasingly exposed to city ways through the opening of new factories, labor-saving inventions, mass-circulation magazines, mail-order catalogs, the visits of traveling salesmen, and changing social customs, all of which caused political and cultural debate and backlash.[3]

How would motion pictures be received by the Cook and Harris company's potential audiences? The uncritical acceptance of this entertainment novelty was not guaranteed. The descendants of New England Puritans and of conservative mid-Atlantic colonial settlers, upstate New Yorkers possessed a long history of ambivalence and hostility toward commercial amusements. The Puritans had fought constant, jealous battles against the theater, fearing its competition as "the Devil's church." Later generations of New Englanders built few theaters in their towns and villages, although they did not ban entertainment. From the 1700s through the late 1800s, settlers migrating westward from New England constructed multipurpose town halls and opera houses (so named because *opera* seemed a more genteel appellation than the disreputable *theater*) in which to hold local community functions; these sprouted on the Main Streets of thousands of towns across the nation.[4]

On the other hand, dominance of a conservative, Protestant, middle-class morality in small towns was neither as monolithic nor as homogeneous as some critics maintained. While the majority of small-town residents of the Northeast in 1900 were still affiliated with some Protestant or Catholic church, active participation was in steady decline. And pious religious values did not necessarily prevent "respectable" amusement in most towns. Standards of public morality could vary between neighboring communities from very restrained to quite loose. Even in the most fundamentalist settlements, illicit pleasures were often tolerated to some extent for men, if not for women and children. For example, in 1900, residents of Antrim, New Hampshire, considered themselves morally superior to the inhabitants of the nearby town of Bennington. The town elders of Antrim discouraged dancing, card playing, breaking the Sabbath, and the operation of taverns and commercial amusements, whereas Bennington allowed them. Consequently, a substantial number of the patrons of Bennington's thriving movie shows, saloons, and dance halls were the men and boys of Antrim.[5]

Although ambivalent about commercial amusements, American small towns in the latter half of the nineteenth century had nourished strong entertainment traditions. Many of their opera house and town hall programs were homegrown and family centered, such as performances by local bands, neighborhood amateur singing, recitals, pageants, tableaux, lectures, and political speeches. Although strangers in town might find little to do, small towns presented almost continuous social activity, if one counted neighborly activities such as picnics and weddings as well as all the church functions, voluntary organization meetings, school programs, benefit performances, and dances to aid the fire company or pay for sidewalks.[6]

The small town's full social calendar did not preclude occasions for commercial amusement; a variety of traveling entertainments passed through even the smallest villages. The circus came to town every year, and a Chautauqua or a tent revival might occur for a week or two in the summer. The railroads brought traveling theatrical companies from New York City, Philadelphia, or Chicago. Well-known actors performed in hundreds of towns on their routes between big cities. Itinerant musical comedy troupes, medicine shows, lecturers, Wild West shows, magicians, stock companies, and exhibitors of mechanical novelties like the phonograph, spanning the talent scale from top drawer to meager, joined the circuit of small-town entertainment. Motion picture exhibition entered the small-town scene as merely one more component of an entertainment lineup that might not have had the sensuousness or "high culture" pretensions of urban diversions but that, nevertheless, had its own vibrant and varied pleasures. Within just a few years, however, movie shows would significantly alter the small-town entertainment scene.

Early Itinerant Film Exhibition

The successful introduction of projected motion pictures in the United States occurred in April 1896 at Koster and Bial's Music Hall in New York City, but films did not long remain the sole property of urban venues. Almost immediately afterward, entrepreneurs purchased territorial franchises to exhibit the latest marvel in vaudeville theaters across the nation. Others took the equipment on the road to fairs and industrial exhibitions. Within twelve months, several hundred movie projectors were in operation throughout the nation. The swift spread of film performances to even the smallest towns was due in part to the easy mobility of the projecting apparatus and in part to enterprising show people's desire to exploit the latest attraction as widely as possible before the "fad" for motion pictures passed.[7]

Lyman H. Howe, a prominent lecturer and purveyor of "genteel" entertainment based in Wilkes-Barre, Pennsylvania, had incorporated motion pictures into his slide and phonograph programs with great success in December 1896. In September 1899, he sent his traveling High Class Moving Picture Company to the village of Cooperstown, New York (population 2,169). Several hundred people at the Cooperstown Village Hall watched nearly two hours of brief films, alternately comic, educational, and fantastic, "all accompanied by realistic Sounds," and listened to separate lectures on travel in foreign lands and laughed at the polite comedy of the monologist.[8]

Cooperstown residents may already have had encounters with motion pictures prior to Howe's show; they might have viewed the performances of other traveling showmen or seen films in a black-top tent at one of the circuses, county fairs, or lakeside amusement parks popular with pleasure seekers in central New York State. More adventurous middle-class people might have seen moving pictures in a vaudeville show while

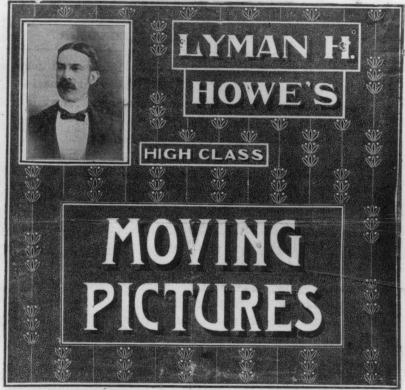

Advertisement for the Lyman Howe troupe's performance in Cooperstown, New York, 1901. Reprinted by permission of New York State Historical Association Library, Cooperstown.

on business or pleasure trips to Albany, Rochester, Buffalo, Syracuse, or New York City and brought home descriptions of the performances. Howe's Cooperstown moving picture exhibition may have impressed Cooperstonians, but it was not exceptional. Itinerant motion picture shows were cropping up everywhere.

Getting started in the business could be as easy as picking up the traveling showman's trade paper, the *New York Clipper*, or reading the Sears, Roebuck catalog. Many ambitious individuals with Horatio Alger–inspired desires to "make good" in a hurry must have been tempted to become moving picture exhibitors when the 1898 Sears, Roebuck catalog trumpeted its new show outfits so enthusiastically:

> Moving-picture exhibitions have been during the past year one of the most popular attractions in the large cities, but the cost of outfits has been so great that as yet few people outside of the larger cities have seen them. Those who are in a position to take advantage of an opportunity of this kind should not wait a moment, but should order an outfit at once, so as to appear before the public at the earliest possible date.[9]

In 1897, Alva Roebuck, the lesser-known partner in the expanding mail-order catalog firm, inaugurated a Department of Public Entertainment Outfits and Supplies, which promoted the fortunes that could be made by traveling entertainment entrepreneurs in New England, the South, Midwest, and West. Roebuck offered combination outfits of magic lantern-slide projectors, moving picture projectors, and "Graphophone talking machine" phonograph players for sale through the catalog, along with complete lecture scripts, slide sets, films, records, advertising posters, and rolls of tickets. All the successful entrepreneur needed was a bit of mechanical ability and showmanship skills. The machines provided the dramatic and musical talent. Roebuck claimed to have created a no-fail system of small-town exhibition. "We furnish with each outfit a book of instructions which tells in the plainest and most simple way how to handle the outfits, how to advertise, how to secure the use of halls, churches, opera houses and everything that is necessary for the exhibitor to know or that would contribute to his success." These low barriers to entry brought many people with no previous entertainment experience into the field of itinerant film exhibition and spurred the proliferation of movie shows in small towns across the nation in the early 1900s.[10]

These beliefs in the promise of technology and reservations about the morality of amusement formed the attitudes that enterprising young people such as Bert and Fannie Cook brought with them to the new field of motion picture exhibition. Their small-town outlook influenced what strategies the Cooks would develop to exploit this new entertainment medium and colored their expectations of what might please their potential audiences.

The Cook and Harris High Class Moving Picture Company

In 1902, B. Albert (Bert) Cook of Little Falls, New York, worked as a singer, film projectionist, phonograph operator, and occasional actor with a small-time concert company that traveled through New York State and the mid-Atlantic area, playing one-night stands in opera houses and lodge halls. At twenty-nine, Bert Cook was already a seven-year veteran of the entertainment business, having started performing in 1895. He possessed handsome physical features, a flair for showmanship, a fondness for mechanical tinkering, some training in photography, and considerable musical talent. Unfortunately, he had neither acting ability, family wealth, nor much of his own capital upon which to draw. He embodied the ambitious-but-poor young showman to whom the Sears, Roebuck catalog appealed.[11]

Bert Cook's twenty-one-year-old wife, Fannie Shaw Cook, was a bright, lovely young woman, an excellent pianist with ambitions to become a famous, wealthy actress. She and Bert had met in the summer of 1900 at Sylvan Beach, a popular resort on the shore of Lake Oneida near Utica, New York, where Bert was employed at a black-top tent moving picture show and tintype photograph parlor. They were married in 1902. Fannie Shaw's family had objected strenuously to the match at first, thinking that Cook was a traveling salesman. While actors and performers were looked upon with suspicion in small towns, apparently there were some occupations held in even lower repute.[12]

The new field of moving picture exhibition attracted Bert Cook, but finding the money to get started was a problem. As early as 1901 he had mentioned "taking on the picture show" in letters to friends. In January 1903 he answered a help-wanted advertisement in the *New York Clipper* placed by Lyman H. Howe, who by this time managed at least two traveling troupes. After much debate with Fannie, Bert Cook ultimately turned down Howe's job offer, determined to try his fortune as an independent exhibitor.[13]

In the spring of 1903, Cook put a deposit down on a film projector of his own but continued to perform in a friend's itinerant variety show. Cook paid off the balance on his Nicholas Power Company Cameragraph moving picture projector in the spring of 1904 and began purchasing films. These constituted a major investment, given Cook's limited means, costing $240 ($.12 per foot for two thousand feet) for the "nice lot of films" he proudly selected. Bert and Fannie Cook honed the presentation of their program during June, July, and August of 1904 at Sylvan Beach, vacation hotels, and local county fairs. As was the common practice in the summer, theaters closed and most entertainers moved their shows out of doors to escape the close confinement of audiences in stuffy town halls and opera houses.[14]

Imitating Lyman H. Howe and other film exhibitors, Bert and Fannie Cook named their new troupe the Cook and Harris High Class Moving Picture Company. Bert served as manager, projectionist, and occasional soloist, and Fannie was musical director, ticket seller, and treasurer. She took the stage name of Harris—a name adopted on a whim, perhaps, or to shield her family in Cooperstown from notoriety. They secured the services of an advance agent to travel ahead of the troupe and contract bookings for future shows. The company at times also included Fannie's brother George Shaw Jr., who worked as assistant projectionist and behind-the-screen sound-effects creator, and an additional pianist or singer to perform when Bert or Fannie was occupied with other aspects of company management.[15]

Bert and Fannie Cook initially modeled their promotional campaigns on those of Howe, whom they at first considered their closest competition. "Howe's moving pictures are in Fireman's Hall [in Cooperstown] Wednesday night and they will no doubt have a good house, as there were several women around all of last week selling tickets," sniffed Fannie peevishly in a letter to Bert, written when she was home visiting Cooperstown. "I will enclose for you one of the [hand]bills they threw around today." The Cooks wanted to duplicate the image of respectable and genteel entertainment that worked so successfully for Howe in attracting small-town, middle-class patrons. However, their emphasis would always be more on entertainment, music, and song rather than educational lectures, which was Howe's focus.[16]

The Cook and Harris company advertising handbills and programs especially resembled Howe's materials. The Cooks adapted for their program covers an illustration of the type Howe favored—an attentive opera house audience captivated by a gigantic motion picture image projected on a stage-filling screen. The moviegoers were drawn in a stiff, naïve folk style, and they were dressed in the plain but neat outfits found more often in the countryside than in the city. The moving picture image they viewed on the screen was an impressive scene of Admiral Dewey's battleship sailing into Manila harbor, which was already four to six years old. A big-city exhibitor probably would have dismissed this program as a dowdy vestige of 1896 movie show advertising, especially since the newest films available for exhibition were brief narratives like *The Great Train Robbery*. Yet small-town people might have been attracted to this image, which through its rendering in an approachable style of artwork managed to convey the wonder and excitement of the small-town moviegoing experience. The Sears catalog had offered a similarly breathless word-portrait of the movie experience for new itinerant exhibitors to clip and use in their advertising to small-town audiences:

> The drop curtain has fallen for the intermission when suddenly the house is darkened and before the eyes of the audience a huge window appears to open. Through it they see a bit of meadow landscape with a forest in the background, from which to a point close by the window stretches a section of railway line on a embankment bed. There appears in the distance, just emerging from the woods, a cloud of white smoke, which within a few seconds shapes itself into the outline of an approaching train, and in another moment what appears to be a real passenger train is rushing by at a tremendous rate. Every detail of motion is clearly defined, and even the rapid rise and fall of the piston rods can be plainly seen. In a twinkling the whole scene disappears, the theatre is again lighted up and before the audience hangs only the drop curtain.[17]

A typical two-hour Cook and Harris company performance featured twenty to twenty-five brief film scenes (Bert carried a complementary number of alternate films in case they played two nights in the same town). In its early years an exemplar of the "cinema of attractions," the program highlighted trick films from the Méliès company, travel scenes and documentary footage from the Pathé Frères company, and hand-colored films of butterfly dances and skirt dances (female dancers twirling in billowing, gauzy costumes). Scenes of speeding locomotives and fire-

The Twentieth Century Production.

THE

Cook & Harris

HIGH CLASS

Moving Picture
Company.

There are Many Imitators, but only One Genuine

M. P. Church, COLUMBIA CENTER

Proceeds to be used for New Cushions

Thursday EVENING **APRIL 20**

ADMISSION

Adults - - 20c
Children under 12, - 10c

TICKETS on sale at PETRIE & SECKNER'S STORE

Advertisement for the Cook and Harris troupe's performance in Columbia Center, New York, 1905. Reprinted by permission of New York State Historical Association Library, Cooperstown.

fights and the "dramatic and spectacular scene in six parts," *Indians and Cowboys,* rounded out the varied mix of film sequences.

At intervals in the program, Bert would sing popular songs accompanied by Fannie on a piano. Slides that illustrated the songs' narratives would be projected while Bert performed. The Cooks and their special-effects assistant also produced musical accompaniment and appropriate sound effects to enhance the drama and realism of the brief films, a practice that had a long history in stock company theatrical productions and that was now adapted for film performances. One review of a Cook and Harris program in Albany reported:

> A noticeable feature of the entertainment, and one that is especially creditable to the manager, is that the audience does not only see the moving picture, but hears some natural noise accompanying it. For instance, when a train approaches a station, he sees it far in the distance, and as it comes into view he hears the rumble, which gradually becomes louder as the train nears its destination, and diminishes by degrees as it slows up and comes to a standstill. The same detail was noticed while the "Indians and Cowboys" pictures were on, for when a gun was discharged the audience saw the puff of smoke and simultaneously heard the report.

The Cook and Harris company, like that of Lyman Howe and other itinerant exhibitors, created an emotional structure from the jumble of images in their performances, carefully orchestrating the program around spectacular sights punctuated by the mounting excitement of comic chase scenes and climaxing with brightly tinted films of fireworks at the finale.[18]

The Cook and Harris company performances were never simply copies of the Howe show, however. The two differed in several crucial respects. The Cook and Harris show featured more elaborate sound effects accompanying the movies than did a Howe performance, and more numerous musical interludes between the film subjects. "The Monotony of a Whole Evening of Moving Pictures is Relieved by the Introduction Now and Then of Some Beautiful Illustrated Song," Cook and Harris's programs proudly announced. The program showed a much wider diversity of film subjects and did not emphasize travel and educational films to the extent of a Howe exhibition, whereas Howe's programs offered more lectures and comic monologue segments. The heterogeneous nature of the early Cook and Harris program illustrates Bert and Fannie Cook's as-

Business stationery for Cook and Harris, Eminent Song Illustrators, 1903.
Reprinted by permission of New York State Historical Association Library,
Cooperstown.

sumption that their audiences had a finite attention span for films and
craved variety in their entertainment, more like vaudeville than a theatrical performance. Bert and Fannie Cook believed in the importance of a
balanced program and offered their audiences equal parts of comedy,
drama, education, adventure, and music.[19]

Attracting the Small-Town Middle Class

The Cook and Harris show had one potential advantage over Howe and
other rival exhibitors—the local ties Bert and Fannie Cook built and
traded on in their home territory. While Howe's attentions were spread
among his various companies that traveled throughout the mid-Atlantic,
northeastern, and midwestern states, Cook proudly advertised that he
was sole manager and proprietor of his company. Bert and Fannie Cook
played up connections to local townspeople wherever possible; their
advertising handbills and programs featured testimonial letters from

satisfied sponsors of Cook and Harris exhibitions in small towns and villages across central and northern New York State, New Hampshire, and Vermont.

Seeking endorsements from "respectable" civic groups was a business tactic that other itinerant shows such as circuses and concert companies had used successfully. Nineteenth-century show people often presented themselves as community citizens who returned to town annually like favorite relatives. The Cook and Harris company, as well as Howe and other film exhibitors, strove to have performances endorsed by fraternal organizations such as the Odd Fellows, Elks, and Foresters, or the Ladies' Aid Society, church fund-raising group, high school, volunteer fire company, or local baseball team. Cook and Harris attempted to ally their business with the most active social groups in a locality, bringing small-town, middle-class respectability to their performance through the place of exhibition, the society sponsoring and promoting the show, and the example set by having group members in the audience. Of course, the support of these sponsoring organizations was negotiated, not given freely. Cook and Harris's advance agent would haggle with prospective sponsors over a contract for the performance on a percentage-sharing basis of the receipts. If box-office receipts were moderate, a sponsor shared 30 percent of the door; if the sponsor dragooned the entire village into attending, the sponsor's share could reach 40 or 50 percent of ticket sales.[20]

Unlike Howe, whose companies played both in small towns and in large cities, the Cook and Harris company rarely performed in towns whose population reached ten thousand. They were village specialists. Records of Cook and Harris's performances in the 1906–1907 season indicate that of 134 engagements in upstate New York, Vermont, New Hampshire, and Quebec, 70 percent took place in villages of under two thousand inhabitants, and 85 percent in towns of fewer than four thousand people. At least 50 percent of the Cook and Harris shows were sponsored by local organizations. In a six months' sampling, 23 percent of the shows benefited social organizations such as a concert band, high-school senior class, firemen, or hospital; 20 percent raised money for an Odd Fellows lodge or other fraternal group; and 7 percent directly benefited a local Protestant or Catholic congregation.

Cook and Harris were not unique, however, in obtaining this level of middle-class endorsement. Howe's itinerant companies also secured many locally sponsored performances because of his solid reputation, excellent show, and connections gained over fifteen years of touring.

Howe's advertising for a show in Cooperstown in 1902 boasted that the sponsor, the Mechanic's Hook and Ladder Company, had "cleared about $100 as [its] share of the proceeds." Other traveling troupes, such as Edwin Hadley's in New England or Marie de Kerstrat's in Quebec, were as successful as Cook and Harris in attaining institutional connections for their shows. If the substantial support of local clubs and churches can be considered an indication of middle-class acceptance, then, at least in the Northeast, small-town, middle-class patronage of film shows in this early era of film exhibition was widespread.[21]

Those exhibitions not sponsored by civic groups—about half—were presented "under the auspices of the management" of a town's opera house. The manager often received 30 percent of the ticket sales as well as rent for the use of the hall. After distributing the sponsor's or hall manager's share, the Cook and Harris company averaged a net income during this period of $35 per night on weeknights and $46 on Saturdays, although sometimes a good Saturday matinee and evening show might earn them between $60 and $80. They played to an average of 150 to 200 people. Tickets cost $.35 and $.25 for reserved and gallery seats, and $.10 per child.[22]

Some may have been skeptical of an alliance between "church people" and traveling film exhibitors, but in practice it was a tolerable and mutually beneficial combination in many small communities. Endorsement of motion picture entertainments brought relatively conservative, middle-class, church-related groups into contact with commercialized amusement in the name of fund-raising and culture. These groups had traditionally taken much of the responsibility for bringing "proper" culture to town, arranging Chautauquas and lyceums. They sponsored civic projects like village beautification, annual town cleanups, the purchase of fire apparatus, street paving, better public health, and law enforcement. Civic and church groups solicited money for their organizations' primary expenses and for luxuries like outings and new meeting-hall furnishings. Religious groups, fraternal orders, and social organizations competed for funds among the small-town population. Groups with ambitious goals or insufficient funding relied heavily on sponsored entertainments such as movie shows (as well as on more traditional bazaars, suppers, and raffles) to squeeze extra money out of their supporters and the rest of the local populace.[23]

Cooperstown's acceptance of moving pictures as appropriate for middle-class audiences, and its loyalty to local talent, was evident during the village's centennial week celebration in August 1907. The village elders engaged Bert Cook to provide free outdoor moving picture shows for four nights, accompanying customary entertainments such as fireworks, band concerts, baseball games, parades, and speeches. The local weekly newspaper, the *Cooperstown Freeman's Journal*, noted with boosterish pride that "the affair was carried on in a most dignified and commendable manner that must have left a good impression of Cooperstown in the minds of our thousands of visitors," and reported that "the moving pictures thrown by B. Albert Cook of Cook and Harris against the First National Bank building were excellent, and pleased a large crowd."[24]

On occasion, Cook exhibited films of regional attractions or events that catered to his local audience's interests, such as moving pictures of Niagara Falls or scenes of the 1909 Hudson-Fulton commemoration in New York City. In January 1908, he showed film of an Elks parade in Albany to a meeting of the local Elks chapter in Saratoga Springs. His advertising urged audience members to attend in order to search for their friends in the pictured ranks. "The Elks Parade given by Mr. Cook's own pictures are taken on the spot in such perfect style that you can recognize many of the members of the Albany Lodge." Receipts from the Lubin Manufacturing Company for parade footage lend doubt to Cook's suggestion that he filmed these scenes himself. Cook's intent, nevertheless, was to extend the connections between his local audiences and commercially available films.[25]

Through its performances and business operations, the Cook and Harris company interacted with many different parts of the small-town community. High-school groups were enthusiastic Cook and Harris show sponsors. Several times proceeds of a sponsored show helped Cooperstown students to finance a big dance, or in the case of the Fairhaven, Vermont, senior class, to fund a class trip to Washington, D.C. Bert Cook successfully traded on his membership in the Odd Fellows and Masons to book his troupe into sponsored shows in small-town lodge halls. The Cook and Harris company also occasionally used hometown connections to procure some measure of protection from rival exhibitors. The president of the Cooperstown Board of Trustees, responsible for renting the town's village hall to itinerant exhibitors, sometimes alerted Cook to rival shows' appearances and favorably adjusted Cook and Harris's booking dates so that they did not follow too closely upon their opponents' heels.[26]

Competing Exhibitors, Recalcitrant Sponsors, and Finicky Audiences

Rivalry among itinerant moving picture exhibitors was already warm when Bert and Fannie Cook launched their troupe in 1904, and it would grow only more intense as part of a nationwide boom in traveling movie shows between 1904 and 1907. In September 1904, Cooperstown residents saw not only Cook and Harris's inaugural performance but also shows by Lyman Howe's troupe (to benefit the Mechanic's Hook and Ladder Company) and the Hadley Motion Picture Company (sponsored by the Baptist church's baraca class.) Three weeks after Hadley's appearance, the American Vitagraph Company gave an exhibition at the Village Hall on Friday, October 27, "with 12 scenes from 'The Last of the Mohicans' and pictures of local schoolchildren leaving the [school] building." It was the fourth elaborate motion picture show presented in a six-week span to a village of twenty-four hundred residents. Despite the many appeals to community interest and local history, the Vitagraph company show suffered from a surfeit of rival film programs as well as from competing social activities on a busy Friday night. The *Freeman's Journal* reported that attendance was light.[27]

The competitive conditions of the itinerant movie-exhibition business are illustrated in reports to Bert Cook from Hugh D. Fryer, the Cook and Harris company's advance agent in the autumn of 1905. Fryer, sixty years old, frequently complained of being old and tired. He does not seem to have been a very successful advance man—he took no for an answer all too often. Fryer wrote to Bert Cook from Carthage, New York, in October 1905:

> I left Boonville yesterday[,] Saturday[,] without being able to make any arrangements for you to appear in that town. I called on Father Pendergrass who had just arrived home and Saturday was Children's Day and he could not talk with me. Saw one or two organizations but they were not favorable to moving pictures as they had been. Foster here with Picture machine lately from Lowville and there was one in town that gave entertainments about once a week.

Rival exhibitor Walter Foster was establishing an exhibition circuit, playing regular dates in fixed locations each week, a movement away from true itinerancy that foreshadowed the establishment of stationary movie shows. Fryer had similar tales to recount from almost every town he visited. "Now Bert perhaps I am not succeeding as well as you expected and am not proving satisfactory in the business," he wrote from the road. "If so don't hesitate to tell me and if you have anyone you think will or can do better send your man along. I shall find no fault. I am doing the best I know how but unless I succeed better than the last two days shall think I am *no good*."[28]

Fryer reported that many potential sponsors had reservations, spurious or legitimate, about engaging the Cook and Harris show. Some organizations demanded ruinously high money guarantees. "Worked all day yesterday to get the Baptist Church people to give me an answer but could get only one night and they wanted 50 per cent at that." Others feared that their profits might be diluted if the movie show overlapped with the entertainments and activities of other organizations. "The YMCA have engaged Dibble [another rival exhibitor] to come here next month and the Methodists are afraid to do anything to conflict with their entertainment." Some groups claimed to have a full schedule booked. "I have been looking up the Elks here but they are to have a week's entertainment the last of November and do not think it advisable to put on anything ahead of it." Other sponsors complained about small proceeds in the past. A fraternal order in Gouverneur, New York, "had quite a time with you when your agent was here before and claim they spent more time in getting it [Cook's exhibition] off than they received pay for[,] as they had a matinee—dance and entertainment but no money for the Lodge." Fryer's best persuasive skills (and probably some whiskey) convinced these lodge members to sign the show contract. "I had them all over to the Hotel after their Lodge meeting and finally prevailed on them to try us once more."[29]

Some conservative organizations rejected show sponsorship in principle. "The Knights of Columbus . . . referred me to Father Reghan the Catholic Priest to see if I could not place it on in their church but as soon as he looked over our courier and saw what it was[,] he objected at once and said he could not think of such a thing." Many disappointments that Fryer met, however, might have demonstrated poor salesmanship skills rather than a dearth of opportunities. The Reverend J. H. Migneron of St. Hubert's Church in Benson Mines, New York, eagerly sought the Cook and Harris show's appearance. Migneron wrote to Bert Cook, "Now, when do you think you would be able to come again in our part of the country? I really think business would be superior now that there are plenty of people all around in the Summer resorts. . . . Kindly let me know by return mail if such arrangement would meet your approval, so that I go to work immediately and have the proper advertisement."[30]

Despite widespread stereotypes of backward, uninformed small-towners, many members of the Cook and Harris show audiences were knowledgeable and critical movie patrons. A Methodist minister wrote of a Cook and Harris performance at his Remsen, New York, church that it was "one of the best we have ever had the privilege of seeing in this town and a good many moving picture companies have been here." In Bert and Fannie Cook's opinion, then, the highest praise their performances could garner in small towns was that they compared favorably with big-city moving picture exhibitions. After their September 1906 show in Coopers-town, Fannie proudly wrote to Bert that "every body spoke well of the entertainment, and said it was far above Howe's, or any that the City people had seen in the cities." Their advertising highlighted testimonials like the following one from an Odd Fellows lodge member in Fillmore: "[P]eople who have seen Moving Pictures in New York, Buffalo and Rochester say that your entertainment was as good if not better than any thing they have ever saw [sic]." A Universalist church pastor from Mid-dleville reiterated that "one who sat near me said, 'I have seen a number of similar entertainments in New York City but this is the best I have ever seen.'"[31]

Not all film subjects popular in the city were necessarily acceptable to small-town audiences, whose tastes, while in many ways similar to those of urban viewers, tended to be more conservative. Surviving records do not indicate how Bert and Fannie Cook made their film pur-chase choices, and probably they rejected outright any controversial sub-jects they felt might not be appropriate for a small-town show. Still, they occasionally encountered negative reactions to popular urban genres like fight films. The Odd Fellows lodge in Attica, New York (population two thousand), put in a special request for a program of prizefight pictures but soon had second thoughts about the propriety of that choice. Both the lodge and the Cooks seemed relieved when the films were unavail-able. The group's representative wrote to Bert: "[I] note that the 'fight pictures' cannot be produced, and we have therefore canceled the item on our copy of the contract. . . . We are just as well satisfied and there would no doubt be some objections in as small a town as this to an exhibition of this kind and as you know our Order will not stand for anything that is not strictly O.K." With no fight films to compromise the respectability of its regular performance, Cook and Harris played to over one thousand people in two nights at the Attica Opera House.[32]

Another threat to the Cook and Harris company's business resulting from the overabundance of exhibitors was the duplication of the limited number of available film subjects. Even had there been less competition from rival show people, the matter of dated films was becoming an issue for the Cooks. Audiences became increasingly reluctant to pay to see the same movies each time a show came to town; whereas repetition of songs might have been tolerated, the appeal of moving pictures seemed to hinge on their novelty. In this way audiences forced changes in the operation of itinerant movie shows. The cost of purchasing new films threatened to raise the Cooks' operating expenses to ruinous heights. Film rental exchanges had begun to open in large cities in 1904, but most itinerants still purchased their film footage. The situation was worse for the Cooks than for rivals like Howe, who shot some of his own documentary film footage. Further, the Cooks' program showcased topical events more often than did Howe's, and their exhibition of film of the great San Francisco fire exemplifies the increasing seriousness of their predicament.[33]

The biggest news of 1906 was the great San Francisco earthquake and fire. The Edison and Biograph motion picture studios raced their cameramen to California to film the scenes of destruction, and by May 15, about four weeks after the disaster, each offered a selection of documentary films of the fire to exhibitors. Bert Cook ordered a print, but since the Cook and Harris company did not travel in the summer, the fire scenes did not debut in their show until the beginning of their fall 1906 season. Cook and Harris advertising for an early September show in Cooperstown defensively tried to allay audience concerns about the currency of the program. "Presenting for the first time in Cooperstown the only genuine pictures of the Great San Francisco Fire. New Moving Pictures, New Illustrated Songs. Everything new and even better than before. Plenty of good, clean comedy. If you enjoy a feast of good things wait for the best."[34]

Within two months, however, moving picture audiences across upstate New York were inundated with San Francisco scenes. In mid-November, an opera house manager in Sherburne, New York, cautioned Cook and Harris's new advance man, Art Richardson, "Will just say that you will have to give our people something 'up to date' to satisfy at all." Richardson in turn railed at Bert Cook: "You had better get the San Francisco Fire off your 3 sheets [posters]; it[']s getting old and stale. And get a new cut [illustration] on your Courier. And get a 9 sheet stand. Hadley has got an all new line of paper [posters] this season—*swell.*"35

By mid-December 1906, Richardson was livid about Cook's seeming reluctance to invest enough money to keep the show current and novel, and threatened that if things did not improve quickly Cook could get another agent:

> This job is too hard. I have no paper to show the society and the minute they see the San Francisco fire they give me [a] wise-look, put their tongue in their cheek and say no I guess not. I lost Vergennes on account of not having paper and the "San Francisco Fire" has been there by both Howe and Foster. Now for god sake get this off your Courier and get some paper. That is one big hoodoo you have got on your show.36

If audiences and opera house managers revolted against what they perceived as tired, old movie shows, and if expensive-to-purchase films became obsolete within three to four months, then itinerant exhibitors' profits would vanish. Surviving receipts from Cook's film purchases from the Pathé company in the spring of 1907 demonstrate what an investment each new print represented. Cook purchased ten short films (totaling a little under two reels of film, or about thirty to forty minutes) at $.12 per foot for $223.92. He ordered hand coloring to be done on three of the prints for an additional $29.00, making the total $252.92. Since Cook and Harris's two-hour show usually featured twenty to twenty-five films, prints were a major investment for them, and they retained them in the program as long as possible. They used *The Lost Child,* described in their advertising as "an exceedingly humorous chase picture, exciting and laughable throughout," in their program from 1904 until as late as December 1906. Films, which arrived COD, were only part of the itinerant exhibitor's operating expenses, as music and accompanying slides had to be purchased or rented, hotel bills and railroad lines paid up front, employee payrolls met, and bills for printing programs and handbills paid.37

After the 1907 season, Bert and Fannie Cook solved their problem of dated films by renting from a film exchange in Pittsburgh, Pennsylvania, thereby assuring a steady stream of fresh subjects for their demanding sponsors and audiences. Although exchanges had been in existence for several years, it is unclear why the Cooks did not begin using them sooner; force of habit, lack of sufficient credit, or the difficulty of coordinating film delivery and local advertising might have delayed the switch.

By May 1908, the Cook and Harris show offered a mix of older purchased and newer rented films; there was a regularly changing, featured one-reel film such as *The Great Boar Hunt.* It was shown with *Alps of Chamonix,* a travel picture; *The Last Witch,* a hand-colored film described as a "great fairy picture in 6 scenes and tableau"; an Elks parade in Philadelphia supposedly photographed by Cook; and at least six other brief scenes, such as *Sea by Moonlight, Haunted House, The Night before Christmas,* and *Three American Beauties in Color.* As before, the films were interspersed with Cook singing the "latest ballads in Illustrated Songs by all the well known publishers." The handbills noted, "As We Are Constantly Adding New Pictures of Notable Events Whenever They Occur, THIS PROGRAM IS SUBJECT TO CHANGE."[38]

Art Richardson was a more capable advance agent than Hugh Fryer. He was able to book the Cook and Harris show into sponsored engagements in many more towns along the troupe's travel route than Fryer, but he gave Bert Cook a great deal of criticism along with the increased business. He constantly lectured Bert on the need for circuslike ballyhoo to attract attention and stand out from other exhibitors. Richardson also boasted of the questionable maneuvers he used to secure profitable show contracts:

> I had a little experience which I gained a few points on a moving picture man, Walter H. Foster, "The Moving Picture King." I got in Fair Haven [Vermont] and landed the High School. Since our [last] visit to Fair Haven, Foster has been there twice and played to big business. Mr. Felix Blei, who owns several theaters throughout Vermont, called me up on the phone and asked me if I cared to play Rutland. I told him no. He asked me if I played Fair Haven (his house) and I said yes. He said I'm sorry but I got Foster booked in two nights ahead of you in Fair Haven. I said all right. I immediately went over to see Mr. Metcalf the manager and he said he would not allow Mr. Foster to play ahead of us. And no Moving Picture shows at all ahead of us or 15 days behind us. He owns the house. So I guess that will hold Mr. Felix Blei for a while.[39]

Although business tactics like these were probably practiced by a significant number of competing booking agents and exhibitors, they did little to smooth relations with theater circuit managers. Blei spitefully returned the favor, and did nothing to prevent "local pictures" from conflicting with Cook and Harris's exhibition at a hall he managed in Bennington,

Vermont, in March 1907. Bert and Fannie Cook earned only $37.55 total for two evening shows and a matinee, far lower than their usual box-office returns for Friday and Saturday performances.[40]

By the end of the fall 1907 season, despite the benefits Richardson brought, Bert Cook terminated him. "Am glad you have finished with Richardson," wrote Fred Waterbury of the Eagle Printing Company in Saratoga Springs, who was now manager of the Cook and Harris show, for "it will save you a great many hundred dollars a year, no matter how good he was at the business. He certainly was not worth the amount he was costing you." Cook turned the position of advance agent over to Fannie's brother, George Shaw Jr., who seemed to work just as efficiently, if not quite as ambitiously. "I told you," Waterbury wrote later to Cook, "you could do better than R. and here is Geo. getting societies to play nearly all your dates and getting tonights [advertising flyers] in a town and saving railroad fares and your own health by less hustling."[41]

Nickelodeons: A New Form of Competition

At this critical juncture in 1907 and 1908, small-town itinerant exhibitors began to encounter a new form of competition that would ultimately prove fatal to most traveling shows—the stationary moving picture theater, or nickelodeon. In February 1907, Fred Waterbury wrote incredulously to Bert Cook: "I see there is a firm, from Rochester or Buffalo, I think, [that] has leased a Broadway [main street of Saratoga Springs] store and will run a moving picture and illustrated song theater on ground floor and slot machines upstairs. I cannot see how it will pay in this small place." Compared with the villages the Cook and Harris show frequented, Saratoga Springs was not small at all; it was a popular resort town with a population of more than eleven thousand.[42]

Waterbury was skeptical about the nickelodeon's potential for success in small towns, despite the rapid multiplication of those small movie theaters in the previous two years in urban areas. Storefront nickelodeon theaters in large cities had begun operating in 1904 and 1905, offering brief (fifteen to thirty minutes long) movie shows at prices as low as five cents, renting films from the new exchanges, and changing their programs semiweekly and sometimes daily. They were generating publicity and enormous profits. Itinerant exhibition had been the most efficient method to reach the large number of people scattered in small settlements across wide distances. Nevertheless, the continued popularity of movie shows in small towns, and changes in the growing movie industry, were bringing about conditions that favored stationary exhibitions over traveling shows. The number of films available for rent was rising, and so a permanent exhibitor could show a wider variety of new subjects to local audiences instead of showing the same stock of films to different audiences across the region.

Like Waterbury and most itinerant film exhibitors, Bert and Fannie Cook saw a finite desire for commercial entertainment in small towns; they assumed that three or four elaborate movie shows per season were all a community could afford or want to see. They believed that too much competition and overexposure would ruin the amusement business for all exhibitors. However, the nickelodeon entrepreneurs, perhaps more attuned to the advance of consumer culture around them, believed that audiences could learn to desire more and more commercialized amusements, seeking movies habitually, every week or even every night.

The Cooks themselves encountered further evidence that the small town's leisure habits might be changing. In the same month that the Saratoga Springs nickelodeon opened, Fannie Cook received a letter from a friend in Groveton, New Hampshire. Congratulating Fannie on the success of Cook and Harris's recent exhibition there, the woman wrote: "Please tell Mr. Cook that I hear nothing but words of praise for the entertainment. One young man said, 'I would go every night if it was here.'" Fannie and Bert Cook probably chuckled to think that anyone would be so profligate.[43]

By 1908, the movement from small-town traveling shows to nickelodeons was evident even in the Sears and Roebuck catalog, which curtailed its promotion of kits for itinerant exhibition of phonograph, slide, and film shows and now concentrated on selling packages for the start-up of stationary movie theaters. Sears and Roebuck's advertising copy describing the features of the firm's nickelodeon outfits, illustrated with a picture of a pressed-tin nickelodeon front, now declared:

> The 5-cent theater is here to stay. It fills a want that has existed in every community for a moderate priced form of clean, up to date amusement. This business offers attractive inducements to anyone with small capital who wishes to establish himself in a profitable and permanent business of his own. Almost any vacant store room can be

made into a five-cent theater by removing the glass front and replacing it with a regular theater front. . . . [T]he low price of admission is an inducement which many people cannot resist.[44]

The most damaging advantage of nickelodeons over traveling shows was their affordability. Charging only 20 to 40 percent of Cook and Harris's general admission price, and offering shorter shows that the audiences could attend more frequently without emptying their pockets or drastically altering their social schedules, nickelodeons quickly began to drain away a vital component of the itinerant-show audience. Nevertheless, the nightly nickelodeon show would not be able to duplicate the excited anticipation of a "special event" that the best itinerant movie shows brought to small towns through advance ballyhoo, the parade of boxes and trunks from the train station to the opera house, and the elaborate two-hour program.

The stationary moving picture show first came to Cooperstown in September 1907, when George Carley, editor of the local newspaper, the *Freeman's Journal,* reported that a pair of businessmen from the nearby town of Oneonta "have rented Fireman's Hall for an indefinite period to have there a moving picture entertainment every night at small prices." The enterprise was certainly indefinite, lasting no longer than a few weeks before folding. In August 1908, Cooperstown resident W. H. Jarvis and a partner named Means thought the time was ripe to try again. "The continuous show by moving pictures has been quite successful in many other towns and Mr. Jarvis believes it will prove so here," Carley noted. "Messrs. Means and Jarvis are showing some excellent moving pictures each evening in Bowne Hall. The films are changed frequently and the entertainments are proving popular."[45]

Nickelodeon managers like Jarvis and Means duplicated many of the strategies that cemented goodwill and community approval in small towns by soliciting sponsors and participating in local fund-raising campaigns. A typical notice in the *Freeman's Journal* stated that Jarvis (Means having moved on) offered

an evening's entertainment of moving pictures for the benefit of Neptune Steamer Co., #3, on Wednesday evening next, at which a variety of fine pictures will be shown. Specialties [songs and vaudeville turns] will be introduced during the intermissions and a full evening's entertainment will be given for the moderate price of 15 cents admission. Come and help the firemen.[46]

Typically, this Cooperstown nickelodeon had several owners in a brief period of time. Jarvis died suddenly in the summer of 1909, and L. H. Spencer, operator of a local summer hotel, bought the successful nickelodeon theater from Jarvis's widow. George Carley, intrigued by the moving picture business, became Spencer's partner, bringing the little theater continuous exposure in his newspaper. In the *Freeman's Journal*'s society columns, Carley faithfully reported Mrs. Carley's "movie parties," at which she and her friends went together to the nickelodeon and afterward retired to her house for tea and bridge.

Carley also gave the local nickelodeon a "real" name, as the paper reported: "The Star Theatre will soon hang its sign out where Bowne Opera House now is. The moving picture business has apparently become a necessity in Cooperstown. The management has made many improvements lately, and the best censored and licensed pictures are now shown, with no flicker to the lights." The name change signaled that the nature of local entertainment was shifting from community events and the welcoming of itinerant shows to an embrace of the commercially operated film exhibition business. Carley greatly reduced the free newspaper space that notices of itinerant exhibitors' shows had previously received, and gave his concentrated support to the Star's programs. A typical Star Theater ad promised, "A two-hour programme will be given that will equal both in quantity and quality any of the traveling pictures." When, in September 1909, the town hall doubled its rental rates for itinerant movie shows because of rising fire insurance premiums, Carley noted that "[i]t will be a good thing for the eyes and ears of the people if some of the moving picture shows are eliminated." As an exception, Carley continued to publish generous reviews of Cook and Harris performances. Itinerant exhibitors found that many small towns, like Cooperstown, were becoming less hospitable and less profitable places in which to perform.[47]

A Cook and Harris program advertisement in 1910 beseeched the reader, "Do not compare this exhibition with any Five or Ten cent small shows; THE COOK & HARRIS Programs are above comparison." But for Bert and Fannie Cook and other itinerant exhibitors, nickelodeons could no longer be ignored. The presence of stationary movie shows, if operated to a standard the community found acceptable, could prevent traveling shows from securing bookings. Traveling exhibitors were restricted to ever-smaller villages that might still be movie "starved." The Cook and Harris company was reduced to performing in settlements of fewer than five hundred people and was increasingly unable to cover its expenses. Bert and Fannie Cook must have received many letters such as the one from the manager of a hall in Middleville, New York. "In reply to your letter of the 15th beg to advise we now have a weekly moving picture which is taking very well. Have been running nearly two months. I do not think it would pay to put on another, do you?"[48]

In the summer of 1911, Bert and Fannie Cook finally bowed to changing conditions in small-town amusement and in the booming film exhibition industry; they shelved their itinerant operation and made the switch to stationary moving picture shows. They found employment operating a nickelodeon in Shaul's Theater in the resort of Richfield Springs, about twelve miles from Cooperstown. In 1914, they returned to Cooperstown and assumed management of the Star Theatre for George Carley. They invested their savings and purchased the nickelodeon from Carley in 1915, and operated the Star as their own. Lyman H. Howe's companies managed to stay on the road longer by concentrating on the educational aspects of travel films, carving out a special niche of middle-class audiences. Although increasingly marginalized from the mainstream movie shows that featured narrative fiction films, Howe's troupes continued to make semiannual appearances in Cooperstown until 1917.

Itinerant movie-show people traveling among upstate New York's many small towns in the early 1900s had constructed a large and diverse audience for motion pictures outside the largest urban centers. Traveling exhibitors like the Cook and Harris High Class Moving Picture Company introduced an audience of small-town middle-class and working-class residents to a new entertainment form in the familiar setting of their own opera houses and town halls, often with the sponsorship and approval of community religious and civic groups. Small-town audiences, in turn, grew accustomed to the idea of moviegoing as a regular habit through the frequent performances and competitive one-upmanship of rival traveling movie shows. The itinerant movie shows themselves were shaped by their audiences' desires to see novel yet not-too-controversial film subjects that would be as good as anything shown in the big-city theaters. The audiences' sustained interest fueled the rapid spread of nickelodeon theaters in small towns.[49]

 2

The Regional Diversity
of Moviegoing Practices

Nickelodeon theaters opened on the Main Streets of practically every town of at least five thousand people in all regions of the country between 1905 and 1910. Villages in the New England, mid-Atlantic, and midwestern states with as few as one thousand inhabitants sprouted nickelodeons, and while the number of theaters was more sparse in the rural South and West, settlements there also acquired regular movie shows. Like Cooperstown and upstate New York, most small towns across the country experienced a steady building of film audiences, not only through the continued showing of itinerant movie shows but also through the establishment of more permanent film theaters. By 1910 an estimated ten thousand nickelodeon theaters were in business across the nation; seven thousand of them were located outside the big cities.

The structures and programs of nickelodeon theaters everywhere were in many ways similar. But outside the largest urban centers, there was a regional flavor to small-town moviegoing. Audience composition, patrons' access to theaters, and frequency of attendance varied from one portion of the country to another. Geography and settlement patterns, and restrictions due to racial and ethnic prejudice, poverty, local customs shaped by religious beliefs, and expectations about gender roles and social class, determined who went to the movies and how often.

To explore some of these differences, a region-by-region profile of small-town audiences and their moviegoing patterns in the nickelodeon era follows. One must keep in mind how, during this period, continuing cultural tensions between urban and rural attitudes, and between native white middle-class and ethnic working-class values, shaped the small-town moviegoing experience. Nonurban areas had a smaller proportion of immigrants among their populations than did the big cities. Thus this profile will not claim to characterize the entire American film audience in the silent film era, but it will complement existing portraits of urban movie audiences that richly document the moviegoing experiences of European immigrants and working-class men, women, and children in industrial cities like Worcester, Massachusetts, and in Manhattan's Lower East Side and Chicago's ethnic neighborhoods.[1]

Geography and settlement patterns were the primary influences on small-town nickelodeon attendance habits, for stationary theaters could operate only where there were sufficient audiences to fill them. While 75 percent of Americans resided outside the largest urban centers in the 1910s, the size of their communities varied from isolated homesteads to village crossroads to bustling manufacturing centers of fifty thousand to one hundred thousand people. On average, villages the size of Cooperstown were still home to one-quarter of the people who lived outside big cities, but settlement was much less dense in the South, where towns of twenty-five hundred people or fewer accounted for only 17 percent of the nonurban population. Many southern families lived on isolated farms with poor roads. Other parts of the country were more thickly settled; in the mid-Atlantic and New England states, villages were home to 40 percent of all people who did not live in the cities. Thirty-three percent of nonurban westerners and 28 percent of nonurban midwesterners lived in small towns; but across the Midwest, settlement could vary from the closely packed towns of Ohio to the sparsely populated Great Plains, where half the counties had fewer than six persons per square mile. The nonurban population was certainly not spread evenly across the land, and that influenced where nickelodeon shows might operate.[2]

Moviegoing in the South

Whenever representatives of the Manhattan-based exhibition-trade press toured nickelodeon theaters south of Baltimore, they were struck by how different the situation was from what they perceived as the New York norm. Not only were the South's patterns of film exhibition and movie attendance distinctly different from those of urban areas, southern states had the lowest density of movie theaters of any other region during the silent film era. As late as 1930, Georgia had only one-third as many movie theater seats per thousand people as any state outside the region. Many southerners, especially small-town and rural residents of the Deep South, were less exposed to movie shows than other Americans in the silent film era. They journeyed farther than people of other regions to movie shows, saw films in smaller auditoriums, and often had only one theater in their town rather than a choice of two or three competing shows.[3]

The greater physical isolation and lower economic status of many rural southerners, compared with those of their midwestern counterparts, kept many away from the movies. The South had the most impoverished farm families among its population; sharecroppers and their families had very little hard cash to spend on recreation. In the South fewer individuals than the national average owned automobiles or had access to good paved roads or public transportation to get into town for a movie show. As late as 1930, eastern social workers professed shock to encounter children in West Virginia Appalachian mountain villages who had never seen a film.[4]

Yet conversely, southern cities in the late nineteenth century had often taken the lead in adopting new communication and transportation technologies, installing telephones, electric lights, and trolley cars at a much faster rate than the rest of the nation. While Alabama cities such as Montgomery and Birmingham may have had only one-third the number of movie theater seats per person of New York City or Chicago, their movie theaters, along with the Balaban and Katz theaters in Chicago, were, in 1917, among the first to install air conditioning. By the mid-1920s, most large urban southern theaters adopted air conditioning; movie houses became associated with cool temperatures in the steamy summer months and were the major source of air conditioning in southern public life before World War II. The difference between northeastern and southern moviegoing experiences was a matter of relative degree instead of absolutes; after all, the movies debuted in southern towns and cities at the same time as in other regions, and almost all southern towns of any size had movie shows in the silent film era. However, southerners in smaller towns might not have seen films as recently released or in theaters as up-to-date as their small-town counterparts elsewhere. This relative lack of access to the movies would begin to change only in the 1940s

Staff of the Jewel Theater in Hartford, Arkansas, show off their popcorn cart, July 7, 1916. Courtesy of Q. David Bowers.

and 1950s, when continued urbanization, industrialization, and the spread of air conditioning increased the number of southern movie theaters constructed.[5]

Racial prejudice was another critical factor shaping the moviegoing experience in the South. Following the spread of Jim Crow laws in the 1890s, African Americans had been segregated and in most cases completely barred from white places of indoor and outdoor commercial amusement. Even apologists for the racial status quo admitted that in most southern communities "public amusements are almost wanting for the Negro."[6]

As one white Mississippi exhibitor complained, New York–based film distributors calculated film rental charges as a percentage of a town's population, white and black totals combined. Most existing nickelodeons in the South (like stores and other commercial buildings) had no second floors or balconies that might accommodate segregated seating. And most southern film exhibitors in the silent film era limited themselves to servicing a town's white patrons, which in some areas totaled only 30 to 40 percent of the population. A Mississippi exhibitor whined that he could hardly stay in business in a town of twenty thousand people because he was charged rental rates "as if" he serviced the entire town. This situation not only blocked blacks' access to movies but also resulted in a poorer quality of show for small-town white movie audiences, as ticket-sales volume was rarely high enough for exhibitors profitably to present "first-run" or spectacular films. Southern movie audiences tended to see scratched, tired prints of older films.[7]

A 1919 regional distribution survey by the First National Exhibitors' Circuit was careful to note the large black population of the South to explain why such a large territory produced such meager revenues. Barring blacks was not good business sense, First National reasoned; the problem would be solved if exhibitors would build balconies for segregated seating. Ironically, the film industry's prodding helped blacks get wider access to movies, but at a terrible cost, for the humiliation of being shunted upstairs offset the films' pleasures.[8]

Thomas Cripps has noted that, despite the continued low box-office totals at southern movie theaters, in the 1920s film studios became increasingly concerned with how southern moviegoers would react to on-screen depictions of black characters. Southern opinion pressured film producers to avoid sympathetic treatment of racial issues or realistic roles for African American characters in the movies for fear that studio-owned southern theaters would be boycotted by white audiences. Even as southern states' editorial clout grew, their box-office returns ranked lowest of any region into the 1940s.[9]

The relative paucity of nickelodeons in the small-town South enabled alternate forms of film exhibition and other cultural outlets to have greater impact there. Itinerant exhibitors continued to circulate among small-town lodge halls and school auditoriums into the 1920s, long after traveling movie shows had been squeezed out of northeastern markets. Theatrical touring companies, vaudeville troupes, and minstrel shows also found welcoming audiences in southern towns not sated by the movies, although one 1920 report noted that four to six road-show attractions per week were inundating towns of twenty-five thousand people. Rural African Americans, denied access to the movies, turned for entertainment to community religious gatherings, revivals, tent shows, medicine shows, "race" records of jazz, blues, and gospel music, and other forms of community-focused entertainment.[10]

African Americans in southern cities were more likely to have access to film entertainment. Black movie theaters opened in Atlanta, Birmingham, Richmond, and Washington, D.C.; these cities also had black vaudeville theaters that incorporated movies into their programs. Some of the nickelodeons serving the black community were black-owned, but most were white-owned with black management. Although in 1913 one black film producer in Chicago claimed that there were more than 200 black nickelodeons across the nation, the number of black theaters across the South was never as large as the population should have warranted. Whereas there were as many as 15 black or segregated theaters in Washington, D.C., in the early 1920s, in 1930 there were only 5 theaters in Atlanta to serve 90,075 blacks, 4 in Birmingham (for 99,077 blacks), 2 in Richmond (for 52,988), and 1 in Nashville (for 42,836). The *Film Daily Yearbook,* which began tracking the number of "colored theaters" in the late 1920s, found 280 black movie houses across the South in 1930 but noted wide discrepancies, listing more than 50 black theaters in Texas, over 35 each in Florida and North Carolina, about 20 each in Georgia, Alabama, and Virginia, but only a few in the heavily black-populated states of Louisiana, South Carolina, Tennessee, and Mississippi. The 461 black theaters listed across the nation represented only 2 percent of the country's 23,000 movie houses. Most of these theaters were small and dilapidated; they were often able to exhibit only worn-out prints of old and inexpensive films. Nevertheless, black movie theaters played a significant part in the leisure-time activities of the southern urban blacks who had access to them in the silent film era.[11]

In a 1927 survey, Howard University sociologist William H. Jones found that going to the movies was an especially popular social activity for the African American population of Washington, D.C. Movies were the only form of white-controlled commercial amusement in which southern blacks could participate. Independent black film companies produced well-received "race films" in the silent era, from *The Birth of a Race,* produced in reaction to D. W. Griffith's portrayal of blacks in *The Birth of a Nation,* through the 1920s films that starred Paul Robeson or that Oscar Micheaux produced and directed. Nevertheless, black films were in too-limited a supply to offer an adequate alternative to white films. Black movie patrons mostly saw mainstream Hollywood releases.

More readily available to exhibitors were talented black musicians, singers, and performers. Black movie theaters in Baltimore and Washington, D.C., interspersed white films with concerts on stage, providing an arena for black performers.[12]

The southern black movie theater could be, at its best, a gathering place for the urban black community, a site at which to see and be seen. Young men performed for the crowds waiting outside Washington's Lincoln Theater, singing, dancing, and otherwise showing off, adapting forms of communal musical entertainment that had been long prominent in the District's alleyways. The Lincoln's manager, trying to maintain "respectable" standards of propriety, made continual and futile attempts to disperse the performers, whom he disparagingly labeled "skunk mollies." The situation for most other southern black moviegoers was far drearier. The contemporary historian Paul Edwards did not find significant black middle-class patronage of Nashville's or Atlanta's dingy, small black movie theaters or of the white theaters. "[B]ecause of the embarrassment to which the race is often subjected in having to enter and leave the large theatre by segregated side entrances usually opening out on adjoining alleys, and to sit, all classes together, in a restricted part of the gallery, a much smaller percentage of Negroes of all classes attend the theatre than is true of whites."[13]

In the silent film era, southern African Americans became increasingly aware that blacks in other regions of the country had what seemed like an abundance of commercial entertainment available to them, and this envy helped fuel small-town and rural blacks' desire to migrate elsewhere. Northern black newspapers with a nationwide circulation, like the *Chicago Defender,* featured pages of advertising for the black movie theaters, cabarets, and vaudeville shows of Chicago's State Street. A *Defender* reader in rural Mississippi wrote longingly to the newspaper that having such plentiful access to movie shows would be "heaven itself."[14]

Religion, Morality, and the Southern White Movie Audience

Mill towns of the New South were more likely to have movie theaters, at least for their white residents, than the agriculture-centered villages of South Carolina and Mississippi, which had larger black populations. Mills and coal-mining companies in North Carolina, Georgia, and Kentucky sponsored movie shows for their workers and built auditoriums in their company towns to provide recreation for workers and their families and thereby to defuse worker discontent. By the late 1910s, North Carolina public officials sent out movie shows by truck and train to deliver educational messages about public health and efficient farming methods to rural families; they also established a program to bring entertainment films to isolated villages without movie theaters. The prosperous years from 1917 to the mid-1920s gave southern mill workers and miners more income to afford movie shows and consumer goods. Their gains began to recede by the mid-1920s, as production speedups, strikes, and depression-like economic conditions affected the South several years sooner than other sections of the country.[15]

Religious beliefs and moral standards shaped the small-town white southern movie audience in the 1910s and 1920s, for even if motion picture theaters were available, many members of conservative religious groups chose not to attend. Southern Baptists, Southern Methodists, and other evangelical sects had long shunned "worldly pleasures" such as dancing, card playing, theater attendance, and gambling. They denounced the movies as the devil's enticement. Southern Methodists sought to ban commercial amusements not only by abstaining from the shows themselves, "but also by stigmatizing such diversion as so potential with evil that no Christian could consistently participate in or encourage them," as one sectarian history related.[16]

Until the late 1950s, elders of the Baptist and Holiness evangelical Protestant churches still did not "think it was right" to attend movies, and the most conservative sects considered the movies taboo; they also proscribed women's activities, particularly rejecting bobbed hair, tobacco use, drinking, and dancing. Some members of these groups (more likely to be male) inevitably were "backsliders who must be saved and sanctified again and again." Although members of southern evangelical sects tolerated the occasional attendance of men or boys at commercial amusements like the movies, they held more stringent standards of public behavior for the girls and women of their communities. Ted Ownby has noted that movie attendance "often carried a strong hint of sinful self-indulgence," and unlike other evangelical cultural taboos, which could be broken in privacy, moviegoing was very much a public recreation.[17]

Urban immigrant women were much in evidence in big-city nickelodeons, but small-town and rural southern women were far more notable for their absence from movie theaters. Edward Ayers's research has

uncovered evidence, however, that, at least in the border states, southerners at the turn of the century had wider contact with consumer culture
through mass-circulation magazines and mail-order catalogs than is generally assumed. In 1918, nevertheless, eastern social surveyors were surprised to find that small-town women in North Carolina subscribed to
fewer women's magazines than women elsewhere and were less likely
than the men in their families to attend the movies. Southern male farmers traveled to the nearest market town or trading center monthly or
weekly to purchase supplies and socialize with other men. Many southern rural women were too heavily burdened with outside paid labor,
housework, and numerous children who could not be left unattended to
spend much time off the farm. On the few occasions poor rural women
and their daughters ventured into town, shopping for necessities absorbed all their time and attention.[18]

Sensational film advertising of "vamp," fallen woman, and white
slavery themes increasingly made the movie show a target for evangelical
ministers and other conservative small-town critics after 1914. Southern
exhibitors were torn between capitalizing on the fact that salacious films
did, in fact, draw large audiences in small towns as well as in the "sinful"
cities and facing the loss of control over film selection to local censorship
committees. In 1917, weary of constantly having to defend the content of
the films he exhibited against conservative attacks, the manager of the
Vogue Theater in Columbia, Tennessee, complained: "Film companies
should quit making suggestive and vulgar pictures, as the small town exhibitor has to fight ministers and local censors continually. Recently a
meeting was held here by one hundred of the best men of our town on
vice conditions, and suggestive pictures were talked about more than
anything else."[19]

By the 1920s, rural evangelicals saw the movies as visually representative of "the decadence of the cities," although movies were not the sole
scapegoat. Freer styles in women's clothing and behavior, jazz music on
the radio, magazines filled with suggestive lingerie advertisements and
stories chronicling the escapades of "sheiks" and flappers—all brought
new threats to what Ownby terms the "stability of evangelical culture
and newly intensified efforts to purify and preserve the virtues of that culture." Initially, conservative elements of southern communities had accepted movie shows, but the eventual encroachments of commercial culture turned evangelicals against the movies, an attitude that persisted
until midcentury.[20]

Moviegoing Practices in the West

In other regions of the United States, patterns of small-town settlement and population density varied more sharply, and these factors influenced moviegoing habits. The West had wider extremes of the rural and the urban than did the South or Midwest. Western settlement generally tended to be more urban than settlement in other sections of the country, with the majority of the population concentrated in cities on the Pacific Coast. The western region had fewer small towns than other areas of the country, with only 1.6 settlements of 2,500 population per 1,000 square miles versus 30 villages of 2,500 population per 1,000 square miles in the mid-Atlantic states. The South and Midwest had 7 and 10 villages of 2,500 population per 1,000 square miles, respectively.

Western farmers and cattle breeders were much more dispersed than their midwestern counterparts, and isolated ranchers' families saw movies only on rare occasions in the early 1910s. One young woman recalled how moviegoing cemented a sense of community; even then, movies were creating the mythology of a "wild west" as well as connecting isolated viewers to a larger popular culture of film:

> Having lived for a number of years on a ranch fifty miles from the nearest town, it was quite an event to attend a movie when I was a child. The first one I ever saw was one in which Tom Mix played. The entire community attended that show, for Tom Mix was a product of the cattle country in which the town lies. Of course, he played only a minor part, but the idea that I knew some one in the movies was enough to assure me that some day, too, I would be an actress.[21]

Sociologist Albert Blumenthal thought the movie theater was a welcome addition to the social life of the Montana mining towns he analyzed in his study *Small Town Stuff*. In many of the most isolated backwaters, nickelodeons were likely to represent for women, children, and teenagers the only gathering place open to them at night and the only alternative to the saloons, poolrooms, and members-only lodge halls that were available solely to the town's men. The movie show's service as a new and inexpensive source of family entertainment, or even as "something to do" in a town with limited diversions, aided the nickelodeons' acceptance by the town's elite.[22]

Many western towns owed their location and growth to the railroads. Being well-linked to transportation lines, many larger western towns and cities had become part of the national theatrical and vaudeville circuits by 1900. Indeed, until the 1930s, people in Portland and Seattle patronized vaudeville as much as the movies. Film cans were even easier to transport across long distances than were scenery, costumes, and companies of actors; this mobility helped bring the movies more quickly and more prominently into smaller, isolated western settlements and to mining and logging camps, where workers were ready to spend their incomes on entertainment.[23]

Western towns grew from a variety of settlement patterns that influenced townspeople's attitudes toward leisure and entertainment. Portland, Oregon, was founded by New Englanders who brought with them long-held conservative cultural traditions and suspicion of commercial amusements. Midwesterners with a fondness for opera houses formed the character of other towns. The large percentage of foreign-born settlers in western cities shaped urban culture in ways that made them similar to the ethnically diverse cities of the East and Midwest.[24]

Movie theaters in the West and Southwest, however, were often sites of white exhibitors' and audiences' discrimination against minority groups. A Galveston, Texas, exhibitor in 1908 proudly boasted in the trade press that middle-class and working-class movie audiences could mix democratically in western theaters. "On the inside, seated alongside of each other, a most cosmopolitan assembly is gathered. The banker and solid business man accompanied by his wife and children dressed in prevailing fashion, will move over and make room for a man in his working clothes or a sailor from one of the ships." Galveston's numerous African Americans and Mexican Americans were doubtless as absent from this exhibitor's theater audience as from his description.[25]

Mexican Americans were discouraged from entering El Paso's white movie theaters. Consequently, small nickelodeons sprang up after 1910 in El Paso's Hispanic ghettos. One Mexican American entrepreneur opened his first movie theater in the *barrio* in 1913 and by 1919 operated six theaters in El Paso plus four others across the Mexican border in Juarez; he became a major film distributor of American films in Mexico. "Carlos" Chaplin's appeal overcame cultural and language barriers, and American-made films constituted the great majority of those shown in Mexican American theaters, which also showed the occasional film produced in Mexico, Central America, or South America. Employees translated the English language subtitles into Spanish and projected the Spanish words

Façade of the Royal Theater, Nacogdoches, Texas, August 1908. Courtesy of Q. David Bowers.

on the screen below the original titles. This popular service received favorable comment in the Mexican American community press.[26]

Japanese American and Chinese American immigrants living on the West Coast maintained very private cultures that emphasized traditional customs and that attempted to limit or mediate their group members' contact with American popular culture. A few Japanese American movie theaters operated in southern California in the silent film era. The relatively small and impoverished agricultural community from which they could draw an audience and the difficulty and expense of procuring Japanese films and talented *benshi* (lecturers or "film explainers" who performed beside the screen) caused the theaters to limp along, showing mainstream American films and remaining barely profitable.[27]

Midwestern Film-Attendance Patterns

In Ohio, Michigan, Wisconsin, Iowa, Minnesota, and the eastern half of Nebraska, small-town dwellers and farm families in the nickelodeon era were much more likely than most of their rural southern counterparts to have regular access to the movies. The networks of small towns in midwestern states were well connected by railroads, trolley systems, and good roads. It was not unusual to find movie shows, even if they only operated one or two nights per week, in tiny Iowa villages of five hundred residents, since the theaters drew moviegoers from the vast surrounding countryside, which was heavily populated with farm families.

Larger trading centers in the Midwest attracted numerous nickelodeons. A traveling salesman wrote a letter to the *Springfield (Ohio) Sun* in 1907, complaining about the paucity of movie shows in the small manufacturing city of Springfield, which supposedly had but a single nickelodeon to serve forty thousand people. Other "up-to-date, live-wire towns" that he visited had plenty: 14 in Dayton, 8 in Muncie, 15 in Youngstown. Even Urbana, with only six thousand people, had 4 nickelodeons. "I have been in more than 400 of them in different towns and cities and I find them very entertaining," he continued, arguing that he preferred going to the movies to sitting alone in hotel rooms and that he found them a more respectable diversion than saloons for a middle-class family man.[28]

Prosperous midwestern farmers had much higher per capita incomes than southerners (at least until the end of the agricultural boom in the mid-1920s), and they were more likely to have discretionary funds for entertainment than southern sharecroppers. Midwesterners also had a much higher rate of automobile ownership than residents of any other region and were building better roads and streetcar lines, which would bring people into town to the movie theaters. A 1919 Paramount report noted that Iowa had the largest percentage of automobile-driving movie patrons of any state in the country. In 1926, 93 percent of land-owning Iowa farmers had cars, and 89 percent of tenant farmers in the state had use of automobiles. In the depression years, however, midwestern farmers would cut back on movie attendance. Surveys in 1935 and 1936

Nickelodeon exterior, Poultney, Ohio, n.d. Courtesy of Q. David Bowers.

showed that only 58 percent of the sampled farm families in Illinois and Iowa went to the movies versus 71 percent of people living in villages of the mid-Atlantic and north central states and 79 percent of small-city dwellers in the north central area.[29]

Midwestern farm women, as isolated in the nineteenth century as their southern counterparts, by the mid-1910s were more likely to use family automobiles to make frequent trips to town. New household technologies did not necessarily give farm women more leisure time, but they ended many home-production functions. Midwestern farm women and their daughters made more trips to in-town stores and local movie theaters as shopping became an increasingly important component of their work.[30]

There were pockets of religious prejudice against the movies and other commercial amusements in the Midwest, for instance, among conservative Swedish American settlers in Minnesota and Wisconsin and in the portions of Illinois, Indiana, Missouri, and Kansas that had originally been settled by southerners. A typical "poor show town" in Indiana was described by a struggling exhibitor as

a town of 11,000 population, badly scattered. About one-third social-
ists; and 2,000 foreigners. Prejudice still exists against motion pictures.
Ministers will not encourage pictures; superintendent of school op-
poses children attending film shows and tried to keep photoplay
magazines out of the library. Ministers oppose Sunday shows but
theatres operate nevertheless. The town is a factory center surrounded
by rich farm lands.

To more conservative small-town midwesterners, the nickelodeon might
represent amoral commercialized entertainment; but movies in the service
of education and religion were acceptable to them, and they flocked to
movie shows advertised as being "uplifting" and "high-class."[31]

The entire Midwest was not equally served by motion picture theaters. In the Great Plains region—the western halves of Kansas and Nebraska, and North and South Dakota—farms were so widely scattered
and population so sparse outside the few small market towns that settlers
had little access to church services or social gatherings, let alone regular
movie shows. The occasional performance of an itinerant film exhibitor
continued to be a special event. Great Plains farm women felt isolated
and culturally deprived. Whereas the movies could not physically reach
them, they enthusiastically adopted the more widespread mass media entertainment of radio broadcasting in the 1920s.[32]

African American migrants to midwestern cities like Pittsburgh, St.
Louis, and Kansas City unfortunately found social conditions little different from what they had left in the South. They were usually barred
from entering white movie theaters or were forced to sit in balconies.
"Segregation to the point of exclusion is the general policy in all of the
large theatres in Pittsburgh," reported sociologist Ira Reid, who noted
that one theater, the Nixon, was less discriminatory. In 1919, blacks sued
exhibitors in Kansas City to be allowed to sit in main auditoriums,
whereas exhibitors threatened to bar blacks altogether, as did most Missouri theaters. "Kansas exhibitors felt 'betwixt and between' the north
and south with reference to handling the negro problem," *Moving Picture World* reported, "for farther north negroes are frequently admitted
to the same sections as white people." Separate black amusement centers
grew up in the larger cities to serve the expanding African American population. In Pittsburgh, seven movie houses in the Hill District served area
blacks. Chicago had between seven and fourteen black movie theaters on
the Stroll, the amusement district of State Street.[33]

Small-Town Moviegoing
in New England and Mid-Atlantic States

In New England communities, the strength of the Puritan tradition among Congregationalists and northern Baptists made many residents of small-town and rural Connecticut, western Massachusetts, Vermont, New Hampshire, and Maine suspicious of commercial entertainments into the twentieth century. A conservative popular culture, emanating from traditional Protestant values and old-line Yankee thrift, served to make the presentation of what amusements did exist, such as lecture series and lyceums, as wholesome, educational, and attractive as possible to overcome traditional prejudice. Movies entered small-town New England, then, as part of a long struggle between different interest groups to influence the popular acceptance of commercial amusements.[34]

Still, nearly every small town in New England had one or more community spaces—town hall, opera house, school gymnasium, or fraternal lodge hall—in which local groups and traveling entertainers could perform. County fairs also abounded, and they served as sites for the new movie shows. As in upstate New York, itinerant film exhibition flourished, and then a number of small town nickelodeons opened. The five thousand people of Amherst, a western Massachusetts farming town with two colleges and several factories, saw many itinerant shows and had regular nickelodeon shows in the town hall. The shows were enthusiastically patronized by farmers, merchants' families, and the occasionally rowdy students. Movie shows were so popular in Amherst that local exhibitors dug out a sloping floor in an old horse stable to create a second movie theater. Four or five additional movie theaters did good business in nearby Northampton, forcing the regionally renowned Academy of Music's theatrical stock company to fold in favor of film screenings.[35]

In Maine, Yankee merchants, part-time farmers, and French Canadian entrepreneurs made up the majority of movie show owners. Tarbell's Theater in Smyrna Mills was operated by a man who was also the local undertaker—his funeral parlor did double duty as a picture parlor. A photographer in the small village of Mattawamkeag (population five hundred) simultaneously operated a nickelodeon, a skating rink, and a photography studio with the assistance of his sons and daughters, who helped with projection, took tickets, and played piano in the tiny theater.[36]

Exterior of the Nickel Theater, Bangor, Maine, n.d. Courtesy of Q. David Bowers.

New England small-town movie theaters also had ethnic audiences. French Canadian Catholic workers migrated to the small towns and larger industrial centers of New England, ultimately constituting 20 to 25 percent of the region's population and creating a counterpoint to the conservative Protestant attitudes and values of older settlement groups. In larger cities like Burlington, Vermont, French Canadian immigrant entrepreneurs opened movie theaters just as they had earlier started grocery stores and other community services. American silent films, rather than French imports, were the norm, but at least among this group, the American films did not act as agents of sweeping cultural change among the young. Exposure to English-speaking culture appears to have helped the young men of second- and third-generation French Canadian immigrant families in Burlington learn to read and speak English more rapidly than their parents; but French-speaking culture was so strongly reinforced in the home, at school, and in social activities that French was still spoken by nearly 10 percent of all Vermont residents as late as 1970. Although the movies proved a great aid in helping young men in this group of French Canadians to adapt to American culture, the movies did not seem to conflict with, or to completely separate children from, traditional culture.[37]

The French Canadians, like other Catholic immigrants to New England (Irish, Italians, and Greeks) held different standards of behavior for their boys and girls, which influenced how much exposure young people had to the movies. Parents exerted only loose control over the social activities of their young men. Boys often earned their own money for the movies through odd jobs or outside employment, and their families allowed them a certain amount of freedom to roam the town's amusement district.

On the other hand, French Canadian families often restricted or forbade movie attendance and other public interactions for their unmarried daughters. One typical case from Maine juvenile court documents in the late 1920s concerned a troubled French Canadian girl living in a small Maine mill town. She was repeatedly denied permission by her mother to attend the movies. The girl rebelled against the conservative restriction, not only continuing to loiter at the movie theater despite her mother's injunctions but eventually running away with the theater manager. When the local courts remanded the young woman to a private reform school on delinquency charges, she suddenly found herself exposed to a steady diet of movies, shown as part of a weekly program of officially approved institutional activities for the female inmates. Her mother must have been most disconcerted. Traditional moral values that shielded young women from adult culture—values that the French Canadians of New England and other ethnic and religious groups attempted to uphold—were often at odds with both the "pulls" of American consumer culture and the "pushes" of changing middle-class social standards and reformers' programs.[38]

The mid-Atlantic region, as demonstrated earlier in the example of Cooperstown, New York, had the highest concentration of small-town settlement of any area of the country and the largest number of movie theaters in small towns. Small-town inhabitants of the mid-Atlantic states felt the influence of the region's big cities. They were more flexible in accepting movies and other commercialized entertainment into their social life than some of the more conservative southerners or midwesterners. Even so, movie exhibition there, as elsewhere, was not without conflict. Small-town exhibitors and the guardians of public morality in the mid-Atlantic region were at loggerheads over the problems of Sunday motion picture exhibition and byzantine local film-censorship regulations.

Conservative ministers and small-town social critics in the mid-Atlantic states sought the passage of blue laws and the enforcement of colonial-era statutes to keep movie theaters and other commercial amusements closed on the Sabbath. Film exhibitors, however, rated Sunday one of their most profitable business days; they continually fought to stay open, incurring fines and even jail sentences. This contest between religious groups and film exhibitors for the allegiance of small-town movie audiences, which was played out in communities in the southern, midwestern, and mid-Atlantic regions, will be further explored herein.[39]

In looking across the country at the situation of some seven thousand nickelodeons outside the big cities and at their nonurban audiences, we see that while most people had access to the movies some groups had relatively more opportunities to attend them—the men and boys of some ethnic groups and the small-town folk of the midwestern, New England, and mid-Atlantic regions. Other groups had relatively less exposure to movies, such as southern blacks, ethnic women and girls, evangelical Christians and other conservative religious society members, and most farm families of the South and West. Outside the South, small-town whites who did not belong to the most conservative religious sects had as much access to the movies as did city folk. And although urban commentators of the day maintained that the movie show's chief appeal was to women and children, we have seen that outside the largest urban areas, women and girls could face more hurdles of social custom and economic restraint to entering movie theaters than did their male kin. While there were very few people who had never seen motion pictures, there was much variety among people of different regions in how large a role movie shows played in their social lives.

"Let's Go in to a Picture Show"

The Nickelodeon

The nickelodeon era has been described as a brief but intense period of business boom, gaudy showmanship, and tumultuous change in film exhibition, wedged between film's beginnings and the rise of the star system, Hollywood, and picture palaces. Stretching the nickelodeon era to its limits would introduce it in 1904 or 1905 with the opening of the earliest stationary urban motion picture theaters. The period's closing is a matter of debate. It might be said to end in 1915 with the release of *The Birth of a Nation* and other spectacular American-made feature films; or in 1914 with the opening of the magnificent Strand Theater in New York City, one of the first true picture palaces; or, further back, in 1912 with the rise to prominence of small-time vaudeville theaters, the hybrid of movie and variety shows. Some have suggested the end of the nickelodeon theater era began almost at the start, with the opening of William Fox's elaborate, upscale Dewey Theater on Union Square in Manhattan in 1908.

From an urban film-exhibition perspective, the nickelodeon era appears momentary. But outside the big cities, many aspects of the era had longer duration. The buildings in which nickelodeon shows were held—opera houses, town halls, converted stores—were in service much longer as community movie theaters in small towns than in the cities. The small-town theaters, exhibitors, audiences, programs, and the entire spirit of the operation retained what might be called a nickelodeon flavor throughout the silent film era.

In 1908, an estimated eight thousand nickelodeon theaters showed motion pictures across the United States. By 1910, that number had mushroomed to ten thousand, with a full seven thousand nickelodeons operating outside the big cities on small-town Main Streets, at country crossroads, at lakeside amusement parks, and at summer beach resorts. Nickelodeons could be started in anything from remodeled stores; older existing opera houses and town halls; spaces cordoned off by curtains or temporary walls in hotels, candy shops, or barrooms; newly built theater structures; and even rehabilitated livery stables. No matter what the structure's origins, to early film audiences across the country, the nickelodeon theater building materially symbolized the excitement, novelty, and mystery of the movie show. All parts of its outer shell were put to use in attracting viewers, from its evocative name written over the entrance to the blinking, glowing lights on the theater's façade and the other colorful exterior decorations. The continuous jangle of its automatic pianos, phonographs, and barkers attracted the notice of passersby. Patrons perused the nickelodeon's melodramatic, vibrant lithographed posters and other advertising materials filling theater lobbies and strewn along the sidewalk in sandwich-board displays.

The nickelodeon movie show was composed of a variety of narrative films of one and two reels in length with melodramatic or comic themes; other film subjects, in the tradition of the earlier itinerant shows, featured travel scenes and visual tricks. The film exhibition was still interspersed with live entertainment such as illustrated songs or a vaudeville act or two. A pianist or a two- or three-member musical ensemble provided simple accompaniment to the movies and performers. At times, exhibitors incorporated into their programs elaborate sound effects; "talkers" creating dialogue behind the screen; hand-colored or tinted films; programs with holiday, local, or other special themes; and a variety of hometown entertainers.

By 1915 in many big cities and smaller cities and towns, the standard movie show evolved into a program centered on a "feature" film of three reels or more in length that "starred" advertised actors. A new generation of urban theaters being built to replace the nickelodeons was larger, seating five hundred to fifteen hundred patrons and having more elegant interior decorations, a corps of ushers, a larger orchestra, and admission prices three to ten times the nickelodeon's price of admission.[1]

In all parts of the country, nickelodeon theaters—urban, small town, and rural—had some obvious differences of decoration and operation, but they shared even more similarities. Some nickelodeons were sparsely adorned, but others had façades garnished with an excess of plaster ornamentation and poster advertising. Some exhibitors eked out a living operating a nickelodeon while working in other businesses, whereas others raked in fortunes due to bonanza locations. Although some distinctions in theater operation and ornamentation manifested themselves in accordance with individual exhibitors' business skills and the communities' tastes, the nickelodeon form could accommodate the majority of these differences.

Spurred by the get-rich-quick hopes of prospective exhibitors and the ease of entry into the field, the proliferation of nickelodeon theaters across the nation was swift. Thomas Tally boasted of starting the boom with his Electric Theater, which opened in Los Angeles in 1902. Hale's Tours (train cars outfitted as small theaters in which "passengers" viewed travel films) were a briefly profitable novelty originating in Kansas City and at the St. Louis World's Fair in 1904. John Harris and Harry Davis claimed credit for originating the term *nickelodeon* with their Nickelodeon Theater, which did fabulous business in Pittsburgh starting in 1905. The huge profits earned by the so-called first urban nickelodeon exhibitors were widely reported, and perhaps were exaggerated.[2]

Between 1907 and 1910, astonished observers counted more than 100 nickelodeons each in St. Louis, San Francisco, and Chicago. Manhattan alone had at least 300, and there were more than 450 in the combined boroughs. Since they were all independent, "mom and pop" operations, no one knew exactly how many existed. Barriers to entering the film exhibition field were low. Novices quickly had a wealth of advice literature to consult, from published guidebooks for prospective nickelodeon owners and how-to manuals on projector operation to the recommendations of suppliers of projectors, seats, screens, and decorative pressed-tin theater façades, all of which could be found in the exhibitors' trade press. By the late 1910s, when movie theater censuses became more precise, nearly 20,000 places were showing motion pictures at least one night a week. The quick and thorough blanketing of urban and small-town America with nickelodeons made movies a shared and almost inescapable part of popular culture.[3]

Despite the many similarities of their nickelodeon operations, urban and small-town exhibitors catered to their audiences' interests in significantly different ways. The tumultuous changes rocking the film industry in the mid-1910s did not impact big-city and small-town nickelodeons at the same time or in equal measure, and greater differences between urban and small-town moviegoing experiences began to appear. During the nickelodeon era, these differences were contained within the broad boundaries of the nickelodeon movie show. Big-city and small-town moviegoing experiences in this formative era were separate but linked, and in many ways were equal. After the nickelodeon period this would increasingly not be so.

Although New York City's nickelodeons, which drew the bulk of positive and negative publicity, were located mainly in the Upper and Lower East Side's tenement districts, this was not a common pattern elsewhere. As Russell Merritt has noted, in other cities and towns "they customarily opened in business districts on the outer edge of the slums, fringing white collar shopping centers, accessible to blue-collar audiences but even closer to middle class trade." Nickelodeon theaters were squeezed tightly into rented store space among shops, grocery stores, offices, apartment buildings, barrooms, garages, and the police and fire stations of Main Streets. Urban nickelodeon theaters largely depended on transients—shoppers, downtown workers, and other passersby—for patronage, whereas small-town theaters needed to attract the attention of a large portion of the community. Both types of exhibitors decorated their theaters primarily to draw customers in from the street, luring them with as many eye-catching exterior and interior decorations and ballyhoo as their needs demanded and budgets and imaginations allowed. The names of nickelodeon theaters illustrated brash showmanship, an appeal to respectability, and the mix of old and new entertainment forms still found in the small-town shows.[4]

Nickelodeon Nomenclature

From the days of the earliest itinerant moving picture company performances, exhibitors deliberated on what they should call this new form of entertainment, which incorporated elements of the lyceum, vaudeville, penny arcade, dime museum, and tent show. When traveling shows became stationary, promoting motion pictures as a novelty would no longer suffice. Exhibitors thought that having a unique name for the product and its site of exhibition would pique public interest, evoke the excitement of the moviegoing experience, and bolster the conservative middle-class patrons' confidence in the good character of the show. Monikers bestowed on the earliest urban motion picture theaters by social critics and the amusement-seeking public—"nickel dumps" and "cheap shows"— were considered highly uncomplimentary by those film exhibitors who possessed pretensions toward legitimacy in the entertainment field. *Cinematograph,* the French term for a motion picture and a movie theater, seemed too cumbersome to most Americans, although another word adapted from the French that did satisfy many exhibitors was *nickelodeon.* It combined the Greek word for theater, *odeon,* which had been in wide use in Europe, with the name of the coin that was the price of admission. The "five-cent theater" sounded somewhat more refined when called the "nickelodeon," or at least so exhibitors hoped.[5]

Searching for an even more refined show-place name than *nickelodeon,* the Essanay Film Manufacturing Company of Chicago in 1910 sponsored a contest for exhibitors. They sought "a term which would be easily remembered, descriptive in character, simple and appropriate." The judges chose the name *photoplay* from among the exhibitors' twenty-five hundred submissions. The winning name was supposedly coined by Edgar Strakosch, a Sacramento, California, theater owner whose own nickelodeons were named Dreamland, Bijou, and Wonderland. Runners-up included *kinorama, mutodramic,* and *photodrome.*[6]

The film industry trade press remained skeptical about the transformative ability of new names. *Moving Picture World* thought it would be much more dignified for movie show places to combine the traditional name *theater* with one of "an enormous fund of names" available that would individualize the house. While *photoplay* would see some use as an elegant term for the films themselves and as the name of a well-known fan magazine, most exhibitors chose to stick with the descriptive name *theater* for their show places.[7]

An examination of the variety of nickelodeon theater names coined by exhibitors to create favorable associations in prospective patrons' minds with the attractions of the movie show provides tantalizing glimpses into the impact of the moviegoing experience on this first generation of film audiences. The names of small-town theaters, similar in many ways to those used by their urban counterparts, convey some of the novel appeal that movies held for nickelodeon patrons and also illustrate the developing new ways for audiences to think about commercial amusement as a component of daily life.[8]

Many nickelodeon owners attempted to cement ties with their local communities by choosing names that created images of the movie theater as a friendly, familiar gathering place close to home. In the cities, creating a local identity was vital for exhibitors who were new to town and who were unknown to local residents. Some exhibitors played on their patrons' loyalties to their neighborhood, town, suburb, or state by naming theaters after their localities. In larger cities, nickelodeon exhibitors associated their theaters' names with landmarks like parks, plazas, or streets and found the names to be easily remembered by their patrons, who might themselves be rural newcomers to the city or recent immigrants.

For movie show operators in small towns, drawing on and furthering established entertainment traditions and local allegiances often meant retaining the name of the original building. Thus a new nickelodeon might be called the Town Hall, Opera House, Lyceum, or Auditorium. Although many of these town hall shows changed names as "real" movie theaters were built, through the 1930s in some of the smallest villages, people continued to attend movie shows in their opera houses. Sometimes the old opera house was just given a new name. It was significant for Cooperstown residents when the Bowne Opera House was renamed the Star Theater; the range of community activities once supported in the space had officially narrowed to focus on the movie show.

To further strengthen the neighborhood theme, nickelodeons might be named the Home Theater, the Community Theater, or the Family Moving Picture Parlor. These comfortable, domestic-sounding theater names offered patrons an image of moviegoing as a daily habit instead of an extraordinary experience. The movie theater, the name promised, could function as their Home away from home.[9]

Other nickelodeon names such as Superba, Ideal, Peerless, Elite, Bon Ton, and Unique assured skeptical neighbors of the high quality of the moving picture show and its appropriateness for family viewing. Sometimes theaters were named for other cities associated with high moral and entertainment standards. Movie theaters and dry-goods stores named The Boston could be found everywhere in the Midwest and West, and in the South the name New York christened stores and theaters that wished to be associated with big-city importance and up-to-dateness. Chicago, besides having a Boston Theater, was also home to a California Theater years before the film industry moved there. Perhaps this name was an allusion to exoticism, to the state's mythic westernness, or to a promise of idyllic living amid sunshine and orange groves.[10]

Other names stressed the pleasure and escapism that tied moviegoing to the expanding world of leisure activities and consumer culture. Many theaters were named Bid-a-Wee, Pastime, Idle Hour, Amuse-U, Amusea, Comedy, Clown, Gaiety, Pleasant Hour, or Revelry. Baltimore had a Teddy Bear Moving Picture Parlor, whose name may have been chosen to capitalize on the popularity of President Theodore Roosevelt and the stuffed toy he inspired. Miriam Hansen notes the use of teddy bears by exhibitors to draw women into consumer culture with toy giveaways and references to frivolity in the theater. The association between dreaming, fantasy, or escape and the viewing of films in darkened rooms was clear to many early theater operators; the name Bijou Dream was adopted for theaters in every urban and small-town setting imaginable. Dreamland, Fairyland, Aladdin, Paradise, Avalon, Eden, and Wonderland were names found on nickelodeons from rural Maine to Des Moines, Iowa, and the West Coast. Following the lead of the Essanay contest, some nickelodeon owners gave their show places names emphasizing the novelty of the new form of entertainment, such as the Electric Theater, Arcade, Novelty, Theatorium, and Cameraphone.[11]

Exotic, foreign place names like Alhambra, Alcazar, or Valencia could be found on nickelodeon marquees in many states, their owners tying in to the first wave of popularity of Spanish and Mexican architecture and culture. In this era, Americans increasingly embraced Mexico as a place of intense sensory experiences—colorful sights, sounds, and tastes—that romantically appealed to those in search of new native inspirations for decoration. Within a few years the fad spread, and movie theater owners across the country adopted Mayan, Mediterranean, Arabic, and Egyptian names and exotic decorative schemes for their ever more elaborate new theaters.[12]

The flashing lights of the nickelodeons' façades and the glowing, pulsating screens that seemed to mesmerize movie audiences were also potent metaphors that managers used for theater names such as Star, Gem, Bijou (French for "jewel"), Aurora, Crescent, Crystal, Comet, Elektra, and Sun. Mythical gods and goddesses, magic, nature, and the supernatural all suggested fresh possibilities for names, for example, the Isis (in Denver and Augusta, Kansas) and the Apollo (in Chillicothe, Ohio.)[13]

Some theater owners dipped into a cache of names already popular

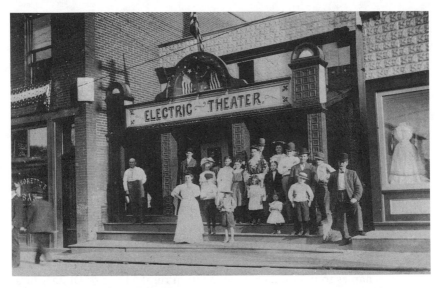

The staff and extended family of the Electric Theater, East St. Louis, Illinois, 1910. Courtesy of Q. David Bowers.

with vaudeville and legitimate theater owners to convey ideas of elegance, European grandeur, spectacle, and respectability, like the Royal, Queen, Princess, Regency, Rex, Empire, Empress, Monarch, Victoria, Strand, Palace, Rialto, Majestic, Lyric, Grand, Century, and Orpheum. A small one-hundred-seat movie theater in Worthington, Indiana, was christened the Hippodrome by an exhibitor with either huge ambitions or a wry sense of humor. It was one of the smallest of well over a hundred nickelodeons across the nation to ape New York City's famous fifty-five-hundred-seat Hippodrome, in 1905 the largest show house in the world.[14]

Paradoxically, while some film exhibitors aimed for elegance, others shunned the thought of connecting moviegoing with luxury, expense, and extravagance. The latter chose names that conjured images of their theaters as informal gathering places, inexpensive, affordable, and likely to be patronized every night rather than just on special occasions. They named their theaters the Nickel, Half-Dime, Nickelette, Big Nickel, Nickeldom, Nickeldome, Nickel-Odeon; and hundreds were simply called the Nickelodeon.[15]

Identification with a celebrity crept into a nickelodeon's name on occasion. Several theaters, such as Baltimore's Bunny Picture Theater,
which opened in 1913, were named to honor the popular Vitagraph
Company comedian John Bunny. When Bunny died suddenly in 1915,
movie theaters in many regions were renamed to commemorate him.
Movie theaters in several cities were named The Blue Mouse to associate
themselves with a famous old Broadway production of that name. But,
although a Baltimore exhibitor in the early 1910s named his house after
his favorite Edison Manufacturing Company film actress, Gertrude Mc-
Coy, the practice of using celebrity names did not catch on. The use of
novelty names for movie theaters declined as the more "serious" names
evoking elegance began to dominate lists of theaters. There were fewer
Bide-a-Wees and Amuseas, and more Strands. Hundreds of exhibitors in
the early period had proudly named their theaters after themselves, but
by the end of the nickelodeon era, family names on theater marquees indicated corporate or chain theaters such as the Stanley, Blank, and
Saenger. In the early 1920s many new theaters in big cities were named for
the film producers or distributors who owned them—Paramount, Fox,
Loews. By the mid-1920s it became rare enough to be commented upon
in the trade press when a new movie theater took its owner's name.[16]

The life span of most nickelodeon names in both small towns and
big cities was brief. Many of the novelty- or celebrity-named theaters
changed their appellations again as soon as the promotional benefits
waned. Many exhibitors altered a nickelodeon's name whenever it was
bought or sold, or at the owner's whim (making accurate censuses of a
town's early movie theaters difficult, for turnovers among owners were
frequent). Some nickelodeons seem to have assumed a new identity with
each new coat of paint.

Theater owners took the naming of nickelodeons seriously, thinking
that the name gave audiences their first impression of a house, that it
could convey some idea about what the moviegoing experience was like,
and that it lent a theater some distinctiveness. *Moving Picture World*
counseled theater owners on the importance of the atmosphere created
by a theater's name and environment to the patrons' moviegoing experience. "It is a wise exhibitor who realizes the importance of helping his
pictures to cast their spell. The picture 'fan' wants to be allowed to drift
comfortably into 'illusion land.'" The trade paper's allusions to make-
believe worlds stemmed from the same impulse of nickelodeon owners to
name their theaters Wonderland or Dreamland. Throughout the silent

film era, exhibitors created a vocabulary to describe the experience of moviegoing and the environments in which it occurred.[17]

Nickelodeon Exteriors

Selling the show, in both small-town and urban nickelodeons, began in the immediacy of the theater building's front entrance. "To a certain extent, a theater is its own best advertisement," wrote a columnist for the exhibitor's journal *Nickelodeon* in 1909. "A picturesque and pleasing exterior, abundantly illuminated with a multitude of incandescent lights, constitutes advertising of the first order."[18]

Bare white incandescent lightbulbs were installed across the small façades of most nickelodeons; lightbulbs outlining doorways and arches, and spelling out the theater's name, were arranged in a celebration of the still-intriguing technology of electricity. The small-town middle class especially envied the many bright lights of the big city; this fact was not lost on either rural or urban film exhibitors, who incorporated as many electric elements into their theater exteriors as possible. "If the house is to catch the crowds, especially when there is so much competition, there must be an attractive front," a 1907 *Chicago Tribune* article advised nickelodeon owners. "Always there must be extensive arrangements for light, and a sign, fairly scintillant with electric bulbs, must extend out over the sidewalk, where it can be seen for blocks." *Moving Picture World* counseled novice exhibitors that "as to lights on the front, aside from expense of operation, there can scarcely be too brilliant an illumination within reasonable limits." The miniature Great White Way of illuminated shop signs and nickelodeon façades made Main Streets resemble Broadway or Coney Island in their residents' eyes, particularly in contrast to the enveloping evening darkness in small-town residential neighborhoods, where many homes had no electricity until the 1920s.[19]

Nickelodeon exhibitors reveled in the excesses of late Victorian decor, adorning their glowing theater façades with painted pressed-tin ceilings and walls crammed with ornamental plaster caryatids, cupids, mermaids, and other gewgaws chosen from the pages of the Decorators Supply Company catalog. There were a few boundaries of tastefulness, nevertheless, for conscientious nickelodeon owners, who were warned that "colored lights . . . seldom look well on a front. Somehow they seem to suggest cheapness and tawdriness."[20]

The Star Theater, Algonac, Michigan, sports bare white lightbulbs on its plain façade and sign, n.d. Courtesy of Q. David Bowers.

A 1913 juvenile novel produced by the Edward Stratemeyer Syndicate, *The Motion Picture Chums' First Venture, or Opening a Photo Playhouse in Fairlands,* captured the excitement generated in small towns by movie theater façades with a description of the opening of the first nickelodeon run by the plucky young film exhibitors-cum-detectives:

> [A]lthough Pep simply pressed a switch of the electric-lighting apparatus, it was with a sense of as much importance as if he was announcing the opening of the Panama Canal. Immediately the front of the new Wonderland burst into a dazzling flood of radiance. The biggest and best electric sign in Fairlands presented its face of fire to the public, glowed, was blank, flashed up again, and began its mission of inviting and guiding the public to the motion picture show.[21]

If these nickelodeon displays were awe inspiring to small-town dwellers, illuminated buildings and flashing, electrified advertising signs had become unexceptional sights for urban dwellers in the shopping districts of large cities by the 1910s. The big city's nickelodeon exteriors joined other urban displays such as billboards, neon signs, and brilliantly lit department store windows and façades to create what historian William Leach has called "commercial guides through the spectacle of American abundance." The big cities' nickelodeon fronts often boasted huge electric and painted signs and three-dimensional terra-cotta figures of butterflies, nymphs, or the Statue of Liberty. Story-high vertical signs overhung the sidewalk with the theater's name spelled out in blinking lights, and rooftop signs attracted passersby, on foot or in streetcars, from blocks away. A film trade journal reporter wrote of the small-town, middle-class visitors' gaping wonder at the transformed urban amusement and shopping districts:

> How different it must seem to a man or woman who has not visited the city for, say, five years—nay, even less—to come here, and in the evening stroll down the avenues and streets. To see tall buildings outlined with lights, huge doorways filled with lighted figures, brilliant paintings, and the ever-present phonograph. But to see the outlay of lights and noise and color is to go back to the Midway at a fair.[22]

Once drawn to the theater front, potential nickelodeon patrons had to be convinced that the show inside was not to be missed. Posters illustrating dramatic moments from current films and upcoming attractions were plastered everywhere—on the fronts of theater buildings, in wall frames, in lobbies, on sign boards, on sidewalk easels, and on neighborhood billboards and fences. Movie posters, like advertising for other consumer goods, heightened the excitement and expectation surrounding the movie show, adding layers of melodramatic, colorful meaning to the brief black-and-white films seen by viewers. Instead of using enlarged versions of the more prosaically posed photographs taken on a movie production set, exhibitors favored the circus poster style—boldly colored lithographs of artists' interpretations of a film's most exciting, sensual, or dramatic scenes. Sometimes nickelodeon-era movie posters—being stock melodramatic illustrations of cowboy-and-Indian fights, shipwreck scenes, out-of-control locomotives, and heroines dangling from precipices— contained more action than the films themselves. Their lurid exaggerations or outright misrepresentations of risqué or violent film action constituted a source of social critics' movie censorship campaigns.[23]

Nickelodeon movie posters and exterior decorations were, for many patrons, the most fascinating elements of the movie theater's contributions to street culture. One Baltimore man remembered childhood days spent entranced by the posters and façade of his neighborhood theater. "Present day youngsters would probably laugh at the looks of the New Gem. But to me it was completely fascinating, what with its painted wreaths and flowers on the outside, its murals of Swiss mountain scenes—and a thrilling painting of the Titanic disaster—on the walls." More than just an enticement into the movie show, lobby decorations and action-packed posters created a spectacle in front of the theater and on the sidewalk that was free to view, at least until the theater manager hustled loiterers away.[24]

Music, verbal banter, and noise were also elements of the nickelodeon's outdoor advertising scheme. Many exhibitors incorporated the trumpetlike horn of a phonograph into their theater façades so that the horn projected its sound toward the street. Other managers had electrically operated automatic pianos installed in such a manner that they could be heard outside as well as inside. Some early motion picture exhibitors stationed barkers outside their theaters' front entrances to coax people inside, and others sent "ballyhoo wagons" to surrounding neighborhoods to promote the show with loud announcements and music. Reports in the exhibitors' trade press noted that, in several cities, neighboring shopkeepers were furious about the obtrusive music and fought to mute nickelodeons' outdoor phonographs. The city of St. Louis passed an ordinance that required anyone desirous of setting up a nickelodeon to obtain signed permission from the owners of neighboring stores and homes, not only next door but also across the street, stating that they would not object to the noise. As phonographs became less of an attention getter, however, most theaters reduced their outdoor use.[25]

The precedent for the attractive nickelodeon exterior as customer lure came from the realm of amusement. Circuses, dime museums, and traveling theatrical troupes plastered the towns they visited with posters, and they used handbills, barkers, and other ballyhoo. Despite their advertising efforts, these shows were often of brief duration in any one town. Nickelodeon managers also adopted promotional techniques from neighboring retail stores, which experimented with decoration of an increasingly theatrical nature, similarly contributing color, excitement, and new, unfulfilled longings to street culture. "It is all well enough to let the store show [nickelodeon] man make the circus display outside his place to attract the crowd," *Moving Picture World* advised new exhibitors. "Many legitimate business places that are not in the amusement field do that." Thus motion picture theaters blended advertising tactics from both amusement and retail sources to attract their audiences, helping to blur the boundaries in consumer culture between selling and entertainment.[26]

Nickelodeon Interiors

Film exhibitors concentrated their decorative efforts on their nickelodeon theaters' exteriors, paying little attention to interior appointments. As one surveyor reported, "[F]ew nickelodeons, no matter how gaudy or alluring on the outside, can be described as more than puritanically simple within. They are little more than academic halls, given over to a direct and vital appeal to the eye from the screen alone." Much of the reason for the plainness of nickelodeon interiors stemmed from exhibitors' practicality; nickelodeon-era film projectors required complete darkness in order to achieve a sharp, bright image on the screen. Some exhibitors kept their theaters pitch black all day and evening, causing patrons to stumble up and down the aisles while trying to find an empty seat among the closely packed rows of kitchen chairs, benches, or theater seats in the little halls that seated between fifty and three hundred viewers. There seemed to be little need or room for interior decoration under the circumstances.[27]

Dark nickelodeon auditoriums posed not only something of a safety hazard but, in the opinion of social critics, also a moral hazard. Wild rumors circulated in some cities that nefarious evildoers stuck young women with syringes or narcotic-tipped pins in the dark theaters and spirited them away into white slavery. In real life, dark movie theaters were popular rendezvous for young courting couples. Inevitably, this aspect of the moviegoing experience was seized upon by popular culture. In 1909, Albert Von Tilzer, a prolific Tin Pan Alley composer, wrote, together with Junie McCree, a follow-up song to his recent hit, "Take Me Out to the Ball Game," entitled "Let's Go in to a Picture Show." Like the earlier song, the chorus of this catchy, waltz-tempo tune is also sung by a spirited young woman who wants to be "out with the crowd" having fun; what is different here is that Mary also appreciates the nickelodeon theater's dark interiors.

> Let's go in to a picture show,
> Because I love it so.
> On the square, there ain't anywhere

Audience in the auditorium of the Boody Theater, location and date unknown.
Courtesy of Q. David Bowers.

> I would rather go.
> There's where ev'ry girl and her beau
> Always go to spoon, you know.
> So let's go in to a picture show,
>   for a good old time.[28]

As Mary convinces her reluctant boyfriend Johnny to give the nickelodeon show a try, she sings rejoicingly that "the house is so dark when
you start in to spark, [with] no fear of lights." Von Tilzer had never actually been to a baseball game before he wrote his famous song; if he
never attended the movies, either, then he was at least attuned to popular
comment on some of the nickelodeon's attractions. Most Tin Pan Alley
songs about new inventions, such as "(Come Away with Me, Lucille) in
My Merry Oldsmobile," celebrated their possibilities for amorous encounters. "Let's Go in to a Picture Show" acclaimed the nickelodeon
both as a site of Main Street community activity "on the square" and as
a semiprivate rendezvous for romance.

Exhibitors responded to reformers' and critics' complaints about the "dangerous" dark conditions of nickelodeon interiors in a variety of ways. They experimented with more efficient projectors that did not require complete darkness and with systems of indirect interior lighting that did not interfere with the audience's view of the screen during the show. As competing movie theaters became larger and more elegant at the end of the nickelodeon era, exhibitors staffed them with corps of uniformed ushers, who wielded flashlights and delivered polite but firm admonitions to calm the behavior of intimate couples.[29]

Even when small-town middle-class and working-class patrons saw nickelodeon theater interiors with the houselights turned up, they seemed to be satisfied with the plain interiors of their towns' movie show houses. Many of their opera houses and town halls were similarly unadorned. In the larger cities, however, the middle class, accustomed to the interior opulence of department stores, restaurants, hotels, and legitimate theaters, all of which began to outdo one another in luxurious decoration in the late 1890s, expected elaborate decoration in places of amusement. The ever increasing elegance of the postnickelodeon picture palaces in big cities and of the next generation of small-town theaters resulted from the desires of exhibitors to seek increased urban middle-class patronage and to outdo their rivals.

Airdomes: Outdoor Nickelodeons

In the summer months, film exhibitors set up airdomes in vacant city lots, at amusement parks, and on small towns' Main Streets. Bert Cook's exhibition of films up against the side of the bank building in Cooperstown was a typical small-town airdome arrangement. Airdomes were, in essence, roofless nickelodeons, offering little of the privacy that Mary so enjoyed when she went "in to the picture show" or that later generations of moviegoers would find in the enclosed automobiles of drive-in theaters. Airdomes developed as a response to the seasonal rhythms that strongly influenced film exhibition during the nickelodeon era. Longstanding theatrical tradition in the days before air-conditioning caused both urban and small-town opera houses, itinerant companies such as Cook and Harris, and vaudeville and legitimate theaters to close during the hot months of summer. Small, poorly ventilated nickelodeons did not draw many patrons in July and August, either. Film industry trade jour-

Drawing of an airdome audience, from *Moving Picture Story Magazine,* August 1913, p. 108. Author's collection.

nals offered suggestions such as slipcovering theater seats in white fabric for a cool look, decorating the exterior and interior with arctic scenes, spraying perfume across the auditorium to quell body odors, installing extra fans, or exhibiting only comedy films in the hope that the audience would laugh and forget the heat. Nevertheless, most nickelodeons either struggled along with sparse audiences or closed until September.[30]

In larger cities, airdomes operated on rooftops or in vacant lots; in smaller towns, any available land on Main Street or out at the edge of town would suffice. Temporary walls were built around the space, folding chairs or wooden benches were set up, a sheet was stretched against a wall or fence, a piano was rolled into place near the screen, and the airdome was ready for business. Some resembled elaborately decorated beer gardens, but others looked quite makeshift. The number of airdomes varied by region. St. Louis boasted over one hundred; Baltimore and New York City had only two or three inside the city limits. Open-air movie shows could be found, however, at many amusement parks only a short streetcar ride from town and at campgrounds, resorts, and beaches.

The airdome was an imperfect answer to film exhibitors' summer problems, as shows could not begin until night fell. Too, rain was a threat, and many Washington, D.C., airdomes reportedly went bankrupt after a summer of rain outs. Urban airdomes also had problems of keeping out nonpaying viewers. Neighbors hung out their windows and small boys climbed trees to see a free show. Ella Lott Goodman and her husband operated the Ideal Theater in the working-class Hampden neighborhood of Baltimore. They also ran an airdome in the summers in an empty lot across the street from the theater. She remembered that "the management's main worry was bad weather. Insurance to cover this was prohibitive because of its cost." The Goodmans gambled and remained uninsured each summer, herding their damp audience into the theater across the street when showers interrupted a performance. The move inside did little to improve the audience's humor, as Mrs. Goodman remembered it. "The patrons were never satisfied with having to spend hot summer evenings inside the Ideal. . . . They used to protest quite strongly. It was a job keeping them in hand, especially when they started throwing things around. People in the theater were sometimes injured. Exhibitions like this led to the Ideal's nickname, the 'Madhouse.'" New technologies of physical comfort, such as the early mechanical air-conditioning systems, first installed in movie theaters in Birmingham and Chicago in 1917, helped to overcome seasonal barriers to year-round film exhibition in the 1920s. In some small towns, amusement parks, and vacation resorts, however, summer airdomes continued to operate for many years.[31]

The Nickelodeon Show

Films, of course, were the heart of the nickelodeon show in both small-town and big-city theaters. The nickelodeon's program of film and either illustrated song or vaudeville skit, or both, lasted anywhere from thirty minutes (in an urban show) to ninety minutes or two hours. The admission price, initially a nickel, soon gave way to ten- or fifteen-cent tickets for adults and three- to five-cent tickets for children. It was still a bargain price. The nickelodeon program's films were a mixture of comedy and melodrama, lots of westerns, historical costume pieces, modern dress farces, slapstick, and fairy tales. Serials had quite a vogue, and each new episode of a ten-or fifteen-part mystery would be anxiously anticipated. Films of current events always found interest among viewers; newsreels began toward the end of the nickelodeon era.

There has been a welcome expansion of scholarship in recent years on the films and film producers of the nickelodeon era. Among the many important new studies available are examinations of films released by the Edison Manufacturing Company, Vitagraph Company, Thanhouser Company, and Biograph Company, and several chronological surveys of developments across the film industry. A detailed discussion of the specific films viewed by American audiences is not attempted here, because for the average nickelodeon patron who attended the shows week in and week out, the overall character of the program and theater had more impact than most individual films, which blurred together into the patron's overall impression of the moviegoing experience.[32]

Film producers in the nickelodeon era released more than one hundred films each week, and a nickelodeon theater that changed its programs three or five times a week would require fifteen to twenty-five films for its programs. Records that might allow us to gauge which films were most often rented or were most profitable are long gone, as is any exact accounting of what films viewers saw in thousands of nickelodeons each week. As a very limited case study, what follows is a random sample of representative nickelodeon film programs presented between 1911 and 1917 by Bert and Fannie Cook, first at Shaul's Theater in Richfield Springs, New York, and then in Cooperstown at the Star Theater, as well as one program shown at the Star under its previous owner, L. H. Spencer. This brief survey of two small-town, upstate New York nickelodeons' offerings cannot speak for trends among all theaters across the nation, but the films chosen for exhibition appear typical of small-town movie shows of the period.

November 1911, Shaul's Theater

Films shown were: *Wifey's New Flat* (Lubin) and *The New Operators* (Lubin), two half-reel comedies; *The Indian Brothers* (Biograph); *Five Bold Bad Men* (Essanay) and *Mr. Wise Investigator* (Essanay), two half-reel comedies; *Capture of Fort Ticonderoga*

(Edison), a "historical" film; *Washington Relies* (Pathé), an educational film; and *Heroes Three* (Edison) and *Mistakes Will Happen* (Edison), two half-reel comedies.

January 1912, Star Theater (operated by L. H. Spencer)

An advertisement announced: "Helen Gardner will be the leading lady in a beautiful mountain drama 'Arbutus.' [T]here will be an Edison, 'The Girl and the Motor Boat'[;] a western featuring Mr. Anderson in 'The Outlaw Deputy'[;] and 'A Tale of Two Cities,' a Vitagraph masterpiece in three reels, which will be repeated from Saturday, when the attendance was light on account of bad weather."

January 1913, Star Theater

An advertisement announced these featured two-reel films: *At Napoleon's Command, The Count of Monte Cristo, The Lady of the Lake, The Olympic Games,* and *The Mills of the Gods.*

January 1914, Star Theater

An advertisement announced these featured two-reel films: *King Robert of Sicily, The Skeleton in the Closet* (Kalem), *The Springtime of Life* (Pathé), *Shipwrecked* (Kalem), *The Clown's Revenge* and *The Burning Rivet,* "a political story in two parts."

January 1914, Shaul's Theater

Films shown were: *A Modern Romance* (IMP), a comedy drama; *Tweedledum as a Suffragette,* a half-reel comedy together on the same reel with *Italian Rivers* (Ambrosio), a scenic film; *In the Wilds of Africa* (101 Bison), a "2-reel sensation"; and *The Retribution of Ysobel* (Frontier), a western comedy. *Her Suitors* (Eclair), a "rich comedy," did not arrive.

January 1915, Star Theater

Films shown were: *The Perils of Pauline,* "the third episode of the most talked about picture story yet made"; *Seed and the Harvest,* a "two part Kalem special feature"; *Fatty's Sweetheart*, a "Vita-graph Laugh"; and "the Selig-Hearst news pictures." One evening was also amateur night.

January 1916, Star Theater

Films shown were: *Neal of the Navy*, "Pathé's greatest American serial featuring Lillian Lorraine and William Courtleigh Jr., ninth episode in 2 parts"; *The Yellow Peril; The House with the Drawn Shades*, a "2 part feature starring Ben Wilson [that] relates a fasci-nating story which lies behind the dusty blinds of a lonely man-sion"; *Eddie's Little Love Affair* and *No Babies Allowed*, both comedies; "and the Pathé news pictures."

January 1917, Star Theater

Films shown were: "[f]eature-length Paramount releases which changed three times a week." They included: *Carmen*, starring Geraldine Farrar; *Still Waters*, starring Marguerite Clark; *The Fatal Cord*, starring Hazel Dawn and John Mason; *Madame Butterfly*, starring Mary Pickford; *The Mummy and the Humming Bird; Zozo*, starring Pauline Frederick; *Bella Donna*, starring Pauline Frederick; *The Girl of Yesterday*, starring Mary Pickford; *Chimmie Faddon*, starring Victor Moore; and *The Gentleman from Indiana*, starring Dustin Farnum. "Burton Holmes travel-ogues were also shown."[33]

The film programs, although spread over a period of six years spanning the tumultuous nickelodeon era, show a number of continuities over time as, until 1917, the shows maintained a mixed five- or six-reel program of comedies, thrillers, educational subjects, and news—something to suit all types of viewers. But the programs' changes in response to the evolution of the film production industry are also apparent, for the shows evolved from a collection of brief split-reel films to a highlighting of special two-part films and, finally, to a focus on a single feature-length star vehicle.

Especially for small-town nickelodeons, the cost of renting films was a major consideration for exhibitors choosing which films to rent. Films from the major firms that formed the General Film Company—Edison,

Biograph, Kalem, Vitagraph, and others—were, not unsurprisingly, the most expensive to rent; so penny-pinching exhibitors had to turn more frequently to independently produced films like those of Thanhouser and IMP, and often switched film services and exchanges. It must have been frustrating for moviegoers in small towns who wanted to see all of a film producer's current releases and their featured players.

The studios released films on certain days of the week, and if a theater was able to afford new releases, it could advertise that it always showed a certain studio's films on a certain regular rotation (a typical poster made available to exhibitors by the films studios trumpeted "Friday is Biograph Day"). Many nickelodeon theaters, such as the Star and Shaul's, changed their programs several times a week or even daily. They could target different days of the week for specific tastes, emphasizing serials on Saturdays and westerns on Wednesdays, for instance; many theaters preferred to offer a mixture of film genres each day. The frequent change of film programs seems to indicate that a significant number of regular patrons attended the movies several nights per week.[34]

This rapid program turnover and scheduling problems at the film exchange, which might necessitate substituting one film for another that did not show up, meant that nickelodeon theaters could not do a lot of advance advertising in newspapers. Very few urban nickelodeons advertised in the big-city papers, though some small-town nickelodeons were able to place notices in the small weekly papers. Most often, nickelodeons advertised only on the theater premises and through printed handbills distributed in residential neighborhoods before the show.

Music and Sound Effects in the Nickelodeon Show

Musical accompaniment, sound effects, vaudeville turns, and illustrated songs were integral parts of nickelodeon entertainment. Live music produced in many varieties played a large role in the movie show of the silent era, for music camouflaged the mechanical whirr and hum of film projectors, and exhibitors claimed that it seemed "natural" to complement the visual component of the show with an aural one. Most nineteenth-century entertainments involving soundless magic lantern slides, shadow plays, and pantomimes had included a spoken lecture or musical accompaniment, or both. It was, therefore, no innovation for audiences when exhibitors linked various forms of aural accompaniment to the silent images on the screen.

Some nickelodeon exhibitors paired mechanically produced music with their filmed entertainment, installing automatic pianos. By 1915, over six thousand photoplayers, the most popular type of automatic piano used in nickelodeons, had been sold. Some of the most elaborate contraptions, including organ pipes that imitated horns, violins, and flutes, could make sound effects and play an orchestra of instruments besides the piano—drums, bells, xylophone—and could play as many as thirty different musical selections on paper rolls without needing to be changed. Although it was probably a more efficient and economical method of providing musical accompaniment for movie shows than the laborious process of locating and retaining talented musicians, the automatic piano could be raucously loud and could not interpret the films' ever more lengthy and fast-paced narratives. Critics complained of ragtime tunes issuing forth from automatic pianos during tender film love scenes. In an example of human talent triumphing over mechanical proficiency, many exhibitors eventually supplemented or replaced their automatic pianos with costlier human pianists. Introduction of elaborate pipe organs by the early 1920s raised the stature of some film accompanists to featured performer at the "mighty Wurlitzer."

Some nickelodeon movie shows continued the practice of interspersing the films with vocalists performing "illustrated songs," a popular component of itinerant shows such as Cook and Harris's. Illustrated songs were popular Tin Pan Alley ballads accompanied by lantern slides projected on the screen and keyed to the song lyrics. Audience members were encouraged to "all join in the chorus." Sheet music of the new tune would be displayed for sale in the theater lobby. Illustrated songs, like other Tin Pan Alley tunes, were alternately lively and comic or melodramatic and pathetic. The combination of song narratives and photographic slides of individuals posed so as to illustrate the lyrics, it has been said, anticipated the development of one-reel film plots. Although illustrated song slides had been used since the 1890s in vaudeville shows, there seem to have been few cries of regret among movie audiences when they faded from nickelodeon shows about 1912. Heavy competition between slide manufacturers and the overly competitive use of song pluggers to promote the tunes onstage in movie houses made song slides unprofitable to produce and distribute. The demise of illustrated songs and audience sing-alongs also may have had something to do with the questionable talents of many vocalists (all too often the exhibitor's wife, daughter, or son) or with nickelodeon audiences' boredom and rising entertainment standards.[35]

Movie audience participation in sing-alongs was briefly revived during the First World War, when the popularity of patriotic "community singing" events swept American movie shows. Movie audiences in St. Louis; Covington, Kentucky; and several other communities, however, were reported to have pummeled German-born theater managers who did not join in "Yankee Doodle in Berlin" sing-alongs or support the liberty loan bond salesmen with what the crowd, whipped into a frenzy by musical propaganda, deemed appropriate enthusiasm.[36]

Live musical accompaniment for nickelodeon films ranged from the automatic pianos to small ensembles of piano, drum, and violin, and the earliest Wurlitzer theater pipe organs. Nickelodeon shows provided many small-town women and men who were church pianists and organists with welcome steady employment. The musical selections heard in nickelodeon movie shows consisted largely of familiar tunes and currently popular songs mixed with whatever bits of ragtime, jazz, classical music, or hymns the accompanist knew. Music publishers soon responded to film accompanists' needs with a series of "fake books." These collections of noncopyrighted music were clearly organized so that harried musicians could quickly flip from one selection to another to accompany a film's love scenes and chase scenes, and to differentiate the ingenues from the villains.

At worst, indifferent theater musicians produced the same tired tunes endlessly, played dirges during chase scenes, or injected their own attempts at humor. One accompanist matched a jazzy popular song, "Oh, You Kid," with scenes of baby Moses being discovered among the bulrushes in a serious biblical film, jarring conservative audience members' nerves. Inappropriate music often brought hoots of laughter from members of the movie audience, but inadequate or poorly performed accompaniments caused sensitive critics and viewers to write complaints to the music columns of the exhibitors' trade papers.[37]

At silent film accompaniment's best, the piano, organ, or orchestra musicians' efforts contributed tremendously to audiences' interpretations of the images shown on the screen. Film producers in the 1920s would provide special scores or theme songs for musicians to use. Skilled pianists and organists adapted scores to the on-screen action to intensify the emotions of love scenes, quicken the chase, or squeeze humor out of a pratfall, and they provided the hoofbeats, train whistles, and slamming-door sound effects that added layers of richness and reality to viewers' interpretations and imaginations.

Sound effects could be as important to the movie show as musical accompaniment. Just as Cook and Harris had done before them, some nickelodeon operators put great effort and imagination into re-creating realistic and exciting sound effects to enhance their films. Sometimes theater musicians would simulate sound effects with their instruments, crashing down on the piano keys or using the novelty effects available on the automatic piano. Sound effects had to be well done and well timed to be effective; nothing could make movie viewers jump in delighted fright more than a well-synchronized, loud gunshot or door slam at a tense moment in the film plot.

We rarely think of human voices connected to silent film, but from the days of the earliest film shows, movie audiences' imaginations had been expanded by the connection of sound effects and human voices to screen images. Itinerant lecturer-exhibitors like Lyman Howe and Burton Holmes had stood beside the screen, providing a running educational commentary on passing foreign vistas, or creating dramatic narratives to link brief film scenes. Despite the success of Howe's companies, and ignoring *Moving Picture World* editor Stephen Bush's campaign to convince more exhibitors to use lecturers to raise the educational level of movie shows, nickelodeon exhibitors did not find that lecturers caught on in stationary movie theaters. Exhibitors claimed that good lecturers were too difficult to find, that their salaries were too high to make the show profitable, that too few film companies provided interesting lecture scripts, and that lectures seemed too educational and dull to nickelodeon audiences. The growing sophistication of film narratives also contributed to the lecture's demise. The more frequent use of action shots, editing, and descriptive titles helped provide the type of context that permitted the audience's imagination to fill in the blanks.

Attempts at synchronizing recorded sounds and film images had been made since the Edison studio's first experiments with the film medium, and they continued through the entire silent film era. Various systems using phonograph records synchronized with films were introduced into individual theaters from 1900 on, but before the Vitaphone system in the mid-1920s, few of them were found to be adequate enough for extended, regular use. "At present we need not discuss the 'pictures that talk,'" commented a theater critic in 1909. "Though scenes from grand opera, vaudeville acts, condensed versions of famous plays, are already given jointly by the picture machine and the phonograph, the synchronizing process has not yet been perfected, nor is the phonograph yet sufficiently free from metallic quality, to give these 'talking pictures' a lifelikeness as vivid as that imparted by the imagination to the merely pantomimic dramas."[38]

A fad for "film talkers"—actors and actresses who were stationed behind the screen and who improvised speeches for film characters—grew both in traveling shows and in stationary theaters throughout the country in 1907. Audiences' desire to have voices emanating from film characters' mouths was strong. At a Brooklyn, New York, nickelodeon, one reporter noted in 1908, "[B]ehind the sheet upon which the pictures are thrown, several men and women carry on the dialogue supposed to be enacted by the characters in the picture, and other sounds, such as cheering crowds, applause, the noise of running, horses, or tramping soldiers are reproduced by these unseen actors." The fad spread so far that one of the troupes from the staid Lyman Howe company was reportedly using talkers in 1908.[39]

The talkers became so popular with movie audiences in Baltimore theaters that they became minor celebrities in their own right, formed their own professional club, and were "stolen" back and forth by rival exhibitors to be the featured attractions of their movie shows. Baltimore exhibitor Harry Lewy reminisced that this gimmick made his theaters very popular. "[W]e really came into our own when we put people behind the screen to talk as the actors' lips moved. They were ingenious, making up their own dialogue. And once we took nine fellows and filmed them moving their lips as though singing. Then we ran the film and played a record with it."[40]

The growing sophistication of narratives in feature-length films in the mid-1910s led to the decline of film talkers, just as it had sped the lecturers' departure. Talkers such as the *benshi* of Japanese cinemas, however, remained essential to the silent film shows of other countries. Numerous dialogue titles inserted in film scenes made talkers superfluous, and in any event, to accentuate feature-length films with live performances was a complicated task. The expense of the talking performers' salaries could not be justified for too long by exhibitors facing higher feature-film rental charges. Talkers also had the unfortunate tendency, like roguish musical accompanists, to spoil dramatic film scenes with continual and misplaced jokes and satire.[41]

A postcard photograph, location and date unknown, with a handwritten notation by an enthralled, unknown movie fan. Courtesy of Q. David Bowers.

The End of the Nickelodeon Era

The steady increase in the popularity of nickelodeons in the years after their introduction meant that by 1910 any town or neighborhood with one successful theater had acquired two or three competitors on the same street. Intense rivalries in local entertainment markets spurred exhibitors' concentration on advertising and audience attraction in every facet of nickelodeon operation.

Increased competition in urban areas and many small towns brought a second generation of permanent theaters, most aptly labeled "small-time vaudeville theaters," to replace the earlier, hastily constructed and improvised nickelodeons. Exhibitors remodeled their old theater buildings or constructed larger, more elegant theaters. Many invested in new structures that combined theaters with rent-producing retail shops. Interiors and exteriors of movie theaters became more elegant, organized, and spacious. Auditoriums became larger, seating five hundred to one thousand or more patrons instead of the nickelodeon's average number of fifty to three hundred. Exhibitors upgraded the entertainment, showing longer, more expensive feature films and often adding several acts of vaudeville to their bills. They also began charging higher admission fees than the lowly nickel, thus losing some of their poorer patrons as steady customers. The higher ticket price and the more sophisticated environment and entertainment, however, attracted a wealthier clientele of middle-class families between 1909 and 1915.[42]

Fierce competition in the big cities' movie theater business spelled the end of the urban nickelodeon era by 1915. The winners in this struggle would be the exhibitors who not only made their theaters larger and more elegant but also bought out the competition. Enterprising exhibitors opened additional theaters in the nearest small towns or adjacent neighborhoods. Chains of theaters were efficient, operated with increasing economies of scale, and brought new levels of standardization to moviegoing by sharing the costs of booking entertainers and films. This second generation of film exhibitors cemented a legitimate place for movie theaters on middle-class Main Street and began to be considered leaders of the retail establishment. In the late teens, film producers and distributors would become increasingly involved in film exhibition, scrambling to build, purchase, or control key theaters in every major city, and purchasing regional chains to ensure the profitable distribution of their films. The influx of film producers and distributors into the picture palace component of film exhibition helped drive a wedge of difference between big-city and small-town moviegoing.[43]

 4

Small-Town Alternatives

Educational, Advertising, and Religious Films and Church Shows

While nonfiction films had predominated in the initial years of American film exhibition, in the nickelodeon era the motion picture manufacturers significantly increased their production of narrative fiction films. Correspondingly, they reduced the number of documentary films of speeding trains, foreign scenery, parades, and public events that they released each week. The new "story pictures" were apparently well-received by both urban and rural audiences in all parts of the nation. However, some viewers who had enjoyed the nonfiction films were dismayed by the loss and petitioned their movie theater managers for their return. "Film manufacturers should note that there is a strong and increasing demand for travel scenes," reported a *Moving Picture World* correspondent in 1908:

> In conversation with an exhibitor he [the exhibitor] said that he had great difficulty in getting such subjects from his rental bureau, although repeatedly requested. He said that his audiences demanded them and that he would like to have at least one such subject for each performance. Probably his case was an exception, as his theater is located in a high-class residential section, but similar remarks heard in

other quarters lead us to believe that the supply of such subjects is not equal to the demand.[1]

Again and again, from the nickelodeon period through the early 1920s, small-town movie theater owners and urban film exhibitors who consciously catered to a middle-class trade wrote to the trade journals complaining that manufacturers ought to supply them with more educational films to meet their audiences' film preferences.

The urgency of rural nickelodeon exhibitors' frustrated appeals to film producers was reflected in the concurrent rise of alternative, church-sponsored movie shows in small-town communities. Some Protestant and Catholic ministers sought to recapture the attention of their straying parishioners, not by merely condemning the movies, but by adopting the movie theater's products and appeal. The ministers began establishing motion picture programs in their own church halls. Their shows featured precisely the types of educational and religious films (produced and distributed by industrial corporations and minor film producers) that the small-town movie theater managers found so difficult to acquire from the film studios, who were reluctant to produce them. Alarmed small-town exhibitors saw church shows become a serious threat to their own theaters. The church-show market appeared to expand rapidly in the 1910s, accompanied by the growth of alternative film producers and distributors to service these new movie outlets.

Although we have established that small-town nickelodeons were usually less elaborately electrified and adorned than their urban counterparts and that small-town theater audiences contained a wider cross section of the town's social strata than did urban audiences, the question remains whether there were significant differences in the film preferences of small-town and urban audiences. While some critics of the day assumed that the tastes of country and city moviegoers must be worlds apart, the film manufacturers maintained that the same movies were popular from the most sophisticated city to the smallest hamlet. The exhibitors' trade journals were largely silent on the topic. Scattered anecdotal evidence can be found in regular columns like *Exhibitor's Trade Review*'s "How Did That Picture Go at Your Theatre?," but few major patterns of difference in audiences' tastes were ever discussed at length. The general climate was that of exhibitor acceptance of the films released by the studios (even though few exhibitors refrained from occasional grumbling about the quality of the films they received). Therefore, an investigation of small-town nickelodeon owners' requests for something different—nonfiction films—will reveal some of the differences between rural and urban audiences' film preferences in the silent film era.

Rural-urban and class-based conflicts between exhibitors, audiences, and special-interest groups over film choice occasionally surfaced in complaints about the dearth of educational, scenic, religious, or industrial films and in protests over the exhibition of particular films. These debates, however, occurred within larger areas of agreement. The most popular films during the nickelodeon and early feature-film years—films such as those starring Charlie Chaplin or Mary Pickford—were sought by exhibitors everywhere, reported the film industry. As the business of film production matured, studios sought to channel diverse audiences' film preferences toward a few most profitable and popular genres. Indeed, the similarity of urban and rural audiences' tastes was largely due to their shared heritage of popular literature and entertainment. Comedies, adventure tales, westerns, and melodramas, all familiar to audiences from decades of exposure to stage melodrama, dime novels, and serialized newspaper fiction, were usually welcomed, in turn, by most film viewers.[2]

The differences between the kinds of narrative fiction films that small-town and urban audiences disliked were minor, but occasionally they became an issue, to filmmakers' dismay. Small-town moviegoers generally had less interest than big-city viewers in high-society films, bold sex comedies, and historical dramas. As Margaret Thorp reported in the 1930s, rural audiences liked films with familiar settings and the continuity of serials. "[T]he subtle, the exotic, the unexpected they do not like at all, and they are frankly annoyed by costume pictures." In one 1922 survey, exhibitors in San Bernardino, California; Greeley, Colorado; Omaha, Nebraska; and Sheboygan, Wisconsin, howled for producers to "give up the society stuff!" On the other hand, theater managers in Ardmore, Oklahoma; Gilmore, Texas; Salt Lake City, Utah; and Bridgeport, Connecticut, begged for more "society pictures with flashy costumes." Thorp noted that "thick and obvious" glamour, plenty of action, and a gripping narrative could help a film overcome most objections from the hinterlands.[3]

Small-town audiences in the late 1920s rejected early talkies drawn directly from hit Broadway shows resplendent with Yiddish humor and barely clad chorus girls, causing headaches for Hollywood film producers. Big-city audiences, on the other hand, had less patience than small-town viewers for films with rural themes, such as those starring Charles Ray. Movies like D. W. Griffith's *True Heart Susie* (1919), about a charming, bucolic girl, and his successful remake of the creaky Victorian stage melodrama *Way Down East* (1920) found fewer audiences as the 1920s progressed. Audiences from Manhattan to Muncie, Indiana, increasingly rejected films like Griffith's for "jazzy" sex comedies and titillating modern stories, and by the late 1920s they more rarely sought out the travel, industrial, and religious films they had once so enjoyed.[4]

Scenics, Industrials, and Advertising and Religious Films

Small-town exhibitors in the nickelodeon period frequently reported to the trade journals that their audiences were especially fond of "scenics," "industrials," and films with religious themes, and that viewers wanted them to be a regular part of movie programs. Scenics were travelogues or panoramic views of historic sights or exotic foreign landscapes. Industrials were brief films telling the story of how consumer products were made, how new farm machinery operated, how crops were planted and harvested; they displayed the wonders of new technology such as Ford Model Ts and electric appliances for the home. Religious films were often motion picture tableaux illustrating biblical themes. To please their patrons, small-town exhibitors programmed movie shows that often featured these types of films alongside, or instead of, narrative fiction films.

In the early years of film exhibition, scenics, industrials, and current-events films had proved successful for itinerant "high-class" exhibitors like Lyman Howe, the Cook and Harris company, and lecturer Burton Holmes. Holmes's supporters claimed that middle-class families in the big cities who had shunned the vaudeville houses, gaudy nickelodeons, and "blood and thunder" melodramas had turned out enthusiastically to lyceums and lecture halls to view Holmes's educational film programs. These film genres did not disappear with the coming of stationary movie shows, as small-town exhibitors continued to seek them throughout the nickelodeon era. Urban nickelodeon exhibitors, however, complained that scenics and industrials bored their working-class audiences and put a damper on the more entertaining portions of their movie shows— comedies, exciting chases, and heartrending dramas.[5]

Social critics crusaded against the sight of pugilists, scantily clad dancers, and slapstick violence in the films typically shown in big-city nickelodeons, and they proclaimed that scenics and industrials were wholesome, instructive, and beneficial for the young and old. In 1910, the manager of the Minersville, Pennsylvania, opera house reported with great satisfaction that the superintendent of the local school district asked to be specially notified when industrial films were shown so that all schoolchildren could be directed to view them.[6]

Testimonials appeared in the exhibitors' trade journals from across the country about the ability of scenics and industrials to improve small-town theater owners' community standing and to attract a better class of audiences. A Knoxville, Tennessee, exhibitor reported that a shared interest in travel films united the diverse elements of middle and working class into one movie audience. An exhibitor in Menomonie, Wisconsin, suggested to his small-town colleagues that they could solidify middle-class nickelodeon patronage by offering free performances of educational films with the sponsorship of local schools, the Tuberculosis Society, or the Red Cross. This would attract conservative patrons who had never seen movies before, and, the exhibitor asserted, "[W]e are sure they will come again." A Washington, D.C., exhibitor argued that middle-class children should be shown educational films rather than being exposed to the low-quality, violent melodramas prevalent in downtown nickelodeons. Scenics, "clean" comedies, and "good education or industrial films" such as Edison Manufacturing Company's *King Cotton,* Selig Polyscope Company's *Industries of Southern California,* or Urban-Eclipse Company's *The Fly Pest* were his recommendations. A theater manager from Portland, Oregon, testified that by highlighting industrial films in a vaudeville-like mix of genteel comedies and dramas, smart western exhibitors were attracting "the educated class" of middle-class patrons to movie theaters. Almost anything exhibitors could interpret as educational was also construed as something the middle class was willing to view.[7]

For the manufacturers of consumer products, industrial films seemed a promising medium of public education and advertising because of the movies' ability to bring the factory and its products to life. Through the presentation of industrial films, traveling salesmen-exhibitors could reach prospective customers in the office, farmers in the grange hall, or curious viewers at agricultural exhibitions or county fairs. In 1904, the International Harvester Company commissioned films to be made of their mechanical threshers and corn pickers working in the fields. Movies were portable, unlike factory showrooms and unwieldy farm machinery; they could be projected on sheets in open fields, if necessary, and could be transported all over the world. International Harvester loaned film prints free of charge "to those itinerant lecturers who travel from town to town and village, suiting their lectures to the interests of the community." One promoter, accounting for the popularity of industrial films with middle-class audiences, claimed, "People flock to see industrial films for the same reason that they are interested in travel pictures—because it is the only way in which many of them can ever hope to see the sights that are pictured."[8]

The more obviously promotional industrials were classified as advertising films; a cleverly made advertising film was as well received by nickelodeon audiences as the most amusing television commercials are today. However, poorly made or annoying advertising films swiftly brought charges of commercial exploitation from admission-paying audiences and from the exhibitors upon whom viewers vented their displeasure. Advertising films had to be shown with caution.

The boundaries between scenics, industrials, and advertising films could be quite fluid; sometimes it was difficult to know where the educational aspects of these films ended and where the promotional parts began. For example, the early scenics portraying spectacular views of landscapes as seen from the vantage point of the cowcatcher on a moving train, which were prominent in early itinerant exhibitions like Howe's and the Hale's Tours, were often actually promotional films commissioned by railway companies and tourist-site organizations to attract new investors and visitors. Incorporation of product advertisements into entertainment was not a novelty with the movies; in the nineteenth century, promotional messages had been incorporated into magic lantern-slide shows and vaudeville and theatrical performances, wherein ads were painted on curtains and printed in the margins of programs.

Middle-class and small-town Americans had great respect for successful businesses and enjoyed learning some of the mysteries of new inventions and the manufacturing processes of their favorite consumer products. Industrial films simply brought viewers closer to the sources of their fascination. For years before the advent of motion pictures, Sears, Roebuck and Company had sold a popular line of stereopticon slide sets illustrated with photographs of the firm's gigantic order-processing operations, including scenes of the merchandise warehouses, the conveyor-belt systems on which workers assembled individual orders, and workers stacking the packed order boxes on the shipping docks. When Alva Roebuck first introduced moving picture projectors and films to the Sears, Roebuck and Company catalog in 1898, he offered itinerant exhibitors an affordable way to add extra subjects to their film programs. "Special $3.00 Films. We have a few very good subjects, taken partly for advertising purposes, such as the employees (nearly 800) leaving our store at noontime for lunch. They are worth $5.00 each, but they will be sold at $3.00 each. The advertisers will pay the balance of the cost. Some are very funny." Selling promotional films at an attractive price fit into Sears, Roebuck and Company's larger strategy of self-promotion mixed with industrial education. It is not easy today to imagine what might have made these films funny; perhaps projectionists would deliberately run the film backward at high speed, causing the hundreds of exiting employees to be inhaled by the Sears building.[9]

In the early nickelodeon era, the Edison, Vitagraph, Selig, and Essanay film studios produced a number of industrials, scenics, public service films, and advertising films for a wide variety of Progressive Era special-interest groups, such as consumer-product manufacturers, the Young Men's Christian Association (YMCA), the Department of Agriculture, and social welfare and political organizations. The films promoted a wide range of social and legal reforms, public health programs, women's suffrage, and birth control, as well as things to buy. Although the film manufacturers must have been pleased with the extra income brought in by the production of these promotional and public service films, they seemed uncomfortable selling the films to exhibitors, if the following catalog copy is any indication:

> Invariably these industrial films are entertaining and marvelous, surpassing in their wonderful developments stories stronger and stranger than fiction, and in many cases they are revelations of wonderland. . . . While necessarily they may advertise an industry, this phase is merely incidental and does not in any way lessen their value as a subject of vast and far-reaching importance, a necessity, in fact, in selecting a program varied with a Biograph or Vitagraph drama and an Essanay or Lubin comedy.[10]

Despite their supposed "necessity" in the film program, wary urban nickelodeon exhibitors often refused to include promotional films in their regular programs. "Washington exhibitors have generally refused to run anything in the way of advertising merchandise of any kind," reported a District of Columbia theater manager. "They have found that it hurts their business, for the fans complain that the theaters are not the place to give publicity to commercial establishments." Even if producers were eager to make industrial films, convincing urban exhibitors actually to pay money to rent films laden with commercial messages turned out to be prohibitively difficult. When city exhibitors caught what they called "snipe advertising" hidden in films (the surreptitious placement of, or reference to, consumer products in a film scene), they cut the film or covered the projector lens until the suspect scene had passed. Although such censorship removed material that exhibitors thought might offend their audiences, abrupt interruptions of the film narrative often angered exhibitors' patrons more than the advertising would have.[11]

Another drawback to the use of scenics and industrials in an exhibitor's nickelodeon program was that they did not particularly appeal to children, an influential part of the middle-class audience. "The desire for culture, which sends adults to see and hear Burton Holmes' Travelogues, has not yet appeared in the younger generation," a writer commented in *Motion Picture Story Magazine*. "To one boy who was bored by a scenic film, it was suggested that it would do him good, as it was educational. 'Aw!' he exclaimed in disgust, 'I get enough of that in school.'" The author suggested that if producers made a "sugar-coated homeopathic form" of travel picture that wrapped exotic scenes in a rollicking adventure plot, it would bring the children flocking. Indeed, other young viewers reported their fascination with the animals shown in scenic films of foreign lands and with the huge machinery at work in industrials. Small-town exhibitors did not incorporate educational films into their programs without careful consideration, then, for they risked either infuriating paying customers with films that seemed too much like blatant advertising or boring the children with scenics and industrials.[12]

The film manufacturers' introduction of weekly newsreel films in the mid-1910s (Pathé and Hearst-Selig were early suppliers) would finally address some of the concerns that both small-town and urban middle-class exhibitors had about the lack of scenic and industrial films in their programs. But even newsreels did not fully satisfy those audiences who continued to desire educational films, which were being produced and exhibited even less often than before. At this juncture, however, new film producers, distributors, and exhibitors operating outside the commercial mainstream began to release alternative newsreels and industrials and to support new exhibition venues for the audiences whose needs were not being fully served.

Ford Has a Better Idea

Films' persuasive influence on the American public apparently piqued the interest of automaker Henry Ford, for he established a Department of Motion Pictures at the Ford Motor Company in 1914. Ford was infamous in advertising agency circles for his reluctance to spend money on advertising in newspapers and magazines; he preferred to arrange free publicity. It seems ironic, then, that the Ford Motor Company invested in one of the most elaborate and expensive attempts to blend educational and advertising objectives: two film series entitled *Ford Animated Weekly* (1914–1921) and *Ford Educational Weekly* (1916–1921). The *Animated Weekly* was a newsreel and the latter series was a topical screen magazine, both of which the Ford company offered for a nominal rental fee of one dollar per week. With a roving staff of six cameramen, Ford's Department of Motion Pictures became the largest industrial film producer in the nation. *Animated Weekly* and *Educational Weekly* reels were seen each week by three million people at over two thousand outlets.[13]

Ford films were more likely to be seen by audiences in small-town and rural theaters and in alternative, church- and community-operated shows than by patrons of big-city theaters. Because of the low rental fees that the Ford company charged, it seems probable that the two weeklies would have been especially attractive to part-time exhibitors and church groups who lacked the funds to rent more expensive films. This would weight the Ford film audience even more heavily toward small-town nickelodeons and alternative shows. Such target marketing made sense, for rural viewers were far more likely to purchase Model Ts and Fordson tractors than the urban middle class (who preferred more expensive and sophisticated automobiles) or the urban working class (who used public transportation). This demographic appeal also paralleled Ford's automobile marketing strategy. By 1912, Ford had a dealer in every town of two thousand people or more. A large percentage of his business was in small towns. As late as 1930, 65 percent of Ford dealers were located in towns of twenty-five hundred or fewer inhabitants, a higher percentage of rural coverage than attempted by other automobile producers.[14]

Watterson R. Rothacker, the most prominent independent producer of advertising and industrial films in the 1910s and 1920s, was a proponent of "the moving picture play which entertains the consumer while his buying instinct is being aroused," calling it "the most subtle advertising ever conceived." The potent power of this new media to "make definite impressions and produce lasting recollections" meant that the manufacturer who used promotional films could have the most effective contact with the public. "Advertising apparently without advertising is decidedly more potent than a direct commercial announcement," Rothacker argued. "These picture plays are far more comprehensive, attractive and convincing than the audible or printed 'how.'"[15]

The *Ford Animated Weekly* and *Ford Educational Weekly* were expertly produced examples of the art of blending indirect advertising into general subject matter. Typical editions of the *Animated Weekly* included Model T car races, promotions for "better roads" campaigns, scenic travelogues, segments on the production of grapefruit or coal, and news footage of dignitaries like President Woodrow Wilson officiating at public ceremonies or shaking Henry Ford's hand. The *Ford Educational Weekly* dropped the quickly dated current-events topics in favor of more general-interest industrial and agricultural segments that would permit the films to have a longer circulation period. *Educational Weekly* films portrayed the processing and packaging of dairy products and fruit, and the production of consumer goods such as lightbulbs, Thermos bottles, soap, and chewing gum; and they featured themes on how electrification and mechanization of the farm (with the help of Delco generators and Fordson tractors) would revolutionize rural life.[16]

The only truly overt signs of Ford company self-promotion in the films were seen in the title credits and subtitles, in which the lettering was superimposed over an image of a Model T grill. Although the Ford company steadfastly maintained that this was anything but a hard sell, its film production staff apparently followed the advice of promotional filmmakers like Watterson Rothacker, who noted that "in arranging a moving picture play of advertising intent, the advertising should be deftly concealed."[17]

Most of the film industry and general public were aware that the films' primary intent was promotion for Ford. One contemporary reviewer of the Ford films commented that "the viewer is entertained so interestingly that he forgets that he is witnessing one of the cleverest advertising plans of these times." The Ford Department of Motion Pictures was future film director King Vidor's first introduction to commercial filmmaking. In his memoir, Vidor recalled that when, as a young man, he set out from Galveston, Texas, to break into the movie business in California, he planned to finance his trip west by shooting film footage of his exploits along the route in a Model T. Vidor mailed the films to Dearborn for freelance consideration by Ford's Department of Motion Pictures. (Although it is not known whether Ford purchased his scenes, Vidor later recalled this as a significant experience.) While Ford films may have been company propaganda, few critics or commentators ever charged that they were poorly made. Even when exhibitors or audience members objected to the obvious or subtle advertising woven into the *Animated Weekly* or *Educational Weekly,* they nevertheless universally praised the Ford films for their interesting subject matter and high production quality.[18]

Competition from Church and Community Shows

Even though the number of scenics, industrials, and religious films shown in mainstream urban motion picture theaters declined in the mid-1910s, the films were still widely available outside the big cities. They were commonly shown at occasional itinerant exhibitions in small towns. Manufacturers still produced industrial films with technical themes for exhibition by sales representatives at business gatherings, industrial fairs, and manufacturing plants. The other most frequent outlet for industrial and advertising films became the shows sponsored by churches, schools, and communities. Church shows represented to some social critics in the 1910s and 1920s a way to remake the moviegoing experience into a more "respectable" small-town, middle-class activity, with the viewing environment and film selections overseen by the clergy or other responsible caretakers of middle class decorum. This was a substantial threat to the small-town nickelodeon. If the cream of exhibitors' audiences was "skimmed off," the nickelodeons' position as a community mainstay would be weakened.

Jealous competition colored much of the religious community's condemnation of the movies and film exhibitors in the nickelodeon era. Movie shows on Sunday afternoons and evenings lured errant parishioners away from church. Automobiles also presented new competition for church attendance, but ministers had little means to deter parishioners from taking Sunday drives. Protestant and Catholic clergy could more easily take measures against movie shows and other commercial amusements, working in many states to reinvoke blue laws. Small retail stores in most towns remained closed on Sundays, but film exhibitors found that Sunday programs were often their highest-grossing performances of the week, and they fought to stay open. The rise of new forms of commercialized recreation exposed changing moral and social habits in American society that alarmed conservative religious groups and that sparked rancorous debates within the urban and small-town middle class on the appropriate balance of commerce, religion, and leisure in their lives.

How did church groups come around to putting on their own movie shows? It is, of course, ironic that a number of Protestant and Catholic congregations embraced motion pictures and revenue-raising film exhibitions, since religious critics were among the first and loudest voices condemning urban working-class nickelodeons and urging film censorship. Nevertheless, as the Cooperstown example and other early episodes of cooperation between small-town church groups and itinerant film exhibitors demonstrated, middle-class religion's response to the movies was shaped by a variety of conflicting factors. Many local churches, both urban and rural, desperately grasped for solutions to shrinking attendance and dwindling funds for church social activities. "The problem of the Sunday evening service has for years been acute in the larger cities," wrote one commentator. "It is now becoming serious in the smaller towns. . . . Perhaps more churches have installed [movie] projection apparatus for this than any other reason."[19]

In the early years of film exhibition, the film industry had made a great show of welcoming Protestant and Catholic groups' interest in the movies as a way to overcome religious prejudice against films and exhibitors. In the early 1910s, *Moving Picture World* regularly published an advice column on church-show operation. The Reverend E. Boudinot Stockton reported on commercial films suitable to illustrate sermons; many of his recommendations were for the producers' standard line of "blood and thunder" melodramas, since, in Stockton's opinion, any film with a theme of redemption from sin or a strong moral at the conclusion would suffice for the minister's purpose.[20]

Ministers' use of film was not simply a capitulation to their parishioners' prurient tastes; it was in line with the methods and goals of the Progressive Era Social Gospel movement. "A new attitude has come on the part of the religious leaders," wrote one promoter of church film shows. "Where official boards condemned before, now they are admitting possibilities. . . . It took years for the church to see that the organ and other musical instruments could be used to the glory of God. Slowly the stereopticon earned its way and today the motion picture has demonstrated its value for religious work." Many of the more liberal Protestant sects advocated church sponsorship of illustrated slide lectures, concerts, and other recreational and educational activities to draw neighborhood people into the church, to teach hygiene, patriotism, and morality to immigrants and isolated rural folk, and to otherwise improve community welfare.[21]

Some minister-exhibitors in the early 1910s praised the limited number of available theatrical films that featured religious themes, such as the Kalem studio's series on the Holy Land and the biblical film subjects released by Pathé, Edison, and Vitagraph. Most theatrical film producers, however, found that religious groups' insistent demands for historical accuracy in biblical pictures swelled their costs of film production to the point of unprofitability. The studios did not forecast a sufficient expansion of the church-show market to make production of religious films profitable, so they chose not to cater to the needs of church shows. Nevertheless, since nationally focused film producers and distributors had no stake to protect in local exhibition, they had no reservations against providing theater owners with rivalry for middle-class audiences from a new clientele of church exhibitors. Film exchanges did not choose sides among competing exhibitors in a community; they were willing to rent their films to any group with cash.[22]

By the mid-1910s, after years of acceptance and even encouragement of church shows, a growing number of small-town movie theater managers began to chafe from the competition of alternative film programs being mounted in church halls. These church shows offered middle-class patrons the local minister's stamp of approval and an already familiar environment in which to experience movies. The appeal was plain—moviegoing could be guilt free, even for the most conservative families. An advocate of church shows explained that, of the many threats of censorship and condemnation that religious and conservative groups posed to the livelihood of movie theater managers, none enraged exhibitors more than churches' attempts to beat them at their own game:

> He [the exhibitor] sees his own house on one corner charging fifty cents admission to see Mary Pickford in "Rebecca of Sunnybrook Farm," and across the street a church with a modest little billboard announcing "Sunday Evening Service: Sermon followed by Motion

> Pictures. Admission Free. Next Sunday, Mary Pickford in "Rebecca
> of Sunnybrook Farm." He visualizes an empty theatre, and all of his
> patrons in church for a "free show."

Furious movie theater managers stopped the pretense of assisting ministers who showed films in their parish halls. By the mid-1910s, if the exhibitors' trade journals published an article about church shows, it was
advice for theatrical exhibitors on how to combat the menace instead of
how to cultivate the local ministers' acceptance and support. More than
ever, the small-town, middle-class movie audience became the prize to be
fought over by commercial and religious interests.[23]

Church shows were more likely to be found in certain regions of the
country and in certain Protestant denominations than in others. The
South, dominated by Baptists and other fundamentalist groups who were
uncomfortable with any movie attendance by their members, largely rejected the use of films in church, but film historian Gregory Waller has
documented the activities of several itinerant black ministers traveling in
Kentucky who used them in their services. Massachusetts was reported to
have a number of church shows, but they were rarely found across the
rest of New England. Congregations in the midwestern, mid-Atlantic,
and West Coast states supported the majority of church shows. By the
mid-1910s, some urban Catholic churches also began using movie shows
in their work with immigrant and working-class children and in Amer-
icanization programs during and after the First World War. A very
unscientific survey of churches' movie programs, conducted by an exhibitors' group in 1922, estimated that anywhere from 4,000 to 25,000
churches showed films; the pollsters could only verify the existence of
1,164 church shows, but they estimated that thousands more operated in-
termittently. New York state alone was said to have 487 church-based
film programs.[24]

Occasionally a movie theater owner still acknowledged that exposure to movies in church might make conservative, middle-class critics
more accepting of theatrical films. An exhibitor in Jamestown, New
York, noted:

> Some local churches show pictures and take up a collection fee in lieu
> of charging an admission fee. It happens that many old and highly es-
> teemed Swedish people (Swedish population in Jamestown predomi-
> nates) attend the churches and are devout worshippers and believe that
> it is wrong to attend theatres at any time. They see pictures in the

church. They realize the entertainment value in them and in a short time they are found in the theatres.

Similarly, a trade journal reporter, discussing the movie shows being held in a Presbyterian church in the conservative town of Montclair, New Jersey, noted sarcastically, "When the people in the cultured town of Montclair decided not to permit a moving picture theater in their enlightened community, how little they supposed that they were helping along the very cause which they were supposedly hindering." More frequently, minister-exhibitors retreated to appeasing movie theater owners with the argument that the church shows were breaking down conservative prejudices and creating new movie fans for the exhibitor instead of stealing the allegiance of the exhibitors' best middle-class customers.[25]

In 1916, the Methodist-affiliated Federal Council of the Churches of Christ in America published a guide to the operation of church movie shows. Its author, Edward McConoughey, offered a plethora of knowledgeable advice and opinions on the many ways enterprising clergy could use films to their benefit. "For the Sunday evening church service the motion picture has proved highly valuable, but this depends upon its sympathetic relation to the whole service," McConoughey wrote. "A motion picture may supplement the sermon, but can never take its place." Yet he knew this was precisely what was happening. He counseled ministers to create as elaborate a theatrical performance around the film as their abilities allowed. "Some ministers have their choir softly sing appropriate hymns as the story is unfolded; others interject a word or two as the film is run; and then with a few inspired words gather up the theme of the story and drive its message home."[26]

Once they found the secret of putting over a good Sunday evening performance, ministers should expand their film programs, McConoughey urged. "On week days the motion picture can be used to gather the children of the neighborhood. The Grace Methodist Episcopal Church of New York . . . has over seven hundred children every Saturday afternoon, with a total for 1914 of over 40,000 in attendance." The church shows' admission prices of one to three cents were often sufficiently low to drive competing movie theaters out of business.[27]

McConoughey instructed the clergy to think and act like businessmen and showmen. Efficient management and profitability were "absolutely essential" if the movie program was to further the church's work. In his enthusiasm, however, McConoughey lost sight of all but the monetary gains to be sought. "In Union Settlement, New York City, motion pictures have been run with profit. The admission, five cents, is the same as that charged by neighboring theaters. The Direction [the minister] has now decided to run costly feature films, charging ten cents admission and to give three entertainments daily." Ultimately, McConoughey hoped the cleansed church show could be merged with the new opulent movie palace to create "cathedrals of the movies" for the amusement-seeking middle class.[28]

Community-sponsored shows were sometimes organized by schools or civic groups with concerns similar to those of movie-showing churches. A typical school-sponsored show was located at Bay City Western High School in Bay City, Michigan. The school received a secondhand projector as a gift, and principal Leroy Perkins set it up in a spare classroom. Perkins reported that he "could get some educational films very cheaply and some without cost." For example, he acquired films "from the government and the Western Electric company at no cost except express charges. Other films, such as the Ford Weekly and Robert Bruce Scenic pictures are secured at small cost." To appease the enraged local movie theater manager, who feared the students might get their fill of movies from the in-class programs, Perkins argued that the shows made students more knowledgeable about and receptive to commercial films. Movies also kept the students quiet and occupied, a benefit that teachers and principals everywhere could find attractive.[29]

When minister-exhibitors could not gather sufficient revenue to rent the latest Mary Pickford film releases by "passing the plate" during the movie show, they could take another route and borrow advertising and industrial films for free from various consumer-product manufacturers. For only a dollar per week a church group could overlook its resentment of the automobile's drain on church attendance and rent Henry Ford's *Animated Weekly*. Because they were less expensive to rent, and perhaps because they caused less competitive conflict with local movie theater managers, industrial and advertising films became the affordable alternatives for many churches' movie programs.

Organizing the Church-Show Market: The Community Motion Picture Bureau

One of the largest obstacles minister-exhibitors faced in operating a successful movie program in their churches was locating a steady supply of suitable films. Many of the theatrical films a church group could secure contained some scene or bit of action that someone might find offensive. Censorship was as complicated in practice as it was in theory for the minister-exhibitor, since cutting and splicing film was a chore; and further, such alteration was not likely to be allowed by the local film rental exchange. One guidebook advocated simply covering the projection lens with a card to achieve brief abridgments, but it did warn that this censorship method, like any other, "has a tendency to arouse curiosity. The average person seeks to do the prohibited thing. That is the weakness of much censorship—it places a premium on the censored picture." If motion pictures in the church were going to be viable, ministers needed reliable distribution systems for appropriate films. A prominent religious writer in 1910 noted that "there seems to be a need for some operating agency through which religious bodies may deal directly with manufacturers."[30]

A number of entrepreneurs sought to solve this problem. In 1913, Warren Dunham Foster, then associate editor of the *Youth's Companion* magazine, founded the Community Motion Picture Bureau (CMPB) as an independent film distributor for the nontheatrical exhibition market. His innovation was to offer a packaged service that reduced the time and energy ministers spent selecting and prescreening films. Foster's aggressive sales force approached small-town churches and women's groups and offered them a complete weekly film program, guaranteed to be "clean," preselected, precensored, and perfect for middle-class family audiences. Foster's programs, the salesmen claimed, would be balanced, with a mix of comedies, scenics, newsreels, educational and industrial films (with emphasis on this category), cartoons, and feature films starring popular, wholesome movie performers.[31]

Foster's wife, Edith, managed the CMPB's censorship and selection department. The CMPB purchased prints of a wide variety of theatrical films (some recent, others several years old) from mainstream film producers and obtained scores of advertising and industrial films that were probably donated freely by consumer-product manufacturers. Edith Foster and her staff sifted through the various movie subjects, creating elaborate scrapbooks of film reviews from the exhibitors' trade journals and compiling a fifty-thousand-card film registration file. The staff screened each film and made editing decisions. The registration file cards show that almost all of Mary Pickford's films passed with high approval, and most Ford company films were acceptable. On the other hand, many of the Biograph company's prints of director D. W. Griffith's older one- and two-reel social-problem films were rejected for inclusion in the CMPB program because the themes were deemed too controversial. Charlie Chaplin's films caused the CMPB selection committee much anxiety; Edith Foster and her staff found them vulgar and violent, but public demand for them was too great for their outright rejection by the CMPB. Chaplin's comedies were included in the CMPB program, but records indicate they must have been extensively edited. The staff even rejected a few advertising films, usually for their low quality rather than their too blatant commercialism. One General Electric industrial film, a tour of its Schenectady plant, was dismissed by the staff as "dull, dull, dull."[32]

The CMPB was a profit-seeking venture, and it charged for its film selection and censorship services. Warren Foster's rental fees must not have been too exorbitant for church groups, however, judging from the howls in the trade press from outraged commercial movie–theater managers, who complained about the CMPB's quick growth and the stiff competition it helped church shows to mount against movie theaters. By 1916 the CMPB was firmly planted in New England and the mid-Atlantic, midwestern, and West Coast states. Its national network of at least fourteen film exchanges included an office at New York's Chautauqua Institute. Foster's field agents even made inroads into the sluggish southern film market, operating two exchanges despite the region's fundamentalist objections to movies.[33]

The CMPB gained a tremendous boost in prominence and revenue during America's involvement in the First World War. The YMCA, which organized entertainment for American military camps in the United States and Europe, contracted with the CMPB to provide all the motion picture exhibition service for American troops in the United States and abroad. For the good of the war effort, studios provided the CMPB with films. The YMCA itself had tried and failed to provide adequate movie service for the troops; its film bureau had been poorly organized, and at least one of the ships transporting the YMCA's collection of films to France was torpedoed and sunk. Practically overnight, Warren and Edith Foster and their CMPB staff trained projectionists and organized an extensive network of mobile film exchanges and projection equipment that brought his patented "clean" shows to fifty-five million servicemen and - women in U.S. military base theaters and in makeshift airdome theaters in France. Edith Foster frantically screened millions of feet of film to assemble programs for camps in the United States and overseas. "I try to get away from my own opinion entirely and to look at the film with the eyes of a soldier," she commented self-assuredly to a *New York Times* reporter. "One who is going to pick out pictures for the army has to know the camps and live the life of soldier at heart before she can be an accurate judge." Her "soldier's eyes" guided her to avoid romance and "eternal triangle" films of sexual jealousy. She decreed that in the American camps the weekly programs would include "[o]ne all-man program— pictures of fighting, racing, adventure in the great outdoors; one comedy and one drama." Over in France, sentimentality and homesickness ruled the camp movie screens, as Edith Foster claimed soldiers sent requests for pictures of home, mothers, and children.[34]

After the war, by 1920, the Fosters and the CMPB claimed that they practically had "control of all nontheatrical business" in the United States, but their downfall was swift. The major film studios, Warren Foster's previous suppliers, began to move in and gain control over the threatening nontheatrical market that the CMPB and other church film distributors had nurtured. The CMPB attempted to manufacture its own films as its suppliers withdrew, but it was too small an organization to produce more than a few films by itself. The CMPB made an agreement in 1920 with film producer Lewis J. Selznick's Republic Distributing Corporation (itself on shaky business footing) to have Republic supply it with films and to act as distributor, but these efforts were too late to prevent the CMPB from being squeezed out by the large studios. Soon, the CMPB found itself nearly put out of business by the increasingly powerful film producer-distributors. Paramount and other studios moved quickly and forcefully to corner the church-show and advertising film markets, and just as swiftly put the alternative shows and distributors out of business to protect the studios' huge new investments in movie theaters.[35]

The Swift Demise of the Church-Show Market

The Ford company's film department and the CMPB were postwar casualties both of the big studios' expansion and of exhibitors' backlash against advertising. A Buffalo exhibitor, asked to sign a new rental contract with Ford in 1920, reported, "I informed the exchange manager that the subjects in this release were very good but that every sub-title was a direct ad for a large manufacturer and that this manufacturer should pay the exhibitor for running the film instead of the exhibitor paying a rental for the film." He cited such scenes as "drug store interiors with all the well known drugs prominently displayed on the counters; bill boards along roads; signs on stores or side of buildings, etc." Henry Ford's vicious postwar antisemitic pronouncements also gravely damaged the film series' reputation among Jewish film exhibitors. Circulation of the *Educational Weekly* and *Animated Weekly* quickly dwindled; in only nine months, the number of outlets exhibiting Ford films plummeted from over five thousand theaters to thirteen hundred. The Ford company discontinued the film series in December 1921.[36]

Newly appointed movie "czar" Will H. Hays met with exhibitors' groups in March 1922 to hammer out a code of ethics in distributor-exhibitor relationships. One of the agreement's three main points asserted, "No paid advertising should be inserted in any feature pictures, comedy, scenic or newsreel." Many consumer-product manufacturers nevertheless retained their enthusiasm for connections to motion pictures. They simply moved outside the movie theater into the broader realm of consumer culture, exchanging on-screen displays of their products for a more indirect approach and associating their goods with the movies through movie star product-endorsement advertisements in the growing number of movie fan magazines.[37]

The Motion Picture Theater Owners of America (MPTOA), a prominent exhibitors' organization, declared in 1920 that "we condemn as unfair competition, the leasing or giving free of charge, or by playing percentage, by any School, Church, Community House, or Charitable Organization, of pictures in conflict with the use of such pictures by a motion picture theatre." The eradication of independent industrial film producers and distributors like Ford and the CMPB spelled an end to many church- and community-sponsored movie shows, even if their loss did not stifle alternative movie shows completely. In 1925, the MPTOA reported that all major studios had closed their nontheatrical sales divisions "and that the furnishing of feature pictures to any such competitive centers is discouraged and will ultimately be discontinued entirely." In a 1925 address to a prominent women's club, Will Hays pled the theater manager's case:

> To show entertainment pictures—the sort we see in the motion picture theatre—either free or at a low price or at whatever price, in school or church, is to set up an altogether unfair, unjust and uneconomic competition to the theatre owner whose livelihood comes from the show-

ing of pictures, who has a large investment in his property, his building, his music and his film rentals, and who pays extra-high taxes, insurance rates and the like from all of which the churches and schools
are free.[38]

While it is possible that church shows might have remained direct competition for exhibitors if the film industry had not been going through a phase
of consolidation, conservative critics were also abandoning their hopes of
harnessing the motion picture for their own uses. By the mid-1920s, fric-
tion between liberal and fundamentalist church factions, moralists' objections to Hollywood scandals, and middle-class audience members' decision that they preferred to see their movies in movie theaters—all
undermined support for church-sponsored movie shows.

When Robert and Helen Lynd in 1924 interviewed YMCA leaders
and church ministers in Muncie, Indiana, about the health of their organizations, all religious groups admitted frustration at trying to attract and
hold the interest of their young people. The Lynds counted 31,000 ad-
missions to Muncie movie theaters each week versus 20,632 persons in
church. The elders complained that youngsters did not seem as interested
as the previous generation in attending both Sunday morning and evening
services, Wednesday prayer meetings, group functions, and the like. On
the other hand, well-attended afternoon and evening movie shows made
Sunday the biggest day at the box offices of Muncie's nine movie theaters.
Exhibitors reported that their Sunday evening shows were filled with children and young couples on Sunday dates. (Doubtless, many other Muncie citizens stayed home from both church and the movies.)[39]

One conservative Muncie mother who capitulated to her children's
Sunday restlessness told the Lynds, "I let them go to the movies because,
while I don't like the idea and was never brought up that way myself, I'm
glad to get them out of the house." Another Muncie mother still banned
her children's participation in Sunday movies, dances, or card games.
Nevertheless, she lamented, "I give way at some new place each year."
The Lynds found middle-class children attending the movies more often
and throwing off Sunday taboos more quickly than their working-class
schoolmates. While one-third of the working-class children they interviewed agreed that it was wrong to go to the movies on Sunday, only
one-sixth of the middle-class youths concurred.[40]

The local YMCA and the Protestant ministers in Muncie established
movie programs in 1924 to recapture the interest of the town's errant

middle-class youth. The largest Protestant church in Muncie, "in an effort to find and hold a crowd," began showing a four-part film series on the life of Abraham Lincoln at its Sunday evening service, the minister presumably lecturing afterward on the president's fine moral example. The Lynds reported that the movie service "lived a brief life before being killed by the strong opposition of one group of church members." Besides, the effort was too little, too late—Muncie's middle-class children had already forsaken their churches for real movie theaters.[41]

Although the Lynds documented significant religious prejudice against the movies in Muncie in 1924, which curbed conservative religious acceptance of moviegoing, several of their interviews revealed that the ban might be of recent vintage. One woman the Lynds spoke with, the wife of a recently converted revivalist preacher, said, "We used to go to the movies once or twice a week, but since February we ain't gone at all, 'cause our church says its wrong—and it saves money, too." The Protestant churches' jealousy of motion pictures might have been due, not to their differences, but to their inherent similarities, the Lynds concluded, slyly pointing out that the appeals fundamentalist churches employed to bring out the penitent yet frenzied revival crowds—the themes of sex and titillation—were the same ones that "the most sensational movies use."[42]

The Lynds reported that one of Muncie's women's clubs organized a program on "the 'problem' of the movies" and discussed motion pictures' influence on the morals and behavior of local youth. One member presented a serious paper entitled "Tendencies of Movies and Their Possibilities." The local women's organizations of Muncie could have taken an instrumental role in policing the theaters and films. They might have pressed forward requests to local theater managers for more educational films or given stronger support to the church shows or the YMCA film series, selecting and thereby channeling the movies into more acceptable forms to fit conservative, middle-class standards. Instead, the clubwomen gave in to their own and their children's fascination with Hollywood glamour and movie fantasy. The Lynds were disappointed, but not surprised, to find that clubwomen devoted most of their discussions of the movie "problem" to "chatty round-table discussion of favorite screen stars, best plays, and why certain ones were chosen by club members." To cap off the situation in Muncie, the town's Rotary Club, that bastion of business respectability, boasted of having a college-educated movie theater manager as an esteemed member.[43]

Despite the outbursts of conservative religious groups, the movies remained a central, accepted part of small-town culture. Conservative, middle-class moviegoers voted with their feet and their dimes and quarters, ultimately supporting mainstream commercial films and regular movie theaters over the precensored offerings of church-sponsored movie shows. By persuasion and by force, the movie industry had secured the loyalty of small-town movie audiences. Movie producers and distributors next proceeded to make small-town audiences dissatisfied with their small-town movie theaters through the siren songs emanating from the new, glittering picture palaces of the big city.

"You Can Have the Strand in Your Own Town"

The Struggle between Urban and Small-Town Exhibition in the Picture Palace Era

"There are so few moving picture houses here [in Manhattan] which attract the most desirable classes," lamented a *Moving Picture World* editorial writer in 1911. "The proud and just boast of many Western and Southern exhibitors, that their patrons come in automobiles, is miles away from being realized in the city and county of New York." Film exhibitors in small towns and medium-sized cities in other sections of the country claimed that there was little comparison between New York City's Lower East Side "nickel dumps," which received all the bad publicity, and their own tidy theaters and respectable audiences. While such comments provided critics with excuses to vent their xenophobic prejudices, they did have a point. Most small-town exhibitors did attract a steady contingent of middle-class patrons along with workers and their families, whereas big-city nickelodeons were perceived to have almost no respectable patronage.[1]

The differences between rural and urban moviegoing expanded dramatically at the end of the nickelodeon period. Small-town exhibitors, social critics, and producer-distributors all thought that the rise of feature films and picture palaces drove a wedge between city and country moviegoing. Such changes, though, could not be attributable to feature films, since the same films appeared in both locations; the picture palaces, however, made quite a difference. In the itinerant and nickelodeon eras, small-town and urban moviegoing experiences had coexisted peacefully (if sometimes grudgingly). Film exhibition had been a disorganized, independently owned and operated small-business field. At the close of the nickelodeon era, however, the maturing film industry built an interconnected system of production, distribution, and exhibition. Now structure and hierarchy entered the picture business, and the balance of equality between urban and small-town film exhibition shifted noticeably, and quickly. The film industry belatedly began to take note of the urban middle class's previous, guilty patronage of big-city nickelodeons and regular attendance at "small-time vaudeville" film programs. The industry only then began to discover the new, more upscale movie theaters and customers. The movie business began to invest in these theaters and to promote them to the public as the new ideal in film exhibition. As one moviegoing experience was promoted as the most desirable, the others inevitably became regarded by the public as inadequate or less preferred.

By the early 1920s, the public saw the small-town moviegoing experience as second-rate when compared with taking in a show at a big-city picture palace. Paramount's advertising propaganda fueled a perception that newer, larger, more elegant theaters naturally offered a better movie show. Certainly the picture palaces offered a richer sensory experience. In most cases, however, the films shown in palaces were still the same as those shown in the older, small-town movie theaters. New films were just shown at palaces sooner, with the organization of the "end-run" distribution system that favored the larger, urban "first-run" theaters. Picture palaces embroidered the moviegoing experience with many nonfilm elements, bedazzling their patrons with impressive stage shows, vaudeville acts, large orchestras, Wurlitzer organs, gloriously opulent decorations, corps of ushers, and all the amenities of theaters with two thousand to five thousand seats. Small-town nickelodeons with three hundred seats could not hope to match such a show, although a new generation of more upscale movie theaters and small-time vaudeville houses that would be the pride of their communities was being built in small towns and medium-sized cities. The small-town moviegoing experience still had a great deal to offer audiences, but big-city picture palaces got all the publicity and attention in the 1920s.

"People Who Do Not 'Need to Go' to the Picture Show": The Urban Middle Class

From the start of the nickelodeon era, New York City had served the film industry as a model of film exhibition and audience demographics. The rationale for this decision was simple; not only was New York the largest city in the nation, but it was the center of the amusement industry, and most film producers and the trade press were then headquartered in Manhattan or its boroughs. New York City's immigrant and working-class nickelodeon patrons monopolized what little attention the film industry had shown its audiences, even though the number of film exhibitors and moviegoers in the largest cities represented only about 25 percent of the national total. Nevertheless, to the film business, the urban segment was the most visible 25 percent of the audience, or the tail that wagged the dog. Like the theatrical and vaudeville worlds, the movie business considered the rest of the country a vast backwater that followed New York's lead.

Most film industry leaders were therefore inclined to pay little heed to the particular situations of exhibitors elsewhere. *Exhibitor's Trade Review* editor W. Stephen Bush, returning from a tour of southern theaters in 1917, chided his colleagues: "We in New York do not always appreciate conditions in the South. We are apt to forget that New York, interesting, picturesque and dominant as it is, after all is only a part of the United States. We fail to get the viewpoint of the 'man in the provinces.'"[2] While Bush's comments found few listeners in New York City, small-town movie theater owners heard him; they were all too cognizant of what one suburban Stamford, Connecticut, exhibitor derisively termed the film industry's "East Side Standard." He claimed the industry myopically geared film production to cater solely to the interests of New York's tenement-district nickelodeons. "The East Side exhibitor has had altogether too much to say in deciding what the public wants and what it does not want," complained the Stamford exhibitor. He charged that so many movie theaters were massed together in New York City's boroughs—450 in one estimate—that they had become "the commercial factor" in film industry decision making. He reminded film producers that the New York film exchanges "supply many out-of-town customers who cater to an intelligent educated trade" in suburbs like his own town, in Rutherford, New Jersey, and even on 116th Street in Manhattan. And he blamed the lack of more suitable films for his middle-class viewers on "The East Side exhibitor [who] has placed the ban on educational or scenic stuff" and who wants only "blood and thunder melodrama."[3]

According to the film industry trade press in the nickelodeon era, the middle-class people of big cities like New York, Boston, Philadelphia, and Chicago stayed away from movie shows, leaving urban nickelodeons to working-class and immigrant audiences. Progressive Era muckraking journalist Mary Heaton Vorse, exposing the horrors of lower Manhattan's tenement district nickelodeons, addressed her urban middle-class readers as "people who do not 'need to go' to the picture show."[4]

Evidence, of course, shows that most of the urban middle class did not ignore motion pictures in the nickelodeon era. In the South, Midwest, and West, the urban middle class attended nickelodeons with enthusiasm. Even in the eastern cities, women on shopping trips and businessmen on their lunch hours were hesitatingly venturing into movie theaters. Cementing the attraction between the urban middle class and motion pictures was the fact that their children attended nickelodeons in droves. The urban middle class acquiesced to the seductions of consumer culture found in the movie theater, but often with guilty hesitation stemming from misgivings about the propriety of nickelodeon attendance and fears about movies' promotion of loosened standards of public morality and behavior.

For all the New York–based film trade press's supposed attention to New York's nickelodeons, the success of small-time vaudeville shows and the opening of elegant picture palaces in Manhattan in 1914 caused a great stir in the local newspapers and in the exhibitors' trade journals. "New Strand Opens; Biggest of Movies" announced the *New York Times*:

> The Strand Theatre at Broadway and 47th Street, the largest and most elaborate moving picture house in New York, which is to be opened to the public this afternoon, threw open its doors last night to a great crowd of invited guests who inspected the theater top to bottom. . . . . The seating capacity of the new theatre, which was originally intended to be a home for big musical productions at popular prices, is almost 3,500 and marks the rapid growth from the rebuilt store moving picture theaters.

S. L. "Roxy" Rothapfel, soon to be the king of movie palace managers, was the first program director of the Strand. During the spring of 1914, it was also announced that Proctor's Fifth Avenue Theater would switch from vaudeville to movie shows and that the Metropolitan skating rink, on Broadway and Fifty-second Street, would be renovated into a "cinematograph playhouse with an expensive pipe organ and private boxes intended to attract society patrons"; it would show D. W. Griffith films and other "elaborate photoplays." On the other hand, in March 1914, theatrical impresario Oscar Hammerstein won an injunction (on appeal) to keep movies out of his Republic Theater. The court ruled that it was "an open question whether motion pictures were not a lower form of dramatic art than high class drama for which the theatre had been leased, and whether the presentation of a film play did not damage the theatre as a place of dramatic presentations."[5]

The New York press and the film industry reacted as if middle-class urban audiences appeared out of nowhere, fully fashioned, at the Strand, Rivoli, Rialto, and other pioneering picture palaces in Manhattan. The picture palaces offered New York City's middle-class audiences what Ben Hall has described as "an acre of seats in a garden of dreams." The palaces also offered middle-class New Yorkers the opportunity to "come out of the closet" and admit their movie patronage in a public manner, the way middle-class moviegoers in medium-sized cities and small towns had been doing all along.[6]

The widely perceived "suddenness" of the shift in the class composition of New York City's movie audiences was due in part to the trade press's shortsightedness. Russell Merritt and Douglas Gomery have demonstrated that the already existing, steady patronage of urban middle-class moviegoers at city nickelodeons spurred film exhibitors' expansion into the larger and more elegant theaters. As a few observers at the time also noted, New York's pattern of film exhibition may have been an atypical case study for middle-class entertainment. Entrepreneurs in Denver, Milwaukee, and dozens of other sizable cities had been encouraged by excellent box-office receipts at local nickelodeons to build upscale motion picture theaters with one thousand or more seats. New York City, however, had a larger and more visible concentration of working-class nickelodeons for critics to disparage and a smaller supply of middle-class and mixed-class movie theaters than any other city in the country.[7]

Film historians have identified a variety of factors that caused the urban middle class to adopt the moviegoing habit in the mid-1910s, including the opening of elegant movie palaces; the establishment of higher ticket prices in palaces, which made their audiences more class exclusive; the release of spectacular and costlier feature-length films; and the emergence of movie stars with "respectable" images, such as Mary Pickford and Douglas Fairbanks. As Merritt, Gomery, and Robert Allen have argued, however, if some segments of the urban middle class had not attended big-city nickelodeons in steadily rising numbers from 1907 and 1908 on, film exhibitors would hardly have begun to finance and construct the second generation of larger and more opulent small-time vaudeville movie theaters and picture palaces in city commercial centers and middle-class residential neighborhoods.[8]

The urban middle class's attitude toward nickelodeons and movie-going exposed its deep ambivalence toward commercial amusement and the encroaching consumer culture. Urban middle-class adults claimed to be chagrined when caught entering movie shows. Nevertheless, even big-city, middle-class audiences had been attracted to the educational, "uplifting" exhibitions of scenic, religious, and industrial motion pictures held in more respectable settings like lecture halls and churches. Their continued interest in motion pictures inexorably drew them into film exhibitions in the cities' vaudeville theaters and nickelodeons.

Unlike the more constricted social world of the small town, the social milieu of the urban middle class provided plenty of class-specific entertainment and activities for enjoyment besides movies. Since the mid-nineteenth century, an increasingly wide range of amusements had become available to the middle class in urban areas such as New York City, from public parks and private clubs to restaurants, cabarets, Broadway shows, the symphony, the opera, and the spreading realm of department stores and other emporiums of consumer goods and luxuries. Middling-level amusement seekers in New York may have cared less for the city's movie theaters because there was so much else to do.[9]

In 1909, *Moving Picture World* published a series of articles for the prospective nickelodeon investor. In "Selecting a Theater Location," author F. H. Richardson clung to older, class-segregated ideas of popular entertainment, writing that "if the neighborhood is a very wealthy one, a nickel house will likely draw no considerable patronage except children, servants and transients." In Richardson's opinion, the urban middle class had not yet become "accustomed to purchasing their amusement" and would need to be "educated to do it." But as an afterthought he wrote that middle-class children could be counted on as steady movie patrons. Another *Moving Picture World* columnist in 1910 fumed in exasperation at the urban middle class's reticence at acknowledging its nickelodeon attendance, "not that educated people do not go to moving picture shows;

they do, as we know by actual observation." He suggested that urban exhibitors should promote educational films to make middle-class adults "see that the picture is something more than a mere trick for entertaining young people."[10]

Michael Davis's 1911 survey of commercial recreation in New York City found that despite their spoken prejudices against going to the movies, middle-class New Yorkers were mixing with working-class audiences in the city's various entertainment venues. Davis estimated that nearly 40 percent of the vaudeville audience, 33 percent of the audience for small-time vaudeville (a combination of variety acts and films, a newer upscale form of movie show), and 25 percent of the nickelodeon audience in Manhattan were white-collar men and women.[11]

Perplexed by the extent of middle-class patronage he found at movies and vaudeville shows, Davis looked more closely at the amusement habits of urban middle-class children. He conducted a survey of middle- and working-class children attending public schools which showed that 62 percent of those children attended the movies once a week or more often. These findings he compared to a survey of fifty-nine upper-middle-class girls who attended "expensive private schools." Of these young women, he reported, forty-four, "or 74 percent, declared they never went to moving picture shows, 10 percent [six students] went 'rarely,' and half of the remainder [nine students] 'often.' The latter were mostly girls under 12, few of the older girls declaring attendance. All these children, however, went to high-priced theatres, the elder girls frequently."[12] Davis had found that middle-class boys and men outnumbered girls and women in movie shows in New York City by a two-to-one ratio. The status-conscious young women he interviewed might have been loath to admit to any interest in the "common" nickelodeon show, but they were quite proud of their many excursions to Broadway theaters, where the middle class constituted almost half the audience. The younger girls perhaps felt less protective of social standing and answered Davis's questions with more forthrightness.

If there were so many other amusements in which the urban middle class could partake, did they need the movies? Part of the answer lies in the fact that not all members of the middle class were equally entertained. Indeed, children were relatively underamused, and nickelodeon theaters exploited this new constituency. Urban middle-class children had parks and school playgrounds in which to play, and toys and libraries and social clubs. But, compared with their parents, they did not enter the work force as early, endured more years of schooling, had larger amounts of after-school time on their hands, and were less burdened with chores in their "modern" households. Urban middle-class adults had an expanding realm of commercialized leisure to entertain them, including restaurants, department stores, theaters, cabarets, and vacation resorts, but these were not places for children. Middle-class youngsters, however, had increasing amounts of small change jangling in their pockets from allowances and gifts, and had a relatively crime-free social environment that permitted them the freedom to roam their urban and suburban neighborhoods unaccompanied. Urban middle-class children represented a wealthy new leisure market waiting to be tapped, and various retail concerns (candy stores, soda fountains, movie theaters) eagerly began to court these young consumers' business. Their movie attendance paved the way for their parents' acceptance of the movies.[13]

Meanwhile, New York City's middle-class families (especially if they were theatergoers) could not escape the frequent references to movies and nickelodeon theaters that surfaced in numerous Broadway musical comedies, reviews, and vaudeville skits. One example is the tune "The Cinematograph Man," from the popular 1909 Broadway review, *The Beauty Spot*. In this song and skit, a Park Avenue swell, feeling run-down and blue, goes to his doctor. The doctor recommends regular visits to the cinematograph (nickelodeon) to see the comedies. The man goes and is so affected by the jerkiness of the poorly projected films that he contracts a kind of St. Vitus's dance. In the song's chorus, the cinematograph man "flickers" across the stage. Irving Berlin contributed the number "At the Picture Show" to the 1912 production starring Eva Tanguay, *The Sun Dodgers,* and dancing girls frenetically performed the jerky, syncopated "Moving Picture Glide" in the Winter Garden Theater's *Passing Show of 1914*. Tin Pan Alley lyricists and Broadway show producers often wove songs dealing with the latest American fads and foibles into their shows, and we can assume from the regular appearance of movie-related songs that middle- and upper-class Broadway audiences were familiar enough with the movies to appreciate the topical humor.[14]

Outside New York City in the other large urban centers, nickelodeons were not as removed from urban middle-class experience as social critics contended. In Boston, Baltimore, and Milwaukee, movie theaters were located at transportation hubs in the downtown commercial districts that straddled the borders of working-class and middle-class residential areas. These nickelodeons were located next to department stores, hotels, smaller shops—the commercial outlets that middle-class women and men frequented. Certainly, an intriguingly decorated nickelodeon, beckoning with posters, music, lights, and decorations to weary shoppers or businessmen on their lunch break, was a temptation they could not resist forever. As Russell Merritt has noted:

> Without feature films and refined theaters, it is unlikely that middle-class audiences would have long remained. But the nickelodeon and its one-reelers had in fact performed the initial task generally credited to imported features, movie palaces, and the First World War. The seduction of the affluent occurred not in the cushioned seats of the Roxy, Strand or the Fox Palace, but on the wooden chairs of the Bijou Dream and Theater Comique.[15]

A columnist in the *Boston Journal* questioned her middle-class readers in 1908: "Have you contracted the moving picture show habit yet? Most of the folks I know have, though for some reason they one and all seem loath to acknowledge the fact. Perhaps it is because it seems a childish pastime and not just the form of amusement one would expect worldly men and women to patronize to any extent." She warned that readers' friends and neighbors might be movie patrons, but "you will not know it unless by chance you happen to see him or her buying an admission at the window, or after groping your way to a seat in the dark find one or the other filling the chair at your side." While waiting outside a Boston nickelodeon to meet a female acquaintance who also sheepishly admitted to the movie habit, the reporter encountered all manner of bourgeoisie—local merchants, businessmen, the butcher, a banker, mothers with their children, department store clerks, a doctor, and three women resting from their shopping—on their way into the nickelodeon. "I was just about to give my friend up and venture in alone when another figure loomed before me which made me feel quite conscious," continued the reporter. "It was that of a woman friend of mine who seemed to shrink within herself when she saw me. She felt as I felt no doubt—like a child caught at the jam-pot." Alluding to the middle class's affinity for nonfiction films, the reporter claimed she especially enjoyed "fascinating views of foreign shores, of mirth-provoking happenings and of events in the news which form the basis of the entertainment."[16]

New York theater critic W. W. Winters also noted the guilty pleasures experienced by urban middle-class moviegoers. He described parties of adventure-seeking folk who went downtown "slumming" to city nickelodeons, rubbing elbows in the darkened halls with the working class, and at least for an hour or two, pushing aside ingrained class prejudices. "Somehow you all enter into the spirit of the thing. Armed with a few stray nickels, a bag of peanuts, a good supply of patience and good humor, and oh! what a time we did have! . . . Don't you slip away from yourself, lose your reticence, reserve, pride and a few other things?" Winters recounted the continuing struggle amusement-seeking urban middle-class people felt between desiring pleasure and exercising restraint. "Of course, it's understood that you had not only no idea of ever going in the 'cheap' places, but, when you were finally inveigled in, that you would go once, but never again. But what's the use? Why not submit gracefully and admit that the five-cent theaters have a place all their own and that, after all, you are going again."[17]

The Urban Picture Palace's Consequences for Small-Town Exhibition

The film industry in the 1910s, like other growing consumer-product manufacturers, began vertical integration of manufacturing and marketing, expanding from film production further into distribution and film exhibition. Film producers became much more interested in film audiences and began to pay more attention to the "new" genteel urban movie audiences. Now that the big-city middle class admitted to itself that, "after all, you are going again," entrepreneurs began to build more elegant movie theaters for it to attend. In the same way that consumer-product manufacturers strove to attract many different types of customers in a nationwide market to their limited number of brand products, the film industry now also wished to have all the diverse kinds of moviegoers act like a nationwide audience. But it was not to be a nationwide audience of equal viewers. The urban moviegoing experience was promoted as the industry standard, and small-town viewers, a "silent majority," were left to follow behind, frustrated and envious.[18]

The evolution of the film industry's attitudes toward its audience, which in turn influenced the image of moviegoers in the wider popular culture, came with film manufacturers' efforts to achieve vertical integration within their industry. Begun hesitantly by studios such as Lubin and Vitagraph, who exhibited their films in their own theaters (Lubin's chain of theaters in Philadelphia and Baltimore, and the Vitagraph theater in

Advertisement for Paramount films, in *Saturday Evening Post*, April 14, 1917, p. 123. Author's collection.

Brooklyn), film producers' efforts to control the distribution and exhibition of their own movies finally began to be realized in 1914, with the growth of the Paramount–Famous Players–Lasky Corporation.

Adolph Zukor and other Paramount executives sensed that large profits could be made in exploiting the urban middle class's interest in motion pictures. The company promoted spectacular, feature-length film adaptations of stage plays starring prestigious Broadway stars. It invested in the construction of a huge, elegant movie palace in the Broadway district of New York, the Strand Theater, which would be dedicated exclusively to the exhibition of Famous Players–Lasky films. Paramount then conducted extensive, nationwide advertising campaigns in prominent newspapers and magazines, which were some of the earliest and most prominent film advertisements ever addressed primarily to moviegoers and not just to exhibitors.

In 1917, Paramount inaugurated an ambitious program of advertising in nationally distributed magazines like *Saturday Evening Post* and *Ladies' Home Journal* to promote the benefits of moviegoing to the middle class. The campaign theme was "You can have 'The Strand' in your own town." Paramount appealed to the aspirations of middle-class, small-town dwellers to run in the same social circles and to be as culturally "current" as their city cousins through the movie theater's agency:

> Last time you were in New York you went to 47th Street and Broadway and joined the big crowd of good-looking, well-dressed people that passed through the gay entrance of the Strand. . . . You sat in the loge and looked over the great orchestra, the sweep of faces in the wide balcony, and then you watched the best motion pictures you had ever seen. . . . You wished that you could have such a theatre at home . . . with pictures like those and a crowd like that. You have the Strand in your town if you have Paramount Pictures! You have the good plays and the good audience.[19]

The same Paramount films would transform any Main Street theater into Broadway, Paramount pledged, and change sleepy villages into "centers of metropolitan animation during the hours that used to yawn." There would be "[n]o more 9 o'clock towns, and no more 9 o'clock people!"[20]

While Paramount proudly proclaimed in its 1920 advertising that Strand Theaters in Manhattan and Middletown "both show the same pictures," the company systematically denigrated the small-town theater in favor of the more opulent picture palace (which, not coincidentally,

Paramount was building or purchasing by the score) as the site of the ideal moviegoing experience:

> Whether you attend a million-dollar palace of the screen in the big city, or a tiny hall in a backwoods hamlet, you will find that it is always the best and most prosperous theatre in the community that is exhibiting Paramount Artcraft Pictures. . . . A theatre cannot be better than the pictures it shows. Good music, wide aisles, luxurious seating and fine presentation have all naturally followed as the appropriate setting for Paramount Artcraft Pictures.[21]

Paramount began to build or purchase movie palaces in other major cities, and other theater-chain entrepreneurs, such as Marcus Loew and William Fox, followed suit. Interested in attracting only a portion of the nation's movie audience, the urban middle class, they nevertheless shaped the popular ideal of the moviegoing experience for viewers across the country.

Although movie audiences in Strand Theaters in small towns and big cities alike may have seen the same Paramount films, certain basic inequalities existed. For instance, they did not view prints of equally pristine quality. Small-town exhibitors had complained throughout the nickelodeon era, to little avail, about the dismal state of the heavily used prints they received from distributors. One Philadelphia exchange manager tried to mollify disgruntled rural theater owners in 1907 by describing the brief life of the fragile one-reel film. He explained that the largest city theaters claimed such a film the first week for a sixty-dollar rental; but only three weeks later, badly worn, it became the only film tiny small-town nickelodeons could afford to rent, at fifteen or twenty dollars. Prematurely old, streaked, and scratched prints were derisively labeled "junk films." One industry critic scolded the small-town exhibitors who screened these cheap but inferior prints, writing that "the audience thinks it's watching a combination snow and rain storm." In 1919, a St. Petersburg, Florida, exhibitor blamed exchanges, complaining that his audiences liked the same films as city folks, yet because his small theater could afford to rent only sixty-day-old prints, his patrons saw nothing but scratched, chopped, patched, and unpleasant-to-view films. The film industry, of course, tried to downplay or minimize these complaints when it was to its profitable advantage. It wanted its relatively small stock of films to be seen by the largest possible number of people in the largest number of theaters. Small-town theaters remained the "end of the line" in distribution.[22]

It became the height of civic responsibility and pride for any town or medium-sized city with aspirations toward big-city status to have a picture palace. In the mid-1920s, Cooperstown got a five-hundred-seat mini-palace, the Smalley, courtesy of onetime Cook and Harris company rival William Smalley, who had become a theater magnate controlling more than twenty movie theaters in central New York state villages. The Palace Theater in Canton, Ohio, was built in 1926 as a monument to successful local druggist and patent-medicine manufacturer H. H. Ink. The Palace was an "atmospheric" theater, its auditorium decorated to look like a Spanish garden in the twilight, its ceiling painted a deep blue and set with tiny lightbulb "stars" that twinkled on cue. It cost one million dollars to build and seated 1,900 people. Just two months later, the Loew's Corporation opened an equally opulent theater, which seated 2,175 people, just across the street. With seating capacity suddenly increased by nearly 50 percent to 9,700, Canton's twelve movie theaters faced stiff competition for patrons.[23]

While the picture palaces, as inheritors of the nickelodeon movie theater tradition, possessed elegant and attractive exteriors, their interiors and attention to audience comfort drew the most notice and comments from audiences and social critics. The picture palaces in many ways built on trends in the decoration of hotels, restaurants, stage theaters, and imposing public buildings like train stations, post offices, and libraries. The picture palace had many things in common especially with the department store, and recapitulated in the 1910s and 1920s the department store's evolution from the dry-goods emporium of the mid-nineteenth century to the fantastical palace of consumption. Like rival department store owners, managers of competing picture palaces vied to introduce more and more luxuries for their clientele—women's retiring lounges, men's smoking rooms, baby nurseries, smartly uniformed ushers, and luxurious furniture, carpeting, and wall hangings for all to admire.[24]

The differences between urban and rural moviegoing intensified with the construction of ever more fabulous picture palaces like the Capitol, State, and Roxy in New York City, the Uptown and Chicago Theaters in Chicago, and those in other big cities in the 1920s. The several hundred first-run urban theaters were owned or controlled by producer-distributors like Paramount–Famous Players–Lasky, Loew's–MGM, Fox, and

Warner Brothers–First National. Although they represented only about 20 percent of the nation's twenty thousand movie theaters in the 1920s, these enormous, opulent theaters soon generated the majority of film producers' profits. Producers found that by maintaining the leading outlets, they could exert a profitable, oligopolistic effect on the mass of independently owned theaters.[25]

The local Bijou on Main Street was increasingly an insufficient outlet for consumer-culture-driven fantasies; as one Iowa exhibitor reported, people in small towns wanted the standards of movie presentation found in the big cities. Even setting their sights higher did not help, for no matter how elegant the large town and small city's minipalaces strove to be, they were continually outclassed by the ever more huge and overblown big-city palaces.[26]

In some ways this increasing disparity would be mitigated by the growing popular culture of film, which was fostered by the fan magazines and by the promotion of movie stars and was available to urban and small-town moviegoers alike. However, the cosmopolitan attitudes promoted in the glamorous society films produced by Cecil B. DeMille and starring Gloria Swanson and Norma Talmadge also contributed to some small-town viewers' sense of dissatisfaction. Theater critic W. H. Bridge, surveying the impact of movies on small-town life in 1921, had noticed that this dissatisfaction had a definite generational dimension. "Undoubtedly the outstanding element in the life of the young in a small town is the movie," he wrote. "It is the big emotion, the adventure, the escape. . . . Home life itself is a dull interval between shows, and must be enriched with perusal of a movie magazine or a practical simulation of the current heroine, with the help of a beauty box."[27]

Robert and Helen Lynd found that both age and class played a role in the small-town movie doldrums. They reported that even as Muncie's youth crowded into its nine movie theaters in the mid-1920s, teenagers constantly complained about the lack of entertainment opportunities and escaped whenever possible by automobile to Indianapolis's ornate picture palaces. Middle-class teens outnumbered working-class young people in the Muncie movie audiences, as the latter seldom had enough money to attend regularly. The Lynds concluded their study with concern that the movies and their sensationalist advertising campaigns emphasizing sexual titillation and conspicuous consumption wore away at the bonds of family, community authority, and small-town tradition.[28]

Having the Strand in one's own hometown seemed a broken promise

Advertisement for Paramount films, in *Theatre Magazine*, December 1919,
p. 432. Author's collection.

for some small-town moviegoers by the mid-1920s. For most movie patrons outside the big cities, the small-town theater was an accepted compromise between urban and rural, whereas for others the picture palace remained an unrealized dream. At least in Paramount magazine ads and in the pages of the fan magazines, moviegoers in rural areas, small towns, and big cities appeared to merge into a nationwide audience, and it suited the film industry's needs to perpetuate this impression. The earlier distinctive forms of vibrant itinerant exhibition and genteel, mixed-class nickelodeon moviegoing available in small towns was subsumed by the growing film industry into what seemed to some critics a diluted, meager version of the favored urban picture palace experience.

But if only one type of exhibition was most sought after, how did the small-town movie theaters endure and not simply go out of business? The answer lies in the creation of movie fan culture. The proliferation of movie fan magazines, the evolution of male and female movie fans, the cults of movie star worship, the spread of movie references to other parts of popular culture, even the linkage of movie stars to consumer culture through product endorsements—all worked to compensate small-town movie fans for any perceived deficiencies in their local experience. One nationwide mass of movie fans shared a common moviegoing culture, whose creation reinforced similarities between the tiniest, most run-down, small-town nickelodeons and the most sumptuous big-city picture palaces.

Despite being overwhelmed by the picture palaces, small-town movie theaters still continued to offer, within a familiar community setting, the considerable pleasures of fantasy-inflected Hollywood movies, mysterious film stars, and movie fan culture.

The Rise of the Movie Fan

Movie fan culture was created through a dialogue between the film industry and viewers. On one side of the dialogue were the commercial practices and promotional efforts of the film producers to publicize films and stars, as well as the exhibitors' efforts to attract the public to movie theaters though local advertising and other on-site activities. On the other side of the dialogue, audience members absorbed the publicity materials provided by the studios, read fan publications, and shared Hollywood gossip with like-minded friends. What they created was a truly popular culture of film. Movie fan culture started with material provided by the film industry and then was re-created as scrapbooks, poems, fan letters to the magazines and the stars, and fan-written film scripts—all created by moviegoers for their own enjoyment. Movie fan culture consisted not only of tangible items and gossip swapped at the lunch table, but it was also present in the fantasies the fans generated from the movies, the movie-influenced attitudes, behaviors, and identities that moviegoers experimented with.

About Movie Fans

Although we all go the movies, we do not all invest moviegoing with the same emotional energy. The movie fan has always been a breed apart from the average person who occasionally drops in at a theater; fans are the most visible and most passionately engaged segment of the film audience. In the "classical Hollywood cinema" period, from the mid-1910s to the 1960s, movie fans were depicted in films, books, plays, and popular song as eccentric, even obsessive people who spent too much time in theaters, who thought and talked incessantly about celebrities, and who perhaps dreamed of "going Hollywood" themselves and becoming movie stars. Since the late 1910s, this depiction of movie fans as deluded daydreamers has been considered feminine, but this was not always so.

The usual depiction of movie fans in the silent film era featured starstruck, teenaged girls mobbing movie stars at film premieres, hysterically fainting at Rudolph Valentino's funeral, or mooning over photos and Hollywood gossip in the fan magazines. The few males among the dedicated movie fans were ridiculous figures—antisocial, emasculated dimwits—like the title character of a popular 1923 novel, *Merton of the Movies,* which became a successful play and film. Merton was a moviecrazed, small-town simpleton who became a Hollywood celebrity only because of dumb luck and the fact that he physically resembled a popular film actor.

Popular culture in the 1920s helped reinforce the image of movie fandom as feminine and obscured the fact that there had existed an era of negotiation over the identity and role of the fan. In the nickelodeon era, both male and female hobbyists experimented with various modes of interaction with the growing film industry. While fans eagerly sought a dialogue with the film studios and film publications, the industry was eventually successful in establishing boundaries of fan participation in the creation of films, scripts, and fan magazines. The new limits truncated most avenues of amateur participation in script production and direct lines of contact between fans and film actors. Much previously acceptable "masculine" interest in the movies—such as the interest in the optics of projection and in the technical aspects of film production—also became marginalized. These boundaries nevertheless encouraged the growth of a rich and multilayered movie fan culture that provided a mediated link between viewers and the glamorous fantasy of movie stars and the film

Sheet music cover, 1913. Author's collection.

industry. Movie fan culture brought new pleasures and meanings to the experience of moviegoing for women and men in the largest cities and smallest towns in the golden age of Hollywood film.

The male movie fan's marginalization occurred in movie fan magazines soon after the close of the nickelodeon period, between 1915 and the United States's entry into the First World War. Despite the male movie fan's disappearance from fan discourse, men and boys continued to have an equal presence with women in the movie audience. After the shift, male enjoyment of the movies was considered to be more detached than female enjoyment, which included absorption in Hollywood gossip; men supposedly reserved their fanlike enthusiasms for more "masculine" interests such as sporting events, wireless radio, and war news.

The subject of media fandom has received increasing attention as scholars employing reader-, viewer-, and listener-reception theories have moved beyond the critical position of audiences as passive spectators and have explored how audiences have used mass media to shape their identities, attitudes, and behavior. Janice Radway, Lisa Lewis, Henry Jenkins, Jackie Stacey, and others have used ethnographic methods to examine such contemporary media audiences as romance-novel readers, Madonna "wannabes," and female science fiction fans, who share their interests at group meetings and conventions and create their own short stories, novels, music, artwork, and videos based on favorite programs. These studies have substantially increased our understanding of how viewers, listeners, and readers appropriate elements of popular texts to create pleasurable and meaningful narratives of romance and adventure for their own personal fulfillment.[1]

Men and boys have often been absent from these pathbreaking studies of fandom, which have focused primarily on the intersections of mass media and feminine culture. In media fan research, it is assumed either that men actively denigrate or have little interest in the subject matter (such as romance novels), or like the legions of male science fiction and rock music fans, they form the dominant audience group from which women and girls differentiate themselves through their fannish activities. Most of these ethnographic studies have also concentrated on contemporary media culture—television, pop music, and fiction. The scholar's interviewing techniques are not easily transferred to historical examination of film audiences, which often requires a reliance on sources much less direct, such as surveys, letters, autobiographical accounts, fan publications, and other past representations of fans in popular culture.

An example of a historical model of a male-oriented media fan culture is Susan Douglas's depiction of the amateur wireless-radio hobbyists of the 1910s and 1920s. The "radio boys" were urban middle-class youth who sought an expressive masculine culture of brainy invention and hands-on technical expertise, of adventure and entrepreneurship, while following in the footsteps of Thomas Edison and the Wright brothers. They assembled their own crystal radio sets from odds and ends and communicated with other enthusiasts throughout the country and around the globe. The popular science press celebrated the radio boys' entrepreneurship but expressed concern when the amateurs clashed with corporate forces that wished to move wireless communication toward commercial broadcasting. The radio boys lost their formative role in the development of AM radio broadcasting as many became listeners rather than communicators, though some radio enthusiasts (primarily men and boys) channeled their energies into the marginal area of shortwave radio communication.[2]

The rise of movie fan culture and of the roles it afforded male movie fans to some extent paralleled the radio enthusiasts' model. Motion picture film cameras and projectors were more complex and expensive to fabricate than broadcasting apparatus, and movie production never offered amateurs the level of accessibility that crystal sets gave to the radio boys. Nevertheless, it was not inevitable that becoming a devotee of motion pictures or reading fan magazines would be seen by the public as primarily a passive, leisure activity for young women or that movie fan culture would seem so inhospitable to the professed interests of male movie fans.

Origins of the Fan

The evolution of the term *movie fan* occurred in the context of long-existing ideas about celebrity, spectatorship, and gender roles in European and American culture. Leo Braudy traces the roots of Western preoccupation with fame and the public person back to Roman times. He finds the advent of the anonymous admirer of famous persons to be a product of the publicity and renown garnered in the eighteenth century by such eminent men as David Hume, Jean-Jacques Rousseau, and Samuel Johnson. The term *fan* itself has two origins; one comes from the world of sports and masculinity, the other from discourse on aberrant psychological behaviors that were often labeled feminine. One early use of the term *fan* dates to the 1700s. British sporting enthusiasts who "fancied" such spectator sports as boxing and horse racing were called "fancies," an effete term that was eventually shortened to the more virile-sounding "fan."[3]

By the middle of the nineteenth century, the term *fan* had gained wide usage in the United States to describe ardent male supporters of baseball. Sports fans loyally rooted for teams with which they shared common geographical or institutional bonds. Spurred by newspapers' coverage of individual performers' efforts, fans began to single out favorite players for admiration. Increased newspaper publicity about heroic sports personalities across the country opened the way for baseball fans to gain interest in teams outside their localities. Being a "sports fan" carried a certain cachet, as the physical exertion on the baseball field and unwavering support in the stands for one's team and community was deemed admirable, masculine, and patriotic.[4]

American middle- and working-class women of the nineteenth century, although representing only a small proportion of the spectators at sporting events, were nevertheless eager participants in the growing fascination with fame. Women and girls were widely criticized for their frivolous addiction to novel reading; indeed, they were disparaged more often for their "fanatical" interests in books and authors than were men with similar interests. Women were prominent in the crowds who thronged the engagements of touring celebrities such as composers, opera singers, statesmen, and literary lions like Charles Dickens, Mark Twain, and Oscar Wilde. Female audience members also participated in the creation of the "matinee idol" of the legitimate stage. Although American women and girls of the Victorian era were increasingly engaged in fanlike behavior, the term *fan* was then rarely applied to them.[5]

By 1900, American theatrical entertainment was firmly entrenched in the cult of personality. Famous actors and actresses toured the country, performing roles geared to exploit their attractiveness and personal magnetism, such as Joseph Jefferson's Rip Van Winkle and Edwin Booth's Hamlet. However, few admirers saw the great stars in person more than once or twice in their lives if they lived outside the major theatrical centers. They often had only photographs, newspaper clippings, or other thirdhand evidence to connect them to flesh-and-blood celebrities. Theatrical promoters began to introduce the stars' names and faces into many areas of consumer culture. Stage performers started to define standards of beauty and sell cosmetics, perfume, shirts, and cigars through testimonial advertisements.[6]

Motion pictures of the prenickelodeon era did not initially contribute much to the growing national obsession with celebrity; presidents, generals, and sports heroes occasionally appeared before the camera while cutting ceremonial ribbons or marching in parades. A few years later, when motion picture producers began to shift the bulk of their production from scenics to story pictures, moviegoers saw theatrical performers more often on film. With a few exceptions, however, these actors were not famous stars of the stage, but journeyman performers. Most film studios operated with stock companies, utilizing the same band of actors and actresses over and over in the roles of ingenue, hero, child, mother. Certain frequently cast actors soon became recognized, and moviegoers across the country became interested in learning the identities of the individuals who played in their favorite film releases each week.

The anonymity of film performers maintained by the major American film producers tantalized and frustrated movie audiences; probably it was a shrewd move by film producers, for it increased moviegoers' clamor to know more. Exhibitors and film industry trade journal reporters began to notice that men and women were seeking out copies of film exhibitors' professional trade journals at newsstands to secure more information about current films and players. Moviegoers wrote to the film studios seeking information on film casts and began to pester their local exhibitors to obtain the names of actors and photo souvenirs of performers they admired. In January 1910, the Kalem company announced it would happily provide exhibitors or individuals with photos of its stock company, but it handed out pictures with no names. Kalem maintained that the performers wished to shield their "good reputations" in the theatrical world and that exhibitors should be reluctant to turn their lobbies into photograph galleries.[7]

Despite the roadblocks thrown up by film producers, some moviegoers, not content with merely uncovering the identities of their favorites, began to attempt to contact the players directly. Viewers wrote to actors they knew only as the "Biograph girl" or "Vitagraph girl" in care of their film studios; others located the studio addresses and haunted the production facilities in Manhattan, Brooklyn, and Chicago. Scornful commentators in the exhibitors' trade press criticized moviegoers who overstepped what they considered the boundaries of propriety. Film studios were flooded with letters from both urban and small-town men bearing marriage proposals to movie actresses. Stage actresses had encountered these unsolicited attentions for many years, and the married lives of stage performers were often kept secret to save the illusion of their availability;

but few in the film industry realized initially that the flickering, soundless, black-and-white images could provoke equally passionate responses in movie viewers. Proposals to film actresses from male admirers soon became expected, though deemed ludicrous by trade press critics; the volume of marriage offers from "forward" female viewers to male film actors, however, shocked them.[8]

At the same time, some American film producers began to publicize the names of their actors and to address movie audiences' interests more directly in advertising campaigns. J. Stuart Blackton, head of the Vitagraph studio, drew on his promotional experience with newspapers and vaudeville to become one of the most enthusiastic proponents of increased producer contact with audiences. In 1910, Vitagraph and other film production companies began to offer souvenir photographs of film performers and other trinkets for sale to movie theater managers, who could either give or resell them to their movie patrons. Trading cards, art prints, cigarette cards, and other customer premiums and bits of advertising had long proven successful in American retailing to promote customer loyalty to particular product brands and stores. Grocery store and department store retailers alike distributed these items for their patrons to collect. Product manufacturers had also participated in premium programs, including spoons, towels, or souvenir cards inside their product packaging. Pictures of lovely young women holding products, which were printed on calendars, postcards, and other ephemera, became popular wall decorations and scrapbook fillers in many middle-class and working-class homes. A number of the women who modeled in consumer-product advertisements subsequently became movie performers, or vice versa. Muriel Ostriche, who posed for Moxie soft-drink advertisements, also starred in Thanhouser company films. Actresses Alice Joyce, Norma Talmadge, and Mabel Normand had backgrounds as models for song slides and advertising art. This overlapping of advertising and motion pictures increased the number of faces on the screen recognizable to movie fans.[9]

The film industry was not unanimous in its support for this new publicity. As one incredulous trade journal columnist commented in February 1910:

> The public, indeed, has its favorite actors and actresses in the silent drama as in the talking play. Manufacturers themselves are recognizing the value of the personalities of the actors and actresses who make the

A small notebook, ca. 1912, that may have encouraged children to daydream about their favorite pastime. Author's collection.

films. They are printing their portraits and distributing them. Some of these portraits have been published in *Moving Picture World*. They are shown in entrances of motion picture theaters. I should not be surprised if before long they do not figure on postal cards. To have your portrait widely distributed on a postal card is the highest pinnacle of histrionic celebrity.[10]

But by November, even the trade journals acknowledged that the machinery of movie stardom had been set in motion, as another reporter noted: "[I]t is only within the last year or so that the personalities of these picture plays have been made known to the public. We are not sure, but we think the *Moving Picture World* when it began to write about 'The Biograph Girl' started the fashion. Now, of course, the veil of anonymity has been gradually turned aside and the public is getting to know more about these moving picture favorites." Even so, only the identities of a few leading players were yet publicized, and the performers themselves were beginning to call for complete cast credits to introduce each reel.[11]

While film performers garnered more attention in 1910, their increasingly devoted, vocal supporters in the movie audience were also gathering notice. During the same year, a newly coined term, *movie fan,* began to be applied to the men and women who regularly and enthusiastically attended nickelodeon shows. Some cultural critics used the term as a sign of their enmity toward working-class film audiences. In a 1910 trade journal article, W. W. Winters wrote of his pleasure-seeking, middle-class friends feeling "deliciously low" while slumming in big-city nickelodeons, but he also chronicled how quickly middle-class people were becoming "fans" themselves. The term gained rapid acceptance in American popular speech. Unlike the association of the term *fan* with baseball spectators, however, *movie fan* from the start accommodated both male and female moviegoers. The designation *movie fan* was flexible enough to apply to a nationwide audience of enthusiastic men, women, and children, blurring many of the class, ethnic, regional, and gender distinctions that had separated audiences for earlier amusements.[12]

Fan Participation in Film Production and Exhibition

The spread of cameras and phonographs into middle-class homes across the United States at the turn of the century made new forms of mass communication and entertainment accessible to hobbyists. Motion pictures, like other Edison inventions, piqued the curiosity of amateur tinkerers as well as business people. *Scientific American* and *Popular Mechanics* magazines published numerous articles on the technology of motion picture photography and projection for the legions of middle- and working-class men and boys fascinated by new mechanical and electrical technology. While it was difficult to build a movie camera from spare parts, by 1898 cameras and projectors could be purchased from several manufacturers or ordered through the Sears catalog. Between 1897 and 1910, Sears's entertainment department outfitted entrepreneurial young men with complete moving picture kits. The relatively easy availability of this new invention started many hobbyists on the road as itinerant motion picture exhibitors.[13]

Among those who sensed the possibilities for exploiting the hobbyist aspects of film exhibition to young tinkerers was Edward Stratemeyer, the undisputed king of boy's adventure fiction. Stratemeyer's publishing syndicate produced over six hundred novels including the Tom Swift and Rover Boys series. In the early 1910s he launched three new series of formulaic juvenile novels that reflected some of the popular interest in movie technology. The Moving Picture Boys series featured four intrepid, honest young men who utilized their movie cameras to shoot newsreel footage, to capture crooks, to foil nefarious plots against local businessmen, and to rescue women and children from disasters. The Motion Picture Chums novels focused on four plucky and entrepreneurial fellows who captured crooks, foiled nefarious plots, and rescued women and children while operating a series of nickelodeon movie theaters. A third series of Stratemeyer juvenile detective novels, The Moving Picture Girls, featured four spunky young heroines who shot newsreels, captured crooks, foiled plots, and saved children with the same verve as such serial queens as Pearl White.[14]

The exhibitors' trade journals took note when they learned of the introduction of toy film projectors, for they saw them as an encouraging sign of the movies' acceptance by urban middle-class parents. Children's toy catalogs offered small-scale film projectors for sale; they had long carried children's magic lantern and stereopticon slide projectors. The inexpensive projectors ran brief strips or short loops of real commercial 35-mm nitrate film, which allowed young exhibitors to put on a show several seconds long. Later, small reels of film could be accommodated, lengthening the show to several minutes. Nitrate film, of course, was highly flammable, so these projectors were not safe toys for young boys and girls. In the 1920s, "home movie" cameras and projectors appeared which used a smaller gauge film made of nonflammable "safety stock." A small selection of condensed versions of older Hollywood films and snippets of cartoons were printed and sold to amateur exhibitors.[15]

In the film trade journals of the day, exhibitors noted with bemusement that members of their audiences sought participation in the production of films as well as consumption. They also felt some disquietude that their customers wanted to embrace a role contrary to that of passive film spectator. The trade journal columnist who wrote under the pseudonym Lux Graphicus struck a rare sympathetic note for fan interest in October 1910:

> Last week it was pointed out in these pages, in reference to the Eclair
> "Behind the Scenes of a Moving Picture Manufactuory" film which
> has just been released, that we all want to know how the pictures were
> made. We like to see the work done. We like to see the producers di-
> recting the actors and actresses acting. On the ordinary stage, there is
> no greater privilege coveted than that of a seat in the wings while the
> performance is in progress. We all like to be privileged spectators of
> anything. We are all curious.

Across the nation movie enthusiasts wanted to become involved in the movies by writing their own scripts, or scenarios, and marketing them to the studios, by learning the mechanical mysteries of film projection, and by reading novelizations and briefer plot synopses of current film releases.[16]

One of the most popular and widely available opportunities for audience participation in the production of films was the writing of photoplay scenarios, as the brief movie scripts of the nickelodeon era were called. Scenario writing provided one way for fans to create their own "fan literature" based on film characters and situations. Tens of thousands of eager amateur writers across the country, middle-class and working-class men, women, and children, joined the silent film scenario-writing craze, which rivaled only the writing of advertising jingles for contests as a national passion during the 1910s and early 1920s. A columnist for *Moving Picture World* reported in 1913 that "the number of scenario writers is estimated at about fifteen hundred. If a census were made of all who had written one or two scenarios the number would approximate twenty thousand."[17]

Among the many appeals of photoplay writing were its ease and quickness; all one had to compose was a synopsis no longer than a few paragraphs of short-story length. Plot formulas were easy to pick up at the nickelodeon show and from the pulp-fiction magazines. One could live anywhere in the nation and mail scenarios to the film studios; indeed, Herman A. Blackman, a successful author of railroad melodramas, wrote while on the job as a train conductor in Marion, Indiana. The financial rewards of scenario writing could be inviting. The studios offered anywhere from five to fifty dollars for each scenario they accepted. These factors made scenario writing especially attractive to audience members who wanted to get into the movies but who did not possess physical beauty or acting talent, or who lived far from the film production centers of New York, Chicago, and California. Scenario writing also allowed thousands of movie fans a creative outlet for their film-inspired fantasies.[18]

Epes Winthrop Sargent, longtime trade journal columnist and story editor for several studios, looked back in his memoirs on the intense identification of silent film viewers with the on-screen action, and scenario writing's service as a vital creative outlet for audience members' fantasies. He complained that the coming of sound to the movies in the late 1920s "deprived many of the former patrons of their sense of illusion":

> In the silent pictures perhaps 75 percent of those attending were wont to put themselves in the place of the hero or heroine, according to their sex. The picture formed a pictorial background to an individual daydream. In the formative days, when scripts were read, this was clearly evident. The amateur author would start off with "John does this" and "John does that," but before a dozen scenes would drop into "then I walked sadly out of the house" or whatever the action might be. They were envisioning themselves in the heroic role.[19]

The appeal of easy money for what seemed like light work was magnetic to Americans from all walks of life. Even movie-struck little boys like future film historian Edward Wagenknecht labored over scenarios. Seventy years later, he recalled waiting anxiously by the mailbox at his home in Chicago for the Vitagraph studio's reply to his submissions. "Fans were encouraged, at least by the movie magazines and the correspondence courses, to try to write film scenarios. As a child, I even tried myself. I sent one such masterpiece to Keystone and one to Vitagraph. Of course they both promptly came back. . . . Both must have been terrible."[20]

Postal sacks full of scripts flooded the film studios each week. IMP

Company studio scenario editor Giles Warren received five thousand manuscripts over a period of several months in 1910 after advertising for submissions in the *Saturday Evening Post, Collier's, Munsey's,* and other middle-class publications. Warren claimed that only fifty of the scenarios were original enough for consideration. Scores of fly-by-night "photo-play-writing schools" and publishers of scriptwriting advice manuals sprang up in such "literary centers" as Fergus Falls, Minnesota, and Everett, Washington, to capitalize on the public's fascination with the movies. The Library of Congress still holds over eighty books on how to write photoplay scenarios from this era.[21]

While one report estimated that perhaps one hundred freelancers, only ten of them untrained writers, earned substantial income from scenario writing, enough amateurs succeeded for American popular culture to support the idea that anyone could write for the movies. The scenario-writing field was especially popular with women, who would be notably successful both as amateur and professional scriptwriters and story editors in the silent era film industry. One lucky amateur, Ida Damon, a secretary from St. Louis, experienced momentary fame as a photoplay author in 1913 when she won a contest sponsored by the Thanhouser Film Corporation to supply an ending for its popular film serial, The Million Dollar Mystery. A scenario-writing school secured her endorsement and proclaimed, "Working Girl Receives $10,000 for Ideas She Thought Worthless." As feature films lengthened and their plots became more complicated, however, studios hired professional writing staffs and adapted famous books and plays for the screen. Still, in 1920, Stephen Bush reported that eight thousand unsolicited scenarios were arriving at California studios each week. A series of damaging court decisions on plagiarized scenarios in the mid-1920s greatly curtailed the movie studios' consideration of outside scripts.[22]

Getting into the Movies

It was not inevitable that film performers would become as extraordinarily famous, mysterious, and inaccessible to film audiences as the movie "gods and goddesses" of the 1920s. Today's soap opera actors and actresses are fairly accessible to their audiences through personal appearances at shopping malls and through television talk shows. Likewise, from the earliest days of the film studios until the mid-1910s, it was not terribly difficult for movie fans, at least those living in or visiting metro-politan New York, to watch a film being made or to meet movie actors, most of whom had the same meager celebrity as traveling stock-company performers. Anyone interested could gawk at crews from Biograph, Kalem, or Essanay shooting on the streets. Movie fans could attend the "general public days" of the annual film industry exhibitors' trade shows in New York, Boston, and Chicago, where they could collect auto-graphed postcards of their favorite film actors and actresses, stationed at various producers' booths. If the fans were lucky, they could watch them dance at the "movie ball."

Visitors to resort villages and residents of scenic areas within easy traveling distance of the film studios also saw movie crews at work. As one exhibitors' trade journal reporter noted in 1909, "Indeed, at the pres-ent time, in the suburbs of New York, Brooklyn, Philadelphia or Chi-cago, any pleasant day you are likely to chance on a big automobile loaded with actors and actresses in full paint and strange array, or to find upon a suburban street corner, or down a country lane, extraordinary ac-tions going on in front of a purring camera."[23]

The Vitagraph Film Manufacturing Company caused quite a stir in Cooperstown, New York, in 1911, when it arrived in town and operated through the summer and early autumn. The company, making use of a Boy Scout encampment on Lake Otsego, filmed a movie based on a local man's scenario and returned to film two additional movies based on James Fenimore Cooper's Leatherstocking tales. Scores of Cooperstown's year-round residents and summer visitors brought picnic lunches to the Vitagraph camp to watch the filming. Some onlookers even played as In-dian extras in crowd scenes. The local newspaper editor, George Carley, who would purchase the village's Star Theater, kept Cooperstown resi-dents informed about the activities of "their friends," the Vitagraph cast members, with weekly updates in his newspaper during that summer. Memories of the locals about their interaction with the movie crew must have been pleasant, for Carley included occasional stories about the cast members in the local news columns for several years afterward.[24]

Other film studios were based outside the big cities, with production facilities in suburban New Rochelle, New York; New Orleans, Louisiana; Jacksonville, Florida. The citizens of New Rochelle had many opportuni-ties to become familiar with the operations of the Thanhouser Film Com-pany. Feature articles about the Thanhouser company and frequent in-terviews with its actors and producers appeared in the local newspaper.

The entire town turned out to watch the conflagration the day the Thanhouser studio caught fire in January 1913. Unfortunately, although the filmmakers were always eager to capitalize on local events in New Rochelle, the crew had been too busy saving film negatives to film the disaster. Not to let such an opportunity be squandered, the following month the Thanhouser company immortalized the day in a re-created melodrama titled *When the Studio Burned*.[25]

In the early days of film production, movie-struck teenagers, young actors, and models like Muriel Ostriche (or Lillian and Dorothy Gish) could haunt the Biograph studio's door and hope to get work. Dozens of mail-order film-acting schools across the nation sold lessons and trade secrets to gullible fans.

Comic songs written for the vaudeville stage offer an indication of the impact of starstruck moviegoers' mad dash for the screen. A number of quickly knocked-off Tin Pan Alley tunes such as "Since Sarah Saw Theda Bara" and "I Want to Be Loved Like the Girls on the Film" satirized the longings of young women to rise from obscurity in the movie audience and become famous movie actresses with handsome lovers and exciting on-screen adventures. The inevitable outcome of these fictional women's efforts was portrayed in a responding sequel to "I Want to be Loved"—"She's Back among the Pots and Pans."[26]

One kind of compromise for movie fans between actually being a part of the movies and merely admiring the film stars was offered to moviegoers at the Bon Ton Theater in the tiny village of Mattawamkeag, Maine, in the summer of 1914. "See Yourself in the Movies!" read the handbills given out by theater owner John Smith's young sons Harold and Carlisle to local residents and visiting vacationers in the hundred-seat movie hall. Smith's daughter Elsie, who accompanied the films, played a rousing march on the piano to warm the patrons up for her father's announcement of the upcoming fun. Smith, a man with good showman's instincts, had arranged for the visit of a friend with a film camera to provide a special treat for Mattawamkeag moviegoers. Starstruck girls and boys in the Bon Ton audience smoothed their hair, straightened their clothes, and read with excitement:

> After each matinee the movie man will be waiting outside to photograph the audience leaving the theatre. These films will be run off next week in addition to other film features, including Mary Pickford, Charles Chaplin, the Keystone Cops films. . . . All the movie man asks

is that the patrons will not stand still but keep moving. Here is a chance for heaps of fun. "Don't forget your facial expressions." Come next week and see if you recognize yourself.[27]

The film, the theater, the audience members who cavorted before the camera—almost all vestiges of that day, which was billed as "an added summer attraction, without extra charge," are long gone. What seems especially remote, when we think about the disengagement of far-flung mass-media audiences from the creation of the product, is the possibility that at least some individuals in the movie audience could have participated in various aspects of the movie show, or could have seen themselves up on the screen, performing and mugging just like their beloved Mary and Charlie. With the end of the nickelodeon era and the rise of feature-length films, however, extraordinarily high salaries and fame had become associated with top movie actors like Mary Pickford and Charlie Chaplin. Many of the film production studios had relocated away from the easily accessible East to the West Coast, and the process of film industry professionalization was well underway. Consequently, opportunities for movie audience members' participation after the initial period of novelty and experimentation in the nickelodeon era became increasingly slim.

Toward a Way to Harness Movie Fans' Interest

Back in New York City in 1910, J. Stuart Blackton, president of the Vitagraph Film Company, perceived that he could enlarge movie audiences by promoting featured performers. Blackton and the Vitagraph company sensed that audiences yearned to know much more about their favorites. He commissioned a Tin Pan Alley firm to write a waltz tune, "The Vitagraph Girl," and arranged personal appearances for Florence Turner, Vitagraph's leading actress, at movie theaters in Manhattan, Brooklyn, and suburban New Jersey. Turner was introduced as each audience applauded, the theater's vocalist then serenaded her with "The Vitagraph Girl," accompanied by musicians and illustrated slides, and the audience joined in the chorus. Blackton promoted his films and performers and sold sheet music all at the same time.[28]

Having attended one of Florence Turner's personal appearances in October 1910 at the small Park Row Theater behind the main post office building in Manhattan, Lux Graphicus of *Moving Picture World* crowed:

I do not want to brag too much about it, but I believe I was the first to draw attention to the great part which personality, beauty and cleverness played in the picture. I foresaw [two years previously] that a natural curiosity would rise in the minds of the public as to the per-sonalities—the corporeal personalities—of the good people who make those "silver shadows" for our entertainment. In other words, the public wanted to see what moving picture actors and actresses were like in the flesh.[29]

Despite Lux Graphicus's euphoria, for every New York movie fan who could revel in seeing movie stars in person, there were millions in cities and towns across the nation with the same desires to somehow be a part of the movies, no matter how vicariously. Blackton had a plan to harness the interests of at least one segment of this seething mass of fans that could bring his studio (and the film industry) increased prestige, a higher-class audience, and additional profits. He looked into launching a monthly literary magazine that would publish novelized versions of pop-ular films and would, he hoped, attract a new strata of educated middle-class male and female fans to the movies. In its formative year, the con-tent of this first fan magazine, *Motion Picture Story Magazine,* was influenced in many unanticipated ways by real movie fans.

Motion Picture Story Magazine and the Gendered Construction of the Movie Fan

In December 1910, Vitagraph studio head J. Stuart Blackton announced the founding of *Motion Picture Story Magazine* (*MPSM*), an innovative kind of fiction publication dedicated to a new audience, motion picture enthusiasts. Blackton's venture was partly a shot in the dark, partly a calculated risk, for it was not immediately clear who made up the target audience, who a movie fan was. How should fans be attracted to the publication, and how should their interests be identified and served? These were all issues with which Blackton and the editorial staff of *MPSM* had to struggle. Blackton and *MPSM* editor Eugene V. Brewster created a publicity vehicle that unleashed fan interest and activities in ways that they could not have dreamed of—and that they became wary of. *MPSM* would change the way some members of the movie audience learned about the movies and made meaning from their moviegoing experiences.[1]

Examining discussions about the movie fan during the nickelodeon era exposes how fluid the notion of the movie fan was. Movie fans did not immediately assume the form that has been so familiar since the 1920s. Fan magazine readers were not necessarily swooning women and giggly young girls romantically obsessed with actors and the glamour of actresses and Hollywood. The gender and social class of the movie fan became hotly contested issues among film producers, theater owners, magazine publishers, and audience members; the debate persisted from the nickelodeon era into the time during which Hollywood and feature filmmaking were becoming established. Ultimately, the image of readers and their interests appeared to be worked out in *MPSM* in the early years of its publication; those years coincided with the first appearance of the movie fan and a broad conversation about fans in popular culture.

In 1911, Blackton was already in the vanguard of American film producers willing to experiment with new modes of publicity and wider forms of audience involvement. Publishing a magazine was a much more complicated undertaking, however, so Blackton hired Brewster as editor of, and partner in, *MPSM,* which was headquartered near the Vitagraph studio in Brooklyn. Brewster was a forty-year-old lawyer, political speaker, and experienced editor of short-fiction magazines.[2]

The idea of a short-fiction magazine based on film story lines was not a radical departure, but rather it drew together several trends in the popular press at the turn of the century. The American reading public voraciously consumed detailed newspaper articles, transcripts of long speeches, dime novels, and monthly fiction magazines devoted to stories about athletics, romance, and western and railroad adventures. Stage plays had been novelized and sold in cheap hardback editions with photographic illustrations of well-known actors in scenes taken from the Broadway productions. Entrepreneurs like Blackton and Brewster saw a vast new supply of action-packed fiction in the translation of movie melodramas to written prose, and they spied an already existing market eager to purchase and read such stories.

Blackton and other members of the film industry were increasingly confronted with evidence that at least some members of the movie audience across the nation were not content remaining merely detached film spectators. By 1910 and 1911, the studios were being deluged with inquiries from moviegoers who wished to know how to write and sell their own scenarios, and how to master the details of film projection and camera operation. Some audience members wanted to collect souvenir pictures of film actors, go on sightseeing tours of film sets, and appear in the movies themselves.

Blackton also noted that movie fans wanted to know as much as possible about the plots of current films, having a desire for translation of visual elements of film to the written word, to re-experience their favorite films in story form. Fans had already begun to seek out plot descriptions in the professional trade journals of movie theater managers. In April 1910, a *Moving Picture World* columnist noted with some surprise the wide readership that trade journal synopses had gained among moviegoers. "Over and over again we hear some such remarks as these: 'Those little stories that you print are just like condensed novels. We enjoy reading them, and if there is a story we like very much, we go and see the picture.'" A Thomasville, Georgia, projectionist reported:

> The *Moving Picture World* was not known here until I induced a local manager of a news company to handle it and now even the kids buy it to read the film synopses. One man said, "When I go to an opera house I have a program telling me of the characters, etc. In a picture show there is nothing but the posters, so every day at lunch time I glance at the titles on the posters, go home and get a copy of the *Moving Picture World,* read the synopsis, and at night I enjoy the photoplay immensely, as I am familiar with the characters and scenes."

This aspect of fan interest seemed to Blackton to be the most profitable to tap and perhaps the least threatening to the balance of power between producers and consumers of motion pictures. It became the focus of his idea for the creation of *MPSM.*[3]

The social status of the prospective *MPSM* readers initially appeared a more important concern than their gender. The new magazine followed the compact size and layout of short-fiction magazines like *Century* and *Munsey's,* which appealed to both educated male and female readers, and the popular science journals like *Popular Mechanics* and *Scientific American,* which had wide middle-class male readership.[4] Blackton and Brewster purposely designed the style and content of *Motion Picture Story Magazine* to attract middle-class readers. Blackton optimistically informed the trade journals that "[p]ersons never having been in a moving picture theater will read in the magazine stories that greatly interest them, and the logical consequence will be that they will make it their business to find out where those stories can be seen in picture form and will go and see them." This would "help raise the standard of the whole motion picture business" and increase attendance at nickelodeons. Drawing in more middle-class patrons would especially help urban movie theaters, which had a much less respectable reputation than most rural nickelodeons across the nation. The small-town middle class were already enthusiastic motion picture supporters, and further courting the interests of this group and their city cousins, Blackton and Brewster hoped, would be one more way to mollify cultural critics who sniffed in disdain that only illiterate immigrants attended motion picture performances.[5]

The inaugural issue of *Motion Picture Story Magazine*, published in February 1911, resembled a staid fiction journal compared with the movie fan magazines of the 1920s. The bulk of the magazine consisted of a dozen seven-page novelizations of one-reel narrative films produced by Motion Picture Patents Company member studios Vitagraph, Biograph, Edison, Lubin, Kalem, Essanay, Selig, and Méliès. Each short story was illustrated with several still photos from the film release. Blackton and Brewster had gingerly noted in announcing the new magazine to film exhibitors that it had been suggested that "a department devoted to personalities of well known picture players" be added to the contents. Uncertain of the reaction of their new readership, the editors tucked a few photographed portraits of film players among the back pages.[6]

Of the more than one hundred film subjects released each month by Motion Picture Patents Company film producers, the films selected for inclusion in the earliest issues of *MPSM* appear to have been chosen for the middlebrow cultural tone of their subject matter. Early issues of the magazine offered plot synopses of recent films on the lives of Molière and Thomas à Becket, and adaptations of Tennyson, Cooper, and Shakespeare. Historical subjects, especially Civil War films such as *A Dixie Mother*, were published frequently in *MPSM*. Also prominently featured, perhaps for their prestige and publicity value, were contemporary, muckraking, message films that featured crusading reporters, brave doctors fighting disease in the slums, and militant suffragettes. The early issues contained few synopses of slapstick comedies or westerns, despite their wide popularity with nickelodeon audiences, perhaps because those films were all movement and had little plot. There were also almost none of the serial-cliffhanger films, because many Hearst chain newspapers and other smaller papers across the nation had begun publishing weekly installments of *The Adventures of Kathlyn, The Million Dollar Mystery,* and *What Happened to Mary?* series in cooperation with film producers and local exhibitors. Brewster and his editorial staff were determined to present a vision of the movies as instructive, uplifting, and wholesome in order for their new magazine to attract and hold a "respectable" male and female readership.[7]

The first issue of *MPSM* was snapped up by movie fans, and the magazine was immediately judged a success. Marketed at movie theaters and newsstands nationwide, subsequent issues often sold out within a week of release, and by 1912 circulation had reached five hundred thousand. Since the magazine was doing so well, the editors had little reason to alter it. The subsequent rapid evolution of the magazine's content, however, suggests either that the editors were dissatisfied or that they were responsive to reader suggestions. Brewster and his editorial staff began to broaden the focus to include more novelizations based on filmed love stories, westerns, and melodramas. They began to select scenarios based on the quality of the finished film rather than on the subject matter. By the April 1911 issue, a photo portrait gallery of film actors and actresses appeared prominently in the magazine's opening pages. New departments debuted, featuring interviews with players and news of their professional activities. Technical articles about scenario writing, film production, and projector optics also appeared in each issue. Although there is only sketchy evidence of readers' direct editorial intervention in the shaping of *MPSM*, inclusion of readers' contributions and solicitation of readers' preferences became much more conspicuous.[8]

Exactly who the magazine's readers were and what interested them was an issue for the editors as well as for firms that advertised in *MPSM*. In the earliest issues, ads for writers' supplies such as typewriters, ink, and carbon paper, appropriate for practitioner-readers of short fiction, gave way to ads for consumer products like Pompeian Skin Cream, BVD underwear, Hershey chocolate bars, Uneeda Biscuits, and Coca-Cola. Letters to the editor from subscribers such as Mrs. R. A. Stratton of Savannah, Georgia, in August 1911, indicated the magazine's success in attracting its unanticipated audience. "My husband brought me a copy of your magazine a day or so ago (knowing my fondness for the Moving Pictures and everything pertaining thereto), and I was never more pleased with anything in my life—am very "keen" on the pictures and know the faces of the players in them as well as I do those of my friends, can even tell when they change from one company to another."[9]

By 1912, *Motion Picture Story Magazine* became a lively, interactive colloquium for the sharing of movie fans' knowledge and creative interests. Besides the plot synopses each month, Brewster provided a variety of features concerned with the growing movie culture: regular columns such as "Chats with Photoplayers" and "Green Room Jottings," behind-the-scenes looks at moviemaking, studio tours, and editorials criticizing poor films and defending the movie industry against attacks by the press and pulpit. Brewster instituted several innovations that gave readers a larger sense of participation in movie fan culture. For example, he started a never-ceasing round of contests wherein his readers could vote for their favorite players and the best films, and he gave readers space to lobby for their candidates. He also crammed the pages full of readers' contributed poems and drawings. Thousands of readers deluged Brewster's offices with bits of doggerel about films and favorite actors, mountains of questions about the films and their players, requests for star autographs, and pleas for advice on how to enter the movie business. By December 1912, a seemingly astounded Brewster noted, "The popularity of this department ['Favorite Plays and Players—by Our Readers'] far surpassed our anticipations." He announced that *MPSM* would give reader contributions on players and films more room, but cautioned, "Even now, we cannot hope to publish one-hundredth part of the verses, appreciations and criticisms that we receive."[10]

Brewster's most outstanding contribution to the creation of a forum for active fan readership was the "Answers to Inquiries" column, which premiered in the August 1911 issue. It was presided over by a staff member known only as the Answer Man. Each month's inquiries column included as many as twenty-five pages of the Answer Man's personal messages to readers. By January 1913, the Answer Man claimed that his office received twenty-five hundred letters a month, and he lamented that he could answer only a small percentage of the correspondence in the magazine. Cartoon drawings showed the Answer Man buried under an avalanche of mail. The Answer Man offered to answer reader queries by mail if the correspondent sent an envelope, and the magazine set up a separate bureau at one point to answer readers' many detailed technical questions about how to operate projection equipment or establish nickelodeon theaters.[11]

The differences between the average reader of *MPSM* and the active fans must be noted, for the active fans represented a small percentage of all readers. They were more motivated to give their opinions, praise, and complaints, and were probably more extreme fans than the passive readers. *MPSM* readers who corresponded with the Answer Man in the early years hailed from both small towns and big cities, were nearly as likely to be male as female, and were interested in a broad diversity of film-related issues. The inquiries column correspondents seemed to represent a geographic cross section of the American movie audience. A contest in September 1911 that awarded monetary prizes for best letters on favorite *MPSM* novelizations illustrated how widespread *MPSM*'s audience was, or at the very least, how widespread *MPSM* editors wished advertisers

"THE SUNSET GUN," A Memorial Day Story—By General Horatio C. King

JUNE   The   15 CENTS

MOTION PICTURE

Story Magazine

THE FIRST KALEM STORY FROM EGYPT IN THIS NUMBER

"Darby and Joan" (p. 118)

Fourteen Complete, Illustrated Stories, from the Best Plays of the Month

Cover of *Motion Picture Story Magazine,* June 1912. Author's collection.

and the public to perceive the audience was. Sixty percent of the eighty-five winning entries came from small-town readers across the country— readers from Pine Bluff, Arkansas; Huron, South Dakota; Durango, Colorado; Washington, North Carolina; and Oswego, New York. The other 40 percent came from urban readers (a quarter from New York City, where much of the film industry, and the magazine's editorial offices, were located); West Coast readers were somewhat underrepresented. Female winners had a slight edge on the number of male winners (forty-five to forty). A survey of reader names in the inquiries column from 1911 through 1916 similarly reveals a fan readership that was almost 40 percent male and 60 percent female. Whether these portraits of the diversity of *MPSM* readers reflected reality or were orchestrated by the *MPSM* editorial staff, it seems clear that the magazine was not yet solely targeted to the female urban readers that dominated fan magazine discourse in the 1920s.[12]

Consumer-goods advertisers judged a significant proportion of *Motion Picture Story Magazine*'s readership to be male, as ads for men's personal products appeared prominently next to ads for women's products in fan magazines from 1911 until the late 1910s. In a typical example, an ad for BVD underwear in sister publication *Motion Picture Classic* was illustrated with a picture of a nickelodeon filled with nattily dressed men who, it seemed, suffered no discomfort in a crowded theater from hot and binding undergarments.[13]

The inquiries column offered more than just the dry recitation of facts in response to readers' questions, although, to save space, the magazine did not include readers' letters, and responses sometimes read like a one-way telephone conversation. The Answer Man nevertheless strove to develop an intimate relationship on a mass scale with the magazine's readers, as he researched their most obscure questions about cast members or technical matters and responded in a confidential, friendly tone. Correspondents held lively debates with him and other readers on such topics as Mary Pickford's acting abilities, the merits or deficiencies of various films, and topical issues such as the war in Europe or national politics. The Answer Man often described his column as an encyclopedia of information about the world of motion pictures, but it also functioned as a meaningful forum for readers' expressions of fannish interests. Eighty years later, film historian Edward Wagenknecht recalled with amused pride that his name appears in the January 1912 issue as winner of a letter-writing prize. The award of a year's subscription may have been small, but it carried enormous importance to an enthusiastic thirteen-year-old movie fan who reveled in the recognition of his knowledge and talents. His participation gave him a stronger sense of connection with movie fan culture.[14]

There were boundaries of permissible discussion in the inquiries column that led to continuing skirmishes between readers and *MPSM* editors. The Answer Man created editorial rules to deflect certain categories of inquiries. He declined to answer some of his readers' most prying questions about players' marital status and personal habits, which the *MPSM* staff judged to be too invasive of players' privacy. In March 1912 alone, the Answer Man claimed to have rejected 104 inquiries as inappropriate. That number included many requests for the names of Biograph film actors. Most studios, responding to public demand, had begun promoting the names of their previously anonymous players in 1909 and 1910, but Biograph remained a particularly stubborn holdout until April 1913, by which time D. W. Griffith and most of the well-known players had already left. The repeatedly stated restrictions on questions did not deter film enthusiasts from continuing to implore the Answer Man each month to spill the facts about an actor's marital status or the identities of Biograph's anonymous players.[15]

While the Answer Man grudgingly remained silent in accordance with Biograph's dictums, he treated rumors of the deaths of prominent players quite differently. The Answer Man addressed such rumors frequently, resuscitating some film actor or actress in almost every issue of the magazine. Typical is the Answer Man's exasperated, negative response, in the August 1912 issue, to a fan's letter asking confirmation of a story obtained from a friend's aunt that Maurice Costello had been run over by an auto and killed. Although many death rumors concerning film players may have been studio publicity "plants," the wild imaginations of movie fans spread the rumors more efficiently and effectively than film producers ever could have done.[16]

Movie fans' continued obsession with death rumors exposed the *MPSM* editors to the dark side of fandom and fame. No wonder then that, following editorial policy and his own preference, the Answer Man remained anonymous. As the most conspicuous, accessible link between the growing legion of movie fans and the film industry, he had himself attained a level of celebrity among the film enthusiasts, and he wisely wanted to control their purportedly kind but dangerously close-to-overwhelming attentions. The Answer Man acknowledged in print only that

"The Answer Man," a popular feature in *Motion Picture Magazine*, July 1920, p. 86. Author's collection.

he was a staff member over seventy years old. But that did not keep correspondents from showering him with tins of cookies and cakes, poems, small trinkets, and pictures of themselves in hopes that he could put them on the inside track to movie stardom.[17]

Limiting the Scope of Movie Fandom

Nickelodeon-era movie fandom, at least as it was depicted in *MPSM* during its earliest years of publication, was both sexually undifferentiated and geographically diverse. Almost everyone was invited to be a fan—men and women, young and old, rural and urban, middle-class suburbanite and industrial worker. To maintain their profits, motion picture producers and theater owners needed to attract every segment of the American public and to deflect cultural critics' concerns that the movies were a low-class entertainment suitable only for immigrants, children, and the uneducated and poor. Thus film exhibitors and producers usually portrayed moviegoers in their publicity materials as adult couples and middle-class families. Beginning in the mid-1910s, however, fan magazines reshaped those images into a more narrowly focused reflection of the movie and magazine audience. They began to portray the movie audience as overwhelmingly dominated by young women. A similar image was also being used by consumer-product advertisers.

From its first issue, *MPSM* had shown respect for movie fans, addressing them knowledgeably, intimately, and confidentially, writing about their interests with a certain admiration for the vast store of knowledge the members of this elite club brought to their study of motion pictures. The editors, writers, and readers even policed the boundaries of movie fandom, taking potshots at those they considered marginal or unworthy film spectators. Stories, poems, cartoons, and tirades railed against audience members who disturbed the fan's concentration, such as the loud and malodorous immigrant, the naïve country bumpkin (usually male) who had never previously seen a film, or the rude woman who refused to remove her hat in the theater or who gossiped during the show.[18]

Although *MPSM* tweaked certain female fans for disturbing others in the audience while they chattered about the stars' private lives, male fans received even more criticism for "inappropriate" levels of interest in the movies. It was men, more than women, who were reproached for being too "fanatical." Young boys were depicted in cartoons as the movies' most rambunctiously overinvolved fans, shown being mesmerized by dramatic posters or tossed about during dreams of cowboy and Indian chases. Ironically, the magazine's first use of the word *fan* was in a satirical poem in the August 1911 issue titled "The Motion Picture Fan." It ridiculed a young man's obsessive interest in the mechanics of film technology and exhibition.

> He's a spunky little fellow, without a trace of yellow,
> He knows his motion picture A, B, C.
> He rivals all the sages, and accurately gauges
> The films that will be pleasing to a "T."
>
> He's very free with strictures, on inappropriate pictures,
> On every mechanism he's *au fait*.
> He can talk about the locus, of the fluctuating focus,
> And let you know the minute it's O.K.

Should he discourse on shutters,—every word he utters,
You'll find he won't make much of a mistake.
His original disclosures, on powder and exposures,
Are anything, believe me, but a fake.

So on *ad infinitum,* you'll find there's not an item,
On which He will not have his little say,
He's business-like, and handy, in fact, he's quite a dandy,
This hero of the motion picture day![19]

This image of the male movie fan had a parallel in middle-class men's and boys' fascination with electrical inventions like wireless radio, which historian Susan Douglas has characterized as a culture of masculinity. *Scientific American* and *Popular Mechanics,* among other publications marketed to mechanically inclined male hobbyists, devoted many articles to motion picture and radio technology. Nevertheless, in the poem in *MPSM* the knowledgeable male movie fan was spoofed as a pedant who bored everyone around him with technical trivia instead of simply enjoying the show. As the movies evolved into a professionalized, commercialized entertainment form, fan magazines replaced this image of the movie fan, intimately knowledgeable about the workings of projectors and the writing of film scenarios, with an image of the fan as a consumer, fascinated with the spectacle of the star system. This redefinition helped distance the audience from film production; it also accommodated women and girls more easily than men.[20]

Despite men's continued visibility in the movie audience and demonstrated interest in movie culture, male movie fans increasingly became the fan magazines' targets for criticism and ridicule of fan behavior. *MPSM* more prominently featured letters from male movie fans that made them appear naïve and foolish. In the September 1915 issue, fans read that William W. Pratt of Punxsutawney, Pennsylvania, claimed to be shocked to learn that the buildings on the back lot of the new Universal City film studio in California were not real, but merely sets:

Now, no one, especially movie fans, likes to admit they have been fooled, and I am not an exception; so the next Universal picture I saw I kept saying to myself, "Oh, that's only a wall and not a house at all," and was wondering what was on the other side of it (a field and a pile of rubbish, no doubt), and I lost all interest in the play. Therefore I shun all Universal pictures and try to find the theaters showing the good old "Generals" and "Mutuals," for if they are faking me I don't know it.

Satiric cartoon panels such as "The Adventures of Flim Flam the Film Fan" also ridiculed male moviegoers like Flim Flam, whose too intense attention to a fan magazine led him into slapstick types of scrapes.[21]

That popular culture poked fun at the foibles of men and women in their interaction with new technologies was nothing new. Humor made at the expense of male movie fans was as prevalent in American popular culture as the jokes and comic songs that had earlier skewered foolish male bicyclists and automobile drivers. However, the movie fan magazines now showed a growing unease and confusion over mens' roles as movie fans and seemed to do their best to discourage them. *MPSM* and its new rival, *Photoplay,* began to reposition themselves, and hence their readership, away from special-interest, fan-interactive publishing and toward the fast-growing, lucrative category of women's magazines, which were incidentally attracting far more consumer product advertising than fan or hobbyist journals.

Several changes were evident as *MPSM* remade itself. In the autumn of 1915 *MPSM* moved away from emphasizing synopses of film scenarios. Movies had passed beyond the one-reel film and brief scenario. By 1916 and 1917, the five-reel and longer feature films were increasingly adapted from popular novels, and novelizations of original film screenplays stretched to book length. Brewster dropped the word *Story* from his magazine's title, simplifying it to *Motion Picture Magazine (MPM).* Technical articles on projectors and scenario writing appeared less frequently, and after 1916, much of the space devoted to readers' poems, drawings, and comments also disappeared. The latter move, which might have relieved those weary of fan doggerel, removed many of the interactive features that let fans contribute to the publication. The magazine still offered the enthusiastic reader contests and opportunities to address inquiries to the Answer Man. But *MPM* now included more features aimed at what mass-circulation magazines portrayed as women's interests—advice columns on etiquette, romance, and beauty; articles about the stars' clothing on-screen and off; details of players' romances and private lives; recipes from their kitchens; and breathless descriptions of what cars they drove and what pets they owned.[22]

In September 1915, *MPM*'s new sister publication *Motion Picture*

Classic, with the same editorial staff, was launched to meet what appeared to be the inexhaustible demand for news and pictures of film actors. *Classic* led the vanguard of fan magazine editorial changes, as it had a larger page size better suited for glamorous photographic layouts of the stars, a greater number of fashion and women's articles, and "only" fifty to sixty questions answered each month by its Answer Man. In *Classic,* Brewster and his editorial staff broke previous taboos on discussing film actors' private romantic lives, with articles like "Cupid, Movie and Company, a Popular Firm."[23]

The restyled movie fan also made her debut in this period. In November 1916, *Motion Picture Magazine* showcased a letter to the editor from an Ohio reader who told the story of "the truest and most faithful" movie fan, eighteen-year-old Mary Curtin, daughter of a Columbus, Ohio, car dealer. Mary "has never been known to witness less than 30 movies a week," marveled the writer, and "the wall of her room has in the vicinity of 450 or 500" movie star portraits. Mary attended the movies every day during her school lunch period. She insisted that dates take her to the movies before going on to fraternity dances, and she often lingered so long at the theater that the dance was already over when she and her escort arrived. Yet Mary was not friendless or introverted; popular and admired for her driving skills, "she has converted many to her habit of almost living at the movies, but none has as yet surpassed her record." This new variety of fan was denigrated by cultural critics for being too absorbed in movies and stars, and was also criticized for being too independent and contemptuous of traditional social rules about women's ambitions and pleasures. Mary's preference for movie experiences over men's company was both a protest against having to fit into traditional women's roles and a notice that men were not necessarily wanted in her world of movie fan culture. She jokingly claimed that "the man I marry must be twice the movie fan I am." When someone warned her she might remain single with those restrictions, "she gave Eva Tanguay's famous cry, 'I don't care!'"[24]

Mary Curtin, movie fan, was a dizzy, off-kilter teenager, but she also represented the New Woman, throwing off traditional roles, daring to do what she wanted. The letter writer mentioned that Mary had traveled all the way to Chicago just to see a film—*The Birth of a Nation*—that had been banned in Ohio. Mary was fiercely independent and quite oriented toward leisure and mass culture. She represented the flapper, a "new and improved" movie fan that would be promoted insistently in the 1920s.[25]

"Feminine Fads and Fancies," a featured article in the January 1917 issue of *MPM* illustrates how Brewster and his editorial staff reconceptualized the magazine's purpose and refocused the image of the movie fan. The wide range of interests practiced by fans in 1911 was reduced to overly intense attachments to film actors:

> Since the *Motion Picture Magazine* and similar publications have begun to draw the public and the player more closely together, the curiosity of the former, regarding the latter, has been hard to satisfy. The more they know, the more they want to know. The Answer Man, kind old fellow, is bowed beneath the burden of questions, ranging from some one's age to some other actress's salary; from one actor's favorite brand of cigarets [*sic*] to another's boot size. But since this curiosity is only human, since the players' lives will almost invariably bear the closest scrutiny, and since the players realize that it is the public who provides "the stuff that fills our pay-envelopes," the Magazine has been endeavoring to tell the public—the great, good-natured, benevolent public, who loves deeply and hates fiercely, without, apparently, rhyme or reason—just what it wants to know.[26]

Photoplay, the movie magazine that took over the mantle of leading fan publication in the late 1910s, began to reinforce feminine aspects of the movie fan image. In the December 1917 issue, an anecdote about the origins of the inquiries department attempted to redefine the appropriate gender and interests of movie fans:

> "Is Broncho Billy married? I'm awfully interested because I just love to see him get the girl in the end." This was the first question ever asked any publication about any film player. The publication was the *Dramatic Mirror* and the query made Frank E. Woods, now production manager of the Famous Players–Lasky studios, the first Answer Man. "As nearly as I can remember," said Mr. Woods, "the writer of the letter was a girl about 16. I published the answer in my column and that started them going."[27]

A columnist for the *Exhibitor's Trade Review* responded caustically in September 1917 to a fan's request for a male star's address. "We received a letter from Evansville, Indiana, which proves that the silly season for screen hero worship by gushing girlies is in full swing." The repetition of stories like these helped reshape popular opinion about who movie fans were and what their appropriate interests were. As the movie industry became more professional, there was less room for amateur authors or tinkerers. Perhaps not coincidentally, all three series of Edward Strate-meyer's juvenile novels—the Moving Picture Chums, Motion Picture Boys, and Motion Picture Girls—were discontinued after 1917. The technologically obsessed male movie fan and the writer of scenarios and film criticism had been displaced in fan magazines.[28]

By the early 1920s, fan magazines were doing booming business. *MPM* was by then one of a dozen publications that, running the gamut from artsy photography journals to tabloidlike weekly gossip sheets, crowded the racks of the nation's newsstands. They included *Cinema Art, Film Fun* (published by the humor magazine *Judge*), *Film Play, Motion Picture Classic* (sometimes simply titled *Classic*), *Motion Picture Journal, Movie Digest, Movie Weekly, Pantomime, Photoplay, Picture Play, Screenland,* and the high-toned *Shadowland.* Male readers still represented about 10 percent of the inquirers in *MPM's* and *Photoplay's* question-and-answer columns. In Cecil B. De Mille's 1920 film *Why Change Your Wife?* the virile husband played by Thomas Meighan reads fan magazines, much to the disgust of his prissy wife, played by Gloria Swanson. Men continued to hold up their share of box-office receipts—adult men represented one-third of the American movie audience (women, children, and teens the other two-thirds)—and surveys indicated that some men continued to read fan magazines throughout the 1920s. Robert and Helen Lynd, for example, found men and boys reading the magazines in the public and high-school libraries in Muncie, Indiana. Movie fan magazines of the 1920s, nevertheless, were the major promoters of the image of a female-dominated movie audience and fan magazine readership. Thus, as the image of the frivolous female fan magazine reader took hold, it became much harder for popular culture to imagine male movie fans or the possibility of their interest in movie magazines or movie fan culture.[29]

While the figure of the male movie fan faded from prominence in *Motion Picture Magazine* and *Photoplay,* one area among the emerging mass media that continued to be open to male interest was radio. The army of amateur radio enthusiasts in the 1910s grew in numbers parallel to those of movie fans and had strong connections to the masculine traditions of mechanical tinkering, invention, and scientific experimentation so dear to American middle-class boys' hearts. Always attuned to the interests of boy culture, Edward Stratemeyer's Radio Boys series of novels included lessons in the technology of radio signal reception and broadcasting. This series, unlike the Moving Picture Chums novels, continued through the late 1920s.[30]

Still, the categories of radio and television fans that emerged in the next several decades do not appear to have been as constricted by gender as was popular culture's notion of movie fans. Because radio and television broadcast such a wide variety of programs at different times during the day, fandom became related to program genre and listening patterns. Female radio fans were widely perceived as being greatly attracted to daytime soap operas, homemaking programs, and beauty advice programs. Adult men were generally perceived as radio and television fans because of the broadcasting of sporting events, news, comedy, and educational programs that would attract them. Popular culture may also have eventually lost some of its ambivalence about the appropriateness for male involvement as fans of mass media.

 8

Photoplay Magazine, Movie Fans, and the Marketplace

By the early 1920s, the queen of the fan magazines, which numbered more than a dozen, was *Photoplay*. Film historian Anthony Slide has called *Photoplay* "the leader in the field" from the late 1910s through the 1930s, literate, informative, and witty.[1]

In the 1920s, *Photoplay* sought to refurbish the popular image of the movie fan. Its editor, James R. Quirk, passionately desired the public to stop thinking that movie fans were merely a mass of gum-chewing, giggling schoolgirls and start regarding them as knowledgeable, middle-class film consumers. Insisting that there was much more about the movies in which to be interested than endless speculation about the love lives of the stars, Quirk educated fans and raised the standards of movie fandom. He commissioned hundreds of feature articles on current issues in film production, interviews with directors and producers, intelligent film reviews, technical advice on scenario writing, and short stories about life and romance in Hollywood from some of the most talented journalists and fiction writers. Quirk promoted an appreciation among his readers for well-conceived plots, sensitive acting, proficient directing, and innovative photography. He even instituted an annual award honoring the year's best film production. In his monthly editorials and in speeches to business groups, Quirk defended movie fans and their interests against the prejudices of conservative social critics.[2]

Broadening the interests of movie fans served another purpose for Quirk, for he was also an enthusiastic proselytizer for the further spread of consumer culture. Quirk advanced a view of fans as a moviegoing intelligentsia while selling the business community on the image of fans as a market segment inordinately influenced by motion pictures. In frequent appeals in the advertising trade press, Quirk argued that the movies had created a breed of "perfect consumers" who had an almost complete dependence on motion pictures to generate their needs and desires. The movies primed them to buy, and the movies focused their vision on what to buy—the glamorous new necessities of life, from cars to candy bars, which they saw on the screen and in the advertising pages of *Photoplay*. Quirk predicted that the persuasiveness of the motion picture medium, coupled with the added weight of product endorsements by movie stars, would fuel an explosive growth of consumer culture led by movie fans.[3]

Photoplay's Rise to Prominence

The successful debut of *Motion Picture Story Magazine* in 1911 and its continuing robust health spurred competition from other magazine publishers. Among the early rivals was *Photoplay*, established in Chicago in 1912. In its early years, *Photoplay* weathered rough times and offered little that was innovative; it nearly ceased publication in 1915. In 1917, a new editor—James Quirk—took over, and the magazine finally hit its stride. Like Eugene Brewster of *Motion Picture Story Magazine*, Quirk had a background in newspapers and special-interest publications, having been managing editor of *Popular Mechanics*. Brewster and Quirk both changed the focus of their publications in the mid-1910s to resemble mainstream mass market magazines more closely.[4]

The movie fan magazines of this period had a tenuous relationship to the film studios, for they were published independently and had no direct financial connection to them. The editorial offices of both *Motion Picture Story Magazine* and *Photoplay* were in New York City, far closer to other magazine publishers' offices than to the stars' dressing rooms. Nevertheless, the fan magazines relied heavily on the studios for material. The tangled connection between the publications and the film studios undoubtedly benefited both; the magazines fueled moviegoers' interest in seeing the newest film releases, and "exclusive" articles written by famous film stars (actually ghostwritten by studio publicists) drew purchasers to the magazines. The fan magazines' freedom from ties to particular studios allowed article authors and readers a bit more latitude to criticize and compare performers and films. At the same time, the magazines' sympathetic and cooperative relationship to the studios brought fan magazines more intimate access to the stars.[5]

As a tangential but highly visible element of the movie business, *Photoplay* did its part to improve the industry's status among film fans and social critics. To give the fly-by-night movie business a sense of its own development, Quirk commissioned journalist Terry Ramsaye to write the first real history of the film industry, which was serialized for over a year in *Photoplay* and reprinted in book form in 1926 as *A Thousand and One Nights*. In 1920, Quirk also instituted the Photoplay Magazine Medal of Honor, which he proudly proclaimed was the "first annual commemoration of distinction in the making of motion pictures." Readers voted on the most meritorious film of the previous year, and *Photoplay* awarded the winning producer a solid gold medallion crafted by Tiffany's. Quirk's efforts at legitimizing the motion picture as a dramatic art form preceded the Academy of Motion Picture Arts and Sciences' first Oscar awards by seven years.[6]

While *Photoplay* after 1917 never provided movie fans the direct participation in the production of movie fan culture that *Motion Picture Story Magazine* had provided for readers in the early 1910s—there was no space for fan poetry or drawings, and there were fewer contests, a briefer question-and-answer department, and many fewer articles instructing fans on filmmaking, acting techniques, and projector operation—*Photoplay* nevertheless offered interested readers an insider's view of the film industry. *Photoplay* featured interviews with directors and set and costume designers, studio gossip, behind-the-scenes photographic essays, a continuing series on scenario authorship, and short stories about life among the moviemakers.[7]

Although even these features seemed increasingly spectator-oriented, limiting fans to a vicarious experience of life in Hollywood, Quirk still offered movie fans some opportunities to voice their own opinions and knowledge. Regular columns such as "Why Do They Do It?" (published until 1925) represented a forum for fans' sharp criticisms of on-screen gaffes, inaccurate costumes, and other negligence of historical detail or narrative logic. The question-and-answer column was also a staple of

Photoplay, though the number of queries answered in each issue was relatively small. Fans still wrote to the film magazines in the 1920s because it gave them the sense of participation in movic fan culture, but film actors were becoming more accessible through their film studios. With the maturation of the star system, studios had established publicity departments to send photographs of the stars to fans, to release stories about stars diligently answering their fan mail, and to announce how many thousands of letters each star received weekly. The studios began to judge players' popularity and negotiate their salaries based on the amount of fan mail they received. So even though it served a less important function for the fan magazines, fan-letter writing remained an active outlet of movie fan culture.

One reason *Photoplay* continued to publish its question-and-answer department was that the names and hometowns of correspondents provided Quirk with a vivid snapshot of the magazine's readership. This evidence could be useful in attracting consumer-product advertisers. In advertisements like "What's in the Book?," which *Photoplay* placed in the advertising industry trade journal *Printer's Ink*, the fan magazine was attempting to persuade account executives that they could stay in touch with the pulse of consumers through reading the "real letters from real folks down in San Antonio, Texas and out in Los Angeles, California and over in Victoria, Australia" and by placing their ads in *Photoplay*. Film historians have questioned the authenticity of fan magazine mail, and no company records survive to verify if the *Photoplay* inquiries column accurately reflected the magazine's wide readership. However, a casual survey demonstrates that editors arranged the correspondents' names and addresses to give the impression that the *Photoplay* faithful represented a cross section of American society. Of 206 letters answered in a typical issue of *Photoplay* in 1917, 9 percent of questioners came from New England, 16 percent each from the South and West, 20 percent from New York City and the mid-Atlantic states, and 26 percent from Chicago and the Midwest. A full 12 percent of letters were from readers in foreign countries. Overall, roughly half the correspondence (52 percent) came from fans in small towns and medium-size cities, and half (48 percent) from readers in big cities.[8]

Unlike editors of *True Story*, the *New York Daily News*, and other growing mass market publications of the 1920s, Quirk appeared not to cater to *Photoplay*'s urban working-class readership. If anything, the staff enjoyed ridiculing working-class moviegoers by reporting silly "overheard exchanges" among the hoi polloi in city movie theaters. *Photoplay* carefully constructed a portrait of moviegoing and fan magazine reading as national phenomena that overcame regional differences and appealed equally to small-town and big-city moviegoers. *Photoplay* supported the mainstream middle-class values of the small- and medium-sized town, but it also represented the new attitude toward leisure, pleasure, and spending associated with the urban middle class of the faster-paced big cities. Through the 1920s, *Photoplay* assumed that its readers were discriminating in their movie choices and that, even though they would not tolerate indecencies, they were liberal in religion and morals, especially when it came to what was portrayed in films. *Photoplay* assumed its readers were a lot like the middle-class citizens of Muncie, Indiana, whom Robert and Helen Lynd described in their survey *Middletown*. While Middletowners held many traditional values, they were also quite addicted to the movies, eager to follow the often scandalous social lives of Hollywood actors and actresses, and increasingly attracted to the pleasures of consumer culture.[9]

Linking Movie Stars and Consumer Goods

Photoplay's content in the late-1910s and 1920s was not solely focused on motion pictures. Articles with a slant toward female readers abounded in the magazine. There were pieces in each issue on clothing styles worn by actresses and actors, giving inside views of the stars' homes, and reporting details of their hairstyles, diets, and use of cosmetics; there were also monthly advice columns on etiquette, manners, fashion, health, and beauty. Within *Photoplay*, the forum for knowledgeable movie fans, was another *Photoplay*, a purveyor of consumer products, attitudes, and behavior that targeted the women who did most of the purchasing and the young people who did most of the desiring. Movie stars acted as role models for consumer behavior on the screen and in *Photoplay* advertisements, while in the articles they were model consumers in private life, too, whom readers could emulate. (Occasionally, though, the magazine criticized performers' self-indulgences and failings.)

The fan magazines were able to make these links between movies, young and female fans, and advertised products more obviously and more directly than could film producers. As noted earlier, most film exhibitors were reluctant to allow anything resembling product advertising

The National Guide to Motion Pictures

PHOTOPLAY

September   25 cents

How They Keep Girlish Figures

Cover of *Photoplay*, September 1925. Author's collection.

onto their theaters' screens. This fear of inciting audience complaints about blatant commercial appeals initially made even the fan magazines a bit hesitant. In September 1916, *Motion Picture Magazine* had published a brief parody for the amusement of its savvy readers, a page from a faux fan magazine named "The Movie Maniac." It satirized *Motion Picture Magazine*'s regular columns, but it also took care to parody the advertising appeals that filled the fan magazines. One such ad noted, "Dolly Darling, leading lady of the Bluster Film Company, attributes her wonderful success to the fact that she eats Puffed-Air Crackers with every meal. Why don't you let Puffed-Air Crackers help you to success?" The *Motion Picture Magazine* editorial staff may have commented on the ludicrousness of movie star endorsements of consumer products, but they certainly did not stop accepting such ads. A few years later, however, with Quirk and *Photoplay* as cheerleaders, the motion picture fan publications moved from being embarrassed about the connections between movies, consumer goods, and advertising to embracing them as an opportunity for influence and profit.[10]

Movie stars' forays into product advertising in the mid-1910s, and the debate it sparked in the film industry, map the further spread of Hollywood into American popular culture. Film producer Samuel Goldwyn liked to recall that the first time he met Mary Pickford, she was seeking advice from Famous Players–Lasky studio head Adolph Zukor about an advertising contract. "They've offered me $500 for the use of my name, but do you really think that's enough? After all, it means a lot to those cold-cream people." Goldwyn was struck by Pickford's seeming financial naïveté, which he said "made you think of a child asking whether it ought to give up its stick of candy for one marble or whether perhaps it could get two."[11]

As Pickford remembered the episode, she asked her lawyer's advice:

"Mary," said my wise attorney, Dennis F. O'Brien, "I think it would be undignified and risky for you to sign this contract, attractive as it may appear. In time you may find your name being bandied about in all sorts of good, bad, and indifferent commercial projects. You are young; there seems to be a bright future ahead of you. For that future you must sacrifice these articles which are now yours for the asking. Your name should stand for motion pictures and not as an advertisement for evening gowns, cosmetics, and perhaps less alluring products of business."[12]

Despite her lawyer's disapproval, Pickford signed the contract to represent Pompeian Skin Cream and indeed was featured in one of the era's most prominent cosmetics advertising campaigns. For ten cents, the Pompeian Manufacturing Company of Cleveland, Ohio, would send customers a "Mary Pickford Art Panel," which, the offer discreetly noted, had "no advertising on front." The pastel print of Mary was lovely enough to grace the walls of the most genteel middle-class home. The Pickford ad series for Pompeian appeared regularly from 1916 to 1921, not only in fan publications like *Motion Picture Magazine* and *Photoplay* but also in the most respected women's magazine, the *Ladies' Home Journal.* It was one of the first major crossover advertising campaigns connecting film stars to consumer products.[13]

Most consumer-product advertisers of the 1910s and 1920s were nevertheless hesitant to tie major products to movie stars. They remained skeptical of the class boundaries of the movie star sales appeal. Like the film industry executives of the nickelodeon period, Madison Avenue–based advertising executives viewed movie audiences and fan magazine readers through the limited perspective of the "East Side Standard," which had earlier characterized moviegoers as urban working class, immigrant, and too poor to purchase much. Consumer-product advertisers also had jitters about movie actors' credibility as product endorsers in the wake of the Hollywood scandals of the early 1920s (the Fatty Arbuckle case; the suspicious deaths of directors Thomas Ince and William Desmond Taylor, which ruined the careers of several actresses; star Wallace Reid's revealed drug addiction and death, among others). Advertisers were worried that the public backlash against "sinful" Hollywood would devastate sales of any product associated with the stars, but just the opposite happened. The enormous publicity surrounding these incidents sold millions of newspapers and intensified the average moviegoer's fascination with the film colony. More movie stars than ever were called upon in the 1920s to lend some of their mystique to consumer products, with results that were often absurd, such as the appearance in *Photoplay* of ads for automobile fenders, "the brand preferred by the movie stars." A manufacturer of grommets also advertised in *Photoplay,* connecting the suave style of stars like Adolph Menjou to the neatness of their laced-up shoes.

As a consequence of advertisers' prejudices against movie fans, however, stars were almost never used to promote expensive, upper-middle-class goods like automobiles or refrigerators; instead, they sold small, impulsively purchased goods like candy, cosmetics, and soft drinks. The Coca-Cola Company had used well-known opera singers and vaudeville performers as their earliest product endorsers in advertisements, but from 1900 to 1915, it adopted the use of anonymous models. Beginning in 1915, however, it used endorsements by serial film star Pearl White and Ziegfeld Follies showgirl Marion Davies in ads placed prominently in the movie fan magazines. Female movie stars were paid to endorse mascara, face powders, depilatories, skin bleaches, and other beauty aids, products that promised to lend the consumer the glamour, physical beauty, and personality of well-known film actors.[14]

Despite the efforts of the film industry and consumer-product manufacturers to join forces, in 1924 at least one contrarian, L. F. Guimond, the director of publicity at Selznick studios, voiced concern about the long-term effects of wanton product endorsements on a star's public image. "I never permit stars I am handling to indulge in the endorsement of beauty preparations, patent medicines and products of that type. Many of these are tie-ups [cooperative advertising efforts] that look good at first glance, but which are found to be actually bad on closer analysis." Guimond based his reasoning on the psychology of the movie fan:

> When a beautiful actress appears on the screen, the conscious or unconscious reaction of the fan is to her natural beauty. When, a little later, the same fan reads in an advertisement in her favorite magazine that "Miss Charming uses and endorses Dr. Fakem's hair-dye," with a picture of Miss Charming and her marvelous blond tresses, and somewhere else sees another star admit that So-and-So's "reducer" helped make her what she is, that fan will feel cheated. She will never see that star in a picture again without remembering her borrowed charms, and the effect will be distinctly harmful.[15]

Advertisers using movie star endorsements, then, walked a narrow path between success and disaster. Fans wanted to think of movie stars as already perfect; but they also wanted to be as much like their favorite stars as possible, and these products held out the hope of effecting the transformation, or at least of temporarily creating the illusion of the star's beauty and glamour. Movie star endorsements carried equivocal messages that traded on the players' mythical, unreal qualities but still offered hope that movie fans could purchase their way toward beauty, love, and popularity. Such longings fueled the restless desire of movie fans to transform themselves through purchased goods that would form the backbone of twentieth-century American consumer culture.

However, it seemed that movie fans required some prodding to make that connection between films, advertising, and consumer desires. Quirk sold his readers from both sides, not only persuading product manufacturers what good spenders *Photoplay* readers were but also promoting the advertisements to his magazine's readers. Quirk constantly preached the benefits of consumer-product advertising, coaxing readers to trust advertising messages. "Read the Advertising!" his *Photoplay* editorial ads exhorted in each issue. Quirk's relentless decade-long campaign told *Photoplay* readers that advertisements were educational and beneficial and that branded products must be the best because they withstood the blinding glare of publicity (like the "best" stars). Patriotically, he urged readers to agree that these "star quality" products made American industry great. Quirk might have shown these institutional campaigns to advertisers to testify to his readers' commitment to consumer culture, but the frequency and directness with which he addressed his readers may betray the fact that fan magazine readers were as wary of ads as the consumer-product advertisers were of gambling their budgets in the pages of *Photoplay*.[16]

Photoplay's Marketing of the Movie Fan

In *Advertising the American Dream,* Roland Marchand profiles New York advertising agency executives of the 1920s, the majority of whom were upper-middle-class men with limited knowledge of the average American's leisure habits. Advertisers tended to select major middle-class-oriented magazines such as the *Saturday Evening Post* and the *Ladies' Home Journal* as the most appropriate forums for their premium consumer-product accounts. This narrow focus led enterprising publishers of magazines attracting new categories of readers to wage long-term campaigns in the advertising trade press to broaden advertisers' attitudes. *True Story* editor Bernarr Macfadden determinedly educated advertisers about the working-class women who read his magazine, and publishers of the *New York Daily News* introduced ad executives to a new breed of urban working-class consumers.

From 1918 through the 1920s, James Quirk also expended much money and ink in the advertising trade press to familiarize marketers with *Photoplay*'s readers. Hoping to counteract the representations of movie fans as a mob of unwashed autograph seekers, *Photoplay* depicted fan magazine readers as comfortable, middle-class moviegoers, young women (and sometimes men) who had plenty of money to spend on consumer goods. Quirk's ads for *Photoplay* in *Printer's Ink* portrayed movie fans as the most desirable group of consumers to reach, people who were addicted to leisure, enjoyment, pleasure, and spending. Quirk's redefinition of *Photoplay* readers as "perfect consumers" occurred in the context of manufacturers' expanding reliance on advertising in the 1920s, their growing awareness of women's purchasing power, and the further market specialization of consumer-product advertising. The same single and married women and men aged eighteen to thirty whom Quirk categorized as movie fans were being increasingly courted by consumer-product advertising agencies. Young adult women were prime decision makers about what to purchase for their families and themselves. More products were being developed for their use. Quirk responded to these shifts in the advertisers' conception of the marketplace by creating a series of attractive profiles of *Photoplay*'s readers to sell back to the advertisers.

Assertive in claiming the allegiance of a middle-class readership that consumer-product manufacturers desired to reach, *Photoplay* initially insisted that the movies' appeal was universal, cutting across class and gender lines. It was "Everybody's Other Business." A 1918 editorial-advertisement in *Printer's Ink* argued that "[t]oday the enlightened eyes of college professors and car conductors and bank presidents and scrub women follow Charlie and Sidney [Chaplin] and Douglas from a common level of interest. 'The Colonel's lady and Judy O'Grady are sisters under the screen.'"[17]

In the economic recession of 1920, Quirk broadcast a variety of arguments likely to be attractive to marketers facing buyer resistance as the sharp effects of the postwar downturn began to be felt across the nation. Motion pictures had not only become the "chief recreation" of Americans, Quirk's ads reasoned; for fans, moviegoing had progressed from a luxury to a necessity they could not do without, even in a recession. "[W]hile with some, economy might be the order of the day, these people would never fail to spend money for recreation. Motion pictures, in other words, have become too much a part of their living to be slighted. And just as pictures themselves have entered the lives of its patrons—so has *Photoplay* with the *devotees* who would not be without it."[18] Advertisers who associated themselves with the siren song of the movie screen could reap sales bonanzas, even in hard times, claimed Quirk.

Quirk's ads in *Printer's Ink* graphically illustrated this idea of the movies' compelling, narcotic power with photographs of well-dressed crowds patiently queuing in front of movie theaters in various cities. "Here's Your Audience!" the *Photoplay* ads cried to potential advertisers. "Something to think about; if they stand in line to see the pictures, they will stand in line to read about them." If these affluent, impatient people in a restless, sped-up American culture were so hooked on moviegoing and fan magazines, *Photoplay* concluded, then advertisers reaching them through the fan magazine, billed as "the next best thing to watching the screen," could sell the goods.[19]

Photoplay's institutional advertising campaigns emphasized the power of movies to create an "ambitious discontent" in viewers, a dissatisfaction with their present lifestyles. "Consider the spending suggestiveness of the moving picture," the *Photoplay* ads counseled advertising executives. Movie fans' minds were "open, receptive and plastic" while watching films or reading about them. The movies broke down old restraints, formed new habits. "[S]ome of them will acquire more longings than they can satisfy for some time to come." One *Photoplay* ad introduced "plain Mrs. Brown," who itched to acquire new dining room furniture just like the enticing set she had seen that evening in a film; her husband Mr. Brown's acquisitive spark was lit while admiring "the silent chug of a certain smart speedster in the same picture." They might, if reached by a canny advertiser, throw old prudent habits to the wind and indulge in purchases to satisfy all their film-generated desires.[20]

Photoplay's marketing ads often referred to motion pictures' "inexorable influence" over their viewers, bending them to the screen's will. This fascination with the screen's power was matched by social scientists' and moral reformers' fears of the same. Both groups held similar assumptions about the human mind's receptivity to external influences, such as those assumptions being advanced by behavioral psychologist John Watson, who worked as an advertising agency consultant. Quirk drew on the rising concern about media influence in his *Printer's Ink* ads, playfully cautioning that not even the jaded advertising executive, his psyche hardened against commercial appeals, was immune to the movies' appeal:

> You remember when you came back from the motion picture theater
> the other night how you caught yourself imitating the ways of the
> hero, the manner in which he carried himself, held up his head, swung
> his arms. Like you, every night, all across the nation men and women

are unconsciously taking over the personalities of those whom they have seen and admired on the screen. And with the new possibilities come new desires for the better things of life—desires that are yours to capitalize on when you use the advertising pages of *Photoplay.*[21]

The movies could inculcate desires in viewers to purchase goods better than any mere printed advertisement, *Photoplay* claimed. For final and incontrovertible proof, Quirk had only to quote F. Scott Fitzgerald, whose short story in the *Saturday Evening Post,* "The Popular Girl," described a young woman's happy absorption of the consumer mentality at the movie theater. "Yanci watched Mae Murray swirl though splendidly imagined vistas . . . she calculated the cost of the apartment. . . . She rejoiced in the beauty of Mae Murray's clothes and furs, her gorgeous hats, her short-seeming French shoes."[22]

This bow to Fitzgerald anticipated a shift in *Photoplay'*s strategy in 1923. Advertisers proved too skeptical of the "inexorable influence" of the movies over the entire film audience to rush to place ads in *Photoplay.* Quirk then backed away from his goal of claiming a uniform and universal middle-class appeal for *Photoplay.* He narrowed his focus to target the most commented upon and most enthusiastic segment of the movie audience—middle-class young people, whom *Photoplay'*s ads symbolized as "Youth." Quirk downplayed the naked power of the medium over its audience and instead promoted the power of the movie fan to influence the rest of society.

In January 1923, Quirk announced in *Printer's Ink* that *Photoplay* was now one of the chief promoters of the "age factor" in selling and advertising. Quirk played on generational issues, claiming that the most devoted moviegoers were young women and men between the ages of eighteen and thirty. This select coterie were (or should be, in Quirk's opinion) advertisers' "preferred prospects: these younger, alert, eager and enthusiastic people who are such good customers for themselves or who dominate the market by their indirect influence on your sales with their elders." Quirk enthusiastically jumped on the bandwagon of American culture's growing fascination with the rising generation. With their rejection of the cautious, conservative habits and values of their patents, in their hedonistic rush to experience pleasure, and in their lack of set consumption patterns, young people exhibited attitudes and behaviors that advertisers found to be, as Stuart Ewen has suggested, the "Industrial Ideal."[23]

Quirk was not the first business entrepreneur to exploit this new market focus on youth; for this new campaign he shrewdly obtained a testimonial from fellow believer Edward S. Jordan, president of the Jordan Motor Car Company. Jordan had made great waves in advertising circles with his "Somewhere West of Laramie" ads for Jordan roadsters; he originated the appeal to youth and style in the somber automobile market. Jordan confidently argued that not only were young people buying more products themselves, but that "[y]outh positively dictates for the family the purchase of furniture, homesites, phonographs and motor cars," and that youth's taste was inherently superior—sons and daughters always pushed for the choice of a more expensive and stylish car than the low-price model their frugal parents might select. The eighteen-to-thirty set represented new prospects without hardened habits of frugality; they had been raised with the twin forces of movies and advertising almost all their lives; they were brought up to spend. Quirk marshaled other endorsements, too, to open manufacturers' eyes to the changing demographics of the marketplace. A spokesman for Kraft cheese testified that in young women "we find the least sales resistance"; the Mineralava Beauty Clay marketing force reported that "from 18 to 26 years of age they buy freely, are most enthusiastic salesmen in selling the older generation and are the most valuable prospects we have for Mineralava."[24]

Quirk's ads proclaimed, "Youth is the Dictator of Style and Fashion," but there was a hitch in his dreams of being a Pied Piper to the "dictators"—young people were not very affluent.[25] Just beginning their careers and setting up households, young women and young couples in the 1920s were at the bottom of the pay scale and could not afford to purchase big-ticket items. At best, Quirk could claim that young people exerted an indirect influence over the purchases of their parents, but who could quantify how often a major family decision such as an automobile purchase was entrusted to teenagers. Young female and male movie fans were most likely able to purchase only clothing, jewelry, cosmetics, cigarettes, and other small, disposable products for themselves.

In 1924, *Photoplay*'s ads in *Printer's Ink* did not even mention movies or moviegoing. Quirk sold his magazine as the younger generation's favorite periodical and as the embodiment of Youth itself. Quirk now downplayed his adult female readers and claimed that the magazine "easily enjoys the largest audience of exclusively younger people of any general magazine" and that it "offers you a definite audience of 500,000 younger people in the 18 to 30 age group—and to . . . many times more of their brothers and sisters and friends who beg, borrow or otherwise appropriate their copies." However, if siblings and friends had to beg a ten-cent magazine, they could not have had much disposable income.[26]

At his most combative, Quirk pitted this younger consuming generation against their frugal elders, contrasting photographs of frumpy old grandmothers and fashionably dressed, laughing young women under headlines such as "Which Group Will You Sell—the Sneering Section or the Cheering Section?" and "What Are They Talking About? The Anecdotes of 20 Years Ago?—Or the Joy of Living and Having?" Older people were largely absent from consumer-product advertisements of the 1920s, and they were only occasionally depicted as purchasers, but almost never were they dismissed as completely as with *Photoplay*'s dark suggestion:

> When you send out your advertising message will it rebound against
> the granite fronts of hardened indifference and crabbed suspicion? Will
> it have to battle with the tight-fisted sneering-sections of the country,
> fighting all the while against prejudice and pre-conceived notions?
> Or—will you talk to the eagerly responsive cheering sections of the
> country, the up-and-coming enthusiastic, youthful readers of the age-
> group between 18 and 30?[27]

Consumer-product advertisers listened to Quirk, but only up to a point. A survey of advertising in *Photoplay* in the 1920s shows that Quirk attracted some but certainly not as many national advertisements as the most popular women's or general-interest magazines such as *Ladies' Home Journal* and *Saturday Evening Post*. Tabulations in *Printer's Ink* rated *Photoplay* in the middle of the market in number of advertising lines sold among general-interest magazines. Indeed, Quirk's ads in *Printer's Ink* in 1925 admitted *Photoplay*'s great success in attracting advertising for women's beauty aids, but they also exposed the magazine's inability to land a substantial number of ads for consumer durables. "The message of the dressing table," interpreted by ad copy accompanying an illustration of a vanity groaning with bottles, boxes, and tins, was that "Miss 1925" bought a lot of cosmetics, soaps, powders, and creams. With wistful optimism, Quirk claimed that, in turn, these products

> point straight to wardrobes of gowns and furs, hats and shoes, lingerie
> and silk hose, jewelry and all other appurtenances that lend to style

and beauty. The fact, then that *Photoplay* carries the largest number of pages of toilet requisites advertising among all national periodicals, *Vogue* alone excepted, bears compelling testimony to its richness as a market for all merchandise that contributes to the adornment and beautification of youth.

Probably only Quirk's persistent salesmanship produced the significant number of national advertisements that did run in *Photoplay,* for while in 1926 *True Story* had fewer than a dozen full-page ads per issue for well-known consumer products, *Photoplay* averaged fifteen to twenty full-page ads.[28]

By 1926, Quirk's institutional advertising campaign for *Photoplay* had come full circle, as the ads in *Printer's Ink* ceased extolling the power of the young "dictators of fashion and style" and again took up the persuasive power of motion pictures to transmit "spending suggestiveness" to movie fans. The *Photoplay* ads themselves resembled little films featuring Mrs. Young, "frequent and ardent attender of moving pictures" (sometimes there is a Mr. Young, too), who sees attractive merchandise in glamourous settings "and is subjected to more buying temptations than she can gratify in a lifetime." The ad reassured advertisers that "*Photoplay* in the home rekindles the yearnings born on the screen" whereupon "your advertising in *Photoplay* identifies your product with her anonymous wishes" and Mrs. Young runs right out and purchases shoes and silverware and whatnot. Motion pictures were the showrooms and fan magazines the helpful sales clerks for the fan's acquisitive desires.[29]

Quirk's plan to market the female movie fan may be judged successful in some respects. The real impact of movie star endorsements may have come more often in perceptions of their persuasive effectiveness than in actual results. Social scientists began to give credit to movie influence, even if advertising executives remained doubtful. Robert and Helen Lynd, for example, believed that the young women of Muncie, Indiana, were slaves to the movies and movie fan magazines, patterning hairdos and dress styles after those of the stars and focusing many of their desires on fantasies rather than on alternative, nonconsumption-oriented ways to change their own lives for the better. Fisk University economist Paul Edwards, surveying the consumption patterns of southern urban blacks in 1929, included endorsement ads in his product awareness tests. He assumed that film stars carried the same cultural authority across geographic, class, and racial boundaries of American society. He was quite disconcerted to find that the black housewives in Nashville whom he polled were not persuaded to purchase a particular brand of hosiery if it was endorsed by a Hollywood celebrity. Indeed, star endorsements made the middle-class black women hostile toward the product. The black women's objection was not necessarily to the star's race; they preferred appeals to a product's quality or style over the association with an actress's glamour. These southern black women found the appeal of Alice White negligible because they paid little attention to the movies; they were barred from whites-only theaters and did not frequent Nashville's substandard Negro movie theaters. That Edwards could have been so nonplussed by the failure of his assumptions suggests either that other female consumers were swayed by the authority stars held in the advertising marketplace or that this was widely perceived to be the case.[30]

By more concrete measurements, Quirk's campaign may be judged to have achieved only marginal success. While movie fan magazines in the 1920s were profitable and did have some middle-class readership, in conservative middle-class popular opinion, they remained a product for the working class. Although monthly circulation for *Photoplay* was half a million copies, whereas the top six fan magazines averaged 1.5 million copies in monthly combined sales, circulation for *True Story* alone was 2 million copies per month, and the *Ladies' Home Journal* sold 2.5 million copies. Movie fan magazines in the 1920s had a niche in publishing, but they did not leap to the level of prominence of some of their competitors. But fifteen years after he began spreading the message, Quirk and his ideas found vindication in the mid-1930s, when consumer advertising executives finally "discovered" the movies as a wondrous new buying motivator.[31]

Movie fan magazines of the 1910s and 1920s were mediating forces between the movie fan and the screen, fleshing out the movie star's character beyond his or her screen roles and contributing to the creation of movie fan culture. For twenty years, *Motion Picture Magazine* and *Photoplay* provided forums for fan interaction through letters to the editor, question-and-answer features, and contests. There was a great deal of interesting material to read in the fan publications—short stories, intelligently written film criticism, and detailed coverage of the film business. *Photoplay* in the 1920s was not only a meeting place for movie fans or a schoolbook of fandom but also one of the most active sites of the legitimation of motion pictures as an art form, setting new standards for film criticism and audience education.

The golden age of movie fan magazines would taper off in the 1930s, hastened by the depression, the premature deaths of influential editors James Quirk and Eugene Brewster, and the fan magazines' increased emphasis on tabloid-style features. Fan magazines became victims of their own efforts to create a middle-class, mainstream popular culture around the movies. In the 1930s, public interest in movie stars outpaced the growth of fan magazines. News from Hollywood gained regular coverage in mainstream outlets such as the *Saturday Evening Post,* women's magazines, the new photo-journalism magazines like *Life* and *Look,* newspaper columns, and radio reports by Hedda Hopper, Louella Parsons, and Walter Winchell. With gossip, stories, and pictures of the movie stars available in so many other places, movie fan magazines became redundant for middle-class readers, and they became less central to the maintenance of movie fan culture.

The movie fan magazine's success in attracting teenaged female readers also contributed to their decline. A veteran movie fan journal, *Picture Play,* founded in 1915, pioneered a new category of mass market magazines when in 1941 it evolved into *Charm,* a fashion and lifestyle magazine aimed specifically at young women of high-school and college age. In 1944, a two-year-old movie fan magazine named *Stardom* followed suit and remade itself into *Seventeen,* a new kind of periodical for younger teenaged girls. Quirk's arguments for youth's influence on consumer purchases and the openness of youth to advertisers' suggestions would become the major marketing themes of this later generation of magazines.[32]

Beginning in the 1920s, movie fans and young people were thought to be synonymous. These movie fans, the younger generation of middle-class and working-class moviegoers, were increasingly subjects for discussion, concern, and scorn in American popular culture. There was always an undercurrent of tension in the movies' and fan magazines' depictions of young fans, an ambivalence that shaded into social critics' fear. In the 1920s, the destructive, moblike behavior of movie fans at celebrity appearances and at Rudolph Valentino's funeral exposed the darker, pathological side of fandom. Some critics and social scientists in the late 1920s argued that movie fans symbolized much that was vulnerable about the younger generation and dangerous about mass society. Nevertheless, young movie fans remained a visible and vocal segment of American society, their numbers continually expanding. In 1928 a group of educational sociologists, psychologists, and social reformers obtained a grant from a small foundation called the Payne Fund; they investigated and quantified what a few of them presumed was the bad influence of moviegoing on young people. In the process of their research they interviewed a group of middle-class college students about their "lifetime" of film experiences. The following examination of these interviews will show how the movie fan culture promoted by the interaction of fan magazines, films, and movie theaters influenced this first generation of middle-class youngsters to grow up at the movies.

Coming of Age at the Picture Show

Middle-Class Youth in the 1910s and 1920s

Now that I have written my memories of the movies I have seen, and have traced their influence upon me, I wonder if, after all, they counted for so much. Could not my actions and ideas have been perfectly natural ones, hastened, possibly, by the inspiration of the movie? Perhaps . . .

University of Chicago undergraduate, 1929

The story of the rise of moviegoing from the turn of the century to the mid-1920s contains interwoven elements of both continuity and change, of loss of local intimacy, flavor, and control but gain of glamour, luxury, and higher performance standards. Motion pictures as an entertainment form and as an industry evolved in this twenty-five-year period from the flash of an amusement novelty, to the growth of a stable, recognizable nickelodeon show, and to the maturation of the Hollywood film industry and the rise of big-city movie palaces. And yet the movies did not represent a complete break from the past; performance styles, theaters, audience profiles, favorite film genres, the roots of fandom, and the early fan magazines—all drew on, rearranged, and expanded on existing practices and ideas about entertainment. Examining early film audiences outside the well-covered urban working-class contingent has demonstrated how quickly all parts of American society were exposed to the movies, how widespread the audience was, and how entrenched the movies became in small-town culture during the nickelodeon era.

This examination has shed light on what film scholars have seen as the pivotal juncture in the history of the American film industry, for motion pictures could have fizzled out at the end of their novelty period as had so many previous amusement fads. The movies also could have remained a small-time entertainment best suited for 250-seat theaters tucked away in small towns, or in big cities, they could have remained tied permanently to "the East Side Standard." But in the 1910s motion pictures evolved from a mom-and-pop-dominated business into a mature, complex industry.

The impetus to transform the moviegoing experience into big-time entertainment came not from a single source but from many, including film exhibitors striving to create larger theaters for demanding audiences, film producers trying to outdo each other in releasing spectacular feature-length films, and fan magazine publishers hoping to tap the full potential of their advertisers and readers. Ultimately, the most important source of change in the moviegoing experience came from movie audiences, for they were the ones buying fan magazines and products endorsed by the stars, making moviegoing a weekly habit, flocking to ever more luxurious picture palaces, and paying higher ticket prices for a more elaborate show. For the tremendous changes in the film industry to happen, the American audiences had to be followed, courted, and appeased, with consideration given to geographical location, class, age, and sex.

The maturation of the movies in the 1920s depended on the support of both segments of the middle class. The urban segment loaned its seal of public approval and filled the movie palaces, and the small-town segment stimulated and sustained the desire for more luxury and a grander scale, demanding to have the upscale theater experience trickle down to its towns. And yet where can compelling evidence be found that the small-town and urban middle class were in the movie audience, shaping the course of the film industry and in turn being affected by the movies in the 1910s and 1920s?

As we have seen, the historical movie audience can be studied indirectly through the complaints of theater managers, the pronouncements of Hollywood studio heads, editorials in fan magazines, suggestions posed by advertisements and publicity releases, and the assumptions of audience reception offered by the films. However, it is difficult to obtain more specific data, since the film industry itself conducted little formal marketing research, and comprehensive records of exhibitors are nonexistent. Luckily, social scientists and educators in the 1920s, concerned about increasing levels of media influence on children's development, began to conduct surveys of young people's moviegoing habits. Examining some of the raw material gathered for one such survey, a cache of documents written by college students about their childhood moviegoing experiences, offers an opportunity to test the strength and extent of the movies' appeal to the middle class from a more direct perspective.

In January 1929, a group of University of Chicago undergraduates in an introductory sociology course were given the unusual assignment of writing autobiographical accounts of their moviegoing experiences and the impact of movies on their developing values and behavior from childhood to the present. Twenty-one of the completed essays have been recovered. Some are dismissive, others are earnest, and still others are the bubbly but frank responses of nineteen and twenty year olds. As one female student wondered, had the movies "counted for so much" with the middle class? To most of these academically elite students, who represented a cross section of rural, small-town, and suburban and urban middle- and upper-class backgrounds, the immediate answer to the question was "certainly not." Another student wrote haughtily, "Considerably influenced by the gospel of H. L. Mencken and George Jean Nathan, I have for the past few years held the complacent attitude that 'the movies were made for morons,' that they were an inferior order of entertainment and that I was possessed of an intellect decidedly too keen to be swayed by such a low order of art." This self-consciously sophisticated young woman's position appeared clear—she did not "need" the movies and, in fact, was quick to deride them and deny any but the most sterling highbrow cultural influences.[1]

Her response might be expected from a student with her socioeconomic background, writing a serious essay for a grade in a social science course. And yet within a paragraph or two of her brave statement, the Mencken devotee let slip that she had seen at least ten films within the last four months, nearly one a week. Despite her criticism, the movies were a ubiquitous part of her life and part of the cultural currency of young people. She could not separate herself from them—and just perhaps she did not really want to.[2]

Another undergraduate was less disingenuous. "I cannot remember ever having been without a movie house." Perhaps liberated by a screen of anonymity, this young woman admitted that the movies had been "a guiding factor" in her life. She argued that motion pictures—embodying "the novelty, speed and finesse which are characteristic of our age"—had indeed played a pivotal role in shaping the attitudes of her generation, with whom the movies had a special bond that came from their having grown up together. Through these students' attempts to explain the movies' influence (or lack of it) on their childhood play and developing sense of identity and sexuality in adolescence, we will learn more about both the middle class's continuing ambivalence about the movies and the strength and breadth of the movies' influence over middle-class culture in the 1910s and 1920s.[3]

To place these documents in appropriate context, it is important to note how and why they were collected, what their purpose was, and what the limitations are in using them today. The essays were collected by Herbert Blumer, a University of Chicago sociologist, as part of his research for the Payne Fund Studies. The Payne Fund Studies was a pioneering series of investigations into children and media influence which sought to measure the long-term impact of film viewing on middle-class children's and adolescents' health, attitudes, behavior, and values. Conducted by respected social scientists and educators at Yale University, University of Chicago, University of Iowa, New York University, and Ohio State University between 1929 and 1932, the research was published by Macmillan in an eight-volume series entitled Motion Pictures and Youth in 1933. The studies received a great deal of attention at a time when film censorship was a hotly debated issue in the popular press. Although social critics and church and parents' groups used the publicity surrounding the studies to promote censorship to protect young viewers from the powerful and morally suspect influence of Hollywood films, the reports themselves went further than any previous research in showing the complexity and limited nature of media influence on children.[4]

In a related book, *Movies, Delinquency, and Crime,* Blumer assessed the power of motion pictures to incite young people to deviant social behavior and sexual misconduct. Whereas other Payne Fund Studies researchers devised statistical methods to gauge the movies' impact on young viewers, Blumer chose nonquantitative life-history and case-study methods then popular with the Chicago school of sociologists. In one of his first attempts to collect material, for the work that eventually became

Movies and Conduct, he gave the autobiographical writing assignment to his own undergraduate students. Enthusiastic about the high quality of the results, Blumer sent copies of twenty-one of the most evocative essays to William H. Short, president of the Motion Picture Research Council and the driving force behind the Payne Fund Studies. Blumer incorporated passages from these twenty-one autobiographies into his final published report, *Movies and Conduct.* Of the several hundred essays Blumer claimed to have collected over several years, only these twenty-one appear to have survived, and they are found in the Motion Picture Research Council Papers in the archives of the Hoover Institution on War, Revolution, and Peace at Stanford University.[5]

When Blumer announced the writing assignment, he handed his students a sheet of general guidelines. First, students were to give a chronological account of their "history of interest in the movies." They were asked what kinds of films they most enjoyed as young children and if those genres had shifted over time; who, as children, they went the movies with; whether the movies influenced their games and daydreams; and whether the movies ever propelled them to "engage in any escapades" or do something wrong. Blumer also asked for details about the movies' effects on students' childhood emotions, especially fear or sadness.[6]

The second category of guidelines covered adolescent forms of imitation prompted by the movies—whether there were any mannerisms, fashions, ways of approaching the opposite sex that the students might have learned from the movies. He asked students how they responded to romantic movies as they reached their teens—if love scenes had aroused them or directly influenced them to translate new sexual urges into changed attitudes or behavior. He assured students that their anonymity would be carefully protected and urged them to be as "conscientious, truthful and frank" as possible when discussing intimate matters. The final category concerned desires and attitudes that the movies might have instilled in them in their teens, such as dissatisfaction with home and parents, yearning for luxury, race and class prejudices, career or college ambitions, and temptations to lie, cheat, steal, or have sex.[7]

Because students followed these guidelines in writing their essays, they may have laid themselves open to charges of bias and dissimulation. Did the students merely fabricate experiences to please Blumer and to receive good grades? The strongest evidence against such an interpretation is Blumer's disappointment at the results. If they wanted to please Blumer, they failed, for beyond expecting articulate, thoughtful statements, Blumer also sought a more incriminating type of information—sex fantasies, temptations to commit crime, and personalities altered by the movies. In correspondence with other Payne Fund Studies participants, he fretted that these students were too straitlaced and too reticent to spill the beans. He was somewhat disappointed, too, not to find the evidence of shocking media influence that he sought in order to make the case for film censorship stronger. The students could have been guided in their answers, acting more prone to draw certain connections between movies and attitudes and behavior because Blumer had asked them to, but they refused to be steamrolled. The quotes found in Blumer's *Movies and Conduct* (widely referenced by media historians in subsequent years) represent not the experiences of a wide cross section of the American film audience but a surprisingly small group of privileged middle-class and wealthy students, highly intelligent and articulate but academically and intellectually prejudiced against popular culture. The students' own past experiences and what they were learning in social science courses, as well as the way Blumer phrased his questions, all worked together to shape the essays; it is likely they would have answered any other questionnaire similarly.[8]

Despite limitations, the material remains useful and insightful for many reasons. Reading the twenty-one complete essays instead of the fragments incorporated in *Movies and Conduct* paints a fuller, more complex picture of the respondents. The students were not so exceptional that their experiences were unlike those of other middle-class children; they could speak for what historian Paula Fass has termed a "major . . . and highly visible subgroup" of the 1920s. Furthermore, other contemporary examinations of media influence on young people corroborate much of the Blumer data. Surveys published by educational psychologists Clarence Perry (1923) and Alice Miller Mitchell (1929) and the Lynds' Middletown research (1929), although not as detailed, lend additional credence to the idea that middle-class children were an important segment of movie audiences in 1910s and 1920s.[9]

Blumer organized his research findings in a chronological format, paying particular attention to the volatility and fragility of children's emotions and the brute power of the film over the child's conscience, which would lead to imitation. Blumer believed that children imitated role models and that outside stimuli prompted them to try on different modes of conduct and schemes of life as they grew. He took a conservative stance that preferred imitation influenced by traditional sources of home, school, and community rather than the outside world. With a few exceptions, Blumer's attitude toward the movies was skeptical; he appeared to find movies variously bland, distasteful, and distinctly dangerous. He discussed film's possession of children's emotions, from fear to the premature stirring of erotic passions. Children's emotions should be kept under restraint, or else emotional control would be lost, he believed. Young teens were particularly vulnerable to the movies' lure, which could break down old restraints and provoke them to dangerous new attitudes and behaviors. Blumer reported with obvious relief that older teens gained what he called "adult discount," a healthy cynicism about Hollywood film, a triumph of rational thought over weak and unruly emotions. Blumer held that the maturing process caused teens to grow out of their movie fan phase and to hold the movies in disdain. The change in these students' attitudes, however, probably owed more to class background, family influence, and the college atmosphere. While *Movies and Conduct*'s strength lies in its evocative examples, even Blumer admitted that this study was slight on analysis and conclusions. He was sympathetic to the Motion Picture Research Council's goals, but perhaps his animus toward the movies was partly show. His attitude was not necessarily shared by his students, either, for despite their disavowals, most of them went to the movies every week.

Moviegoing middle-class children of the 1910s and 1920s, like these University of Chicago students, were the backbone of a nationwide audience for commercial amusement that spanned divisions of class, gender, and ethnicity. Their attraction to the movies overcame regional and geographic boundaries, too; students' essays showed that children from big cities, small towns, inner-city Chicago, Indiana farms, and western ranches were equally enthralled. Whether they saw movies daily or only on occasion, whether in an elegant movie palace or in a meager country nickelodeon such as one autobiography writer's beloved Dinky Theater, middle-class children adopted the movies as their own and shared many movie-influenced attitudes and behavior patterns that had been unknown to their parents' generation.

How typical were the experiences of these University of Chicago students compared to other young people? Fass argues for the representativeness of college students' opinions both numerically and culturally. Sixty percent of American teens were in high school in the 1920s, twenty percent of eighteen to twenty-two year olds attended some postsecondary school, and college enrollments tripled. American culture focused a spotlight on college students as trendsetters. So the young people who wrote moviegoing autobiographies for Blumer were on the one hand very representative of middle-class attitudes toward the movies. On the other, they were a self-consciously elite group bound to bring some prejudices to any discussion of film.[10]

First Impressions: Learning How to Watch Movies

Despite the widely assumed affinity of young people for motion pictures, most of the University of Chicago students recalling their earliest encounters with the movies claimed that they were not necessarily born a generation of moviegoers but had to be educated to it. As their essays make clear, going to the movies in the silent film era was a complex social activity involving patterns of performance and audience behavior that could seem confusing, even frightening, to the uninitiated.

Between sixteen and twenty-one years old in 1929, the autobiography writers were born between 1908 and 1913, at the height of the nickelodeon era. With their older brothers and sisters, they represented the first generation of middle-class children to have grown up with the movies. They were taken to their first movie shows by their parents when they were mere toddlers; most reported their first conscious memories of attending movie shows at ages two, three, or four. But even in the familiar company of mother and father, brothers and sisters, the students were far from being instantly entranced with the movies and often remembered their initial moviegoing experiences as unpleasant. As youngsters, they were unable to read the silent film subtitles, incapable of sitting quietly for two hours to concentrate on the show, untutored in the ways of interpreting film plots, and distracted from the movie by other aspects of the theater.

Several male students, who later became dedicated fans, remembered their ambivalent reactions to their earliest moviegoing experiences. "My parents very seldom allowed me to go to the movies with them on account of the fact that I generally was bored to the point of extreme restlessness by most of the movies they attended," wrote one young man. In researching his assignment, he interviewed his parents, who reminded him that he used to race up and down the theater aisles and annoy other patrons. Another recalled, "[T]he mere mention of the word 'show' was enough to make me hide, so great was my dislike for them." Even if they could read, children might not have been able to comprehend the lengthy subtitles or grasp the humor of drawing-room dramas and comedies their parents enjoyed. A third student could remember only that he had been much more interested in watching the orchestra's drummer than the screen. In order to become full-fledged members of the movie audience, young viewers had to learn to order, balance, and interpret the many aural and visual components of the silent-era movie performance.[11]

More disconcerting for very young moviegoers than the live elements of the program were the characters on the screen, whose actions seemed terrifyingly real. First-time moviegoers could be perplexed or frightened by their incomplete understanding of scenes of violence, suspense, or horror in adult films. Several of the college students explained such misunderstandings as their not yet having learned how movies "worked." As one young man described his inability to differentiate between fantasy and reality during his first movie experience, "I cheered the hero and hissed the villain and wept with the heroine. In fact I wept so hard that I beat it for home and mother. My tender nature couldn't see these hardened crooks lock up such a sweet young thing and beat her at every turn. . . . I worried about the cruelty of these heartless loggers for days and days and fretted to think that such acts could go unpunished." The autobiography writers implied that viewers had to learn to distance themselves from the on-screen story and to anticipate that a Hollywood-style happy ending would inevitably rescue the actors and themselves from harm.[12]

For some young children, exposure to vivid screen images triggered emotional reactions. Herbert Blumer's concerns about the volatility and fragility of children's emotions led him to focus on such incidents, for here might be evidence of the movies' deleterious impact on young people. Several of the college-aged writers did remember being terrified by particular movie characters. Lon Chaney's revelation of his monstrous disfigurement in the 1925 film *The Phantom of the Opera,* in particular, caused both younger and older children to cry and to have nightmares. Yet there were no simple, direct connections to be drawn between disturbing film images and emotional harm, for children polled in other surveys praised the film. "It was a good play because it made me feel spooky," was one typical response. Several students remembered remaining upset for days after viewing such innocuous films as Mary Pickford's *Daddy Long-Legs* (1919), in which an especially vicious orphanage matron threatened the heroine.[13]

The students, social scientists in training, also interpreted some of their more abstract fears and prejudices as coming from the movies. Fear of the unknown, shaped and peopled by horrifying movie images, could form young viewers' opinions. The unfamiliar ethnicity of some screen antagonists served to intensify the villainy of their actions and to crystallize racial prejudices in the minds of young children. One male student's childhood fear of movie characters he called Mexican "greasers" fed a prejudice against Mexican American immigrants, he claimed, that remained with him through adolescence. Several female students recalled transferring their terror of villainous Chinese characters on screen to an off-screen avoidance of their hometown Chinese restaurants and laundries.[14]

Despite the movies' powerful tendencies to shape viewers' perceptions of unknown people and places, their effects on young children's attitudes seemed to be neither universal nor uniform. The students argued that movies did not inevitably breed fear and hatred (and these conclusions were confirmed by other Payne Fund Studies). The student who wrote of her movie-inspired mistrust of Chinese people had a much more sympathetic reaction toward the African American characters in D. W. Griffith's 1915 film, *The Birth of a Nation,* despite the film's dismal portrayal of them as rapacious villains. She recalled that her anger at the film's white characters' behavior toward blacks quizzically moved her to save pennies from her allowance to donate to poor black children whom she encountered on the street.[15]

The college students were also quick to cite film situations and genres that had nurtured their escalating interest in the movies. As children learned how to watch films, the pleasurable factors of identification and participation began to displace negative ones. "I greatly enjoyed seeing children act because I could put myself in their place (in my imagination) more easily than I could older folks," wrote one female student. These young viewers became enamored of the movies at age six or seven as they found empathetic characters like children, animals, and fairy-tale heroes and heroines, and as they discovered the simple but strong appeal of serial queens, cowboys, comedians, and chase scenes.[16]

The Movies' Most Enthusiastic Fans

Serials, westerns, and slapstick comedies were the film genres that the student writers reported having most enjoyed as children. Indeed, in the

An enthusiastic crowd of children gathers to play and gawk at the western movie posters in front of the Princess Theater, date and location unknown. Courtesy of Q. David Bowers.

1910s and 1920s, these genres played a major role in building a large and loyal youthful movie audience. Their uncomplicated narratives featured rapid action, physical humor, and nail-biting suspense. Motion pictures added new interest to old plots that had been popular in nineteenth-century fiction and melodrama. The young essayists did, though, conflate their own interests with the context of the times; they claimed that westerns and serials became popular at the same time that, as children, they discovered them, and as their tastes changed, these film genres declined. While they did enjoy serials at their peak, westerns and comedy shorts flourished long after these young people graduated to more romantic and sophisticated films.

Serials enjoyed a great vogue in the mid-to-late 1910s. Brief one- and two-reel films, usually shown in one episode per week, serials built narratives around lost treasure, a kidnapping, or some other escapade that pitted brave heroines and heroes against villains. The characters in these high-action stories needed the full twelve to twenty episodes to solve the mystery. Each episode ended abruptly with the heroine or hero caught in a seemingly deadly disaster (a car crash, burial in an avalanche, a fall from a cliff), with the action suddenly interrupted by a title card announcing "Continued Next Week."

Instead of being frightened by the serial's on-screen violence and the potential dangers threatening the actors, as toddlers in the audience might have been, growing children were totally absorbed in the action and found the experience exhilarating. "I would 'yell' out 'kill 'em' if the hero was fighting with the villain, or if my hero was hurt I'd immediately shed tears—my emotions were easily aroused," recalled a young woman. "I lived within me each action that was demonstrated on the screen." Serials not only engrossed children while they were in the theater but also influenced their thoughts and games at home. A male student described how serials dominated his conversations with friends between episodes:

> We discussed pro and con all the probabilities of the manner in which the hero would escape the terrible predicament the villain plunged him into just before the "To Be Continued Next Week" caption was flashed on the screen. We conjectured upon the identity of the 'mysterious rider' and prophesied the downfall of the villains in language heated with the illusion of reality.[17]

Much of children's extraordinary fascination with outlandish, convoluted serial plots stemmed from their continuing process of learning to distinguish between fantasy and reality. The perceived naturalness and truthfulness of films' visual images carried a powerful authenticity. "Those serials were very real things to us fellows," wrote the same young man. "We accepted all that was in them with a perfect faith and never doubted the reasonableness of any of the incidents for a second."[18]

It is here in their discussion of their adolescent interaction with the movies that the University of Chicago writers' material most directly addresses psychological interpretations of film spectatorship. Although the experiences related by students are too fragmentary to act as standalone evidence, there is nothing in their accounts that disproves or contradicts current theories of film reception. The data, though frustratingly incomplete, is particularly evocative of feminist film theory's hypotheses about how gender and identity are constructed and acted upon in the act of film viewing.[19]

Interestingly, according to the students' essays, both young male and female viewers wanted to emulate the serial queens' daring feats. The serial heroines of the 1910s were extraordinary role models, particularly vigorous and independent Progressive Era new women. Rarely before or since have on-screen female characters solved as many mysteries or escaped death as courageously and confidently as did the heroines of such serials as *The Perils of Pauline, What Happened to Mary, The Hazards of Helen,* and *The Adventures of Ruth.* One essay writer, an athletic girl as a youth, found cliff-hanging serials to be an especially effective outlet for the frustrations of living in a small town under a conservative father's restrictions. For her, vicariously living the serials represented rebellion against prescribed behavior for young women and a way to ameliorate the contradictory tensions between childhood and adolescence. "Alberta Vaughn was our favorite serial star. She gave me an inkling of what I could with that sense of adventure of mine. . . . All summer this long-legged girl in her 'teens, who should have been learning to bake and sew for her future husband, ran wild, climbing fences and trees, and telephone poles, and riding on the gasoline tank of a yellow puddle-jumper."[20]

While playing, children could pretend to be different characters and could experiment in harmless fashion with good and evil and alternative values. Supporters of the movies suggested that on-screen role models provided positive and educational aspects for children's development, such as "the richer compensations of vicarious experience" and "the stimulation of ambition and widening of horizons." Critics of the movies were skeptical of what kinds of ambitions children absorbed, citing statements similar to one made by one University of Chicago student that the "robber" was a more sought-after role in his childhood movie-inspired games than the "cop," since the crook got to devise and carry out the crimes and was considered to be the game leader.[21]

There were more regional variations in the western's popularity than among other film genres, as surveys showed that cowboy heroes Tom Mix and William S. Hart were especially popular in New England and the West. Nevertheless, cowboy and Indian pictures found enthusiastic fans among all age groups in every section of the country. Another student writer, of Russian Jewish parentage, who grew up in a poor section of northwest Chicago, recalled in detail his long fascination with westerns. Being an only child, frail, studious, and harassed by neighborhood bullies, he spent his afternoons and evenings alone, watching cowboy and Indian films at the local nickelodeons. After a show, he reenacted the film for hours on end in the privacy of the enclosed yard behind his parents' market and apartment building, riding a fish-barrel "horse."[22]

Several of the female University of Chicago students reported having felt as attracted to westerns as the boys, and many wrote that they played cowboy in their youth. Sometimes they took male roles; on other occasions they played cowgirls or western heroines. One essay writer remembered that while growing up on a ranch she and her brother tried to duplicate all the fancy riding and roping tricks Tom Mix and William S. Hart performed in their films. She was attracted to active western heroines who rode, fought, led companies of cowboys, and shared romance with gunslinger heroes. She wrote of her favorite films that "even while realizing their absurdity and their unlikeness to real Western life, I enjoyed them to the utmost and they at least served to fill my thoughts and provide ideas for execution between our infrequent trips to town."[23]

Westerns, serials, and comedy films in particular seemed to offer opportunities for preadolescent children to bend or subvert preconceived gender roles, for girls to assume the cowboy hero's place or for boys to imitate Pearl White's heroics as Pauline of the serials. Pretending to be Charlie Chaplin was a universally favorite game. One female University of Chicago student remembered admiring young male characters in the movies and wishing to be like Peter Pan and Little Lord Fauntleroy, portrayed in films by actresses Betty Bronson and Mary Pickford. She recalled admiring the luxuriously curly hair and other androgynous features of the characters and envying their freedom to do as they pleased.[24]

More often, movies in this era presented viewers with contradictory messages about gender roles, with whose ambiguities even young girls were forced to wrestle. A college woman ruefully remembered that as a young teen she saw the movie *Humoresque* and was inspired to be as dedicated a violinist as the boy in the film; at home she received criticism for "making so much noise" rather than praise for practicing. The young woman who grew up on a ranch playing interchangeably at Tom Mix and cowgirl heroines remembered that, soon after her family moved to an urban area, she was exposed to a greater number and wider variety of films than the strictly western fare shown in her rural movie house. Rather than broadening her horizons, these new film genres confronted her with role models that emphasized constricted, traditional guidelines for feminine behavior:

> After witnessing "Tom Sawyer" I was quite humiliated that I had ever imitated any of the heroines of western pictures. How unlady-like and

boisterous I had been! My utmost desire was now to become the sweet, pretty dainty type of girl . . . that "Tom" so enthusiastically endorsed. So for a short time I gave up all active life; even went so far as to play with a doll for one day.[25]

Movies probably were not the root cause of this girl's confusion. Combined with her new world of town life, however, where the activities of men and women, boys and girls, were more firmly divided into separate spheres of work and home, and where decorous behavior was expected of growing girls, the movies served more as a reinforcer of existing gender roles than as a vehicle for experiment or change. This young woman soon abandoned her dolls and returned to an energetic imitation of cowgirls, but only with a sense of the anomalies expressed in movie depictions of life. Hollywood films of the next several decades would continue to offer stereotypical, restrictive roles for female characters as well as images, models, and occasional moments that made for challenges to those roles.

Obviously, children's reactions to these films were not identical. While many young girls enjoyed westerns, one high-school-aged student interviewed by Blumer admitted that cowboy pictures had always put her to sleep as a child (despite the noise of the enthusiastic audience, presumably). She was attracted instead to "women's" pictures, preferring to spend her playtime dressing up like elegant movie actresses. Some boys dismissed fairy-tale films like *Cinderella* as stuff for sissies; one young man remembered being sorely disappointed to find that *Little Women* was not a movie about pygmies. Also, with the exception of Charlie Chaplin's popular films, many girls did not care for the more rough and violent of the Keystone-style slapstick comedies.[26]

Movies and Adolescence

Most of the University of Chicago students, typical of young moviegoers, outgrew their fascination with nonstop action, car chases, and pie throwing at ages twelve and thirteen. Surveys showed that adolescents (and adults) continued to enjoy westerns, serials, and comedies, but maturing children's obsessive interest in these genres lessened as they discovered other film categories—romances, melodramas, mysteries, and crime stories—that addressed their newfound interests brought on by the social and physical changes of adolescence.[27]

Teenagers' movie attendance patterns did not drastically change

A deck of playing cards (ca. 1917) featuring a different movie star on each card. Author's collection.

from the habits they had established in childhood, except that they began to avoid the afternoon shows patronized by children and instead made evening movie performances into popular dating destinations. From small towns to big cities, movie theaters were rendezvous points for young people, where they went to be with friends, to look over the cliques from rival schools, and to flirt. "We never stopped to reason why we went," reminisced one female University of Chicago student. "[W]e knew it was a form of amusement—we loved the pictures—and besides, there were always the high school boys there, too, a row or two behind us, and aware of us." Clarence Perry's 1922 nationwide survey had found that the majority of middle-class teenagers were movie fans. Forty percent of the 37,500 high-school students Perry queried went at least twice a week, and 45 percent more than once every week. Perry's research showed that young people chose films more often by their alluring titles or by the attractiveness of the posters decorating theater lobbies than by good reviews. They habitually attended a favorite theater, no matter what film was showing.[28]

At later childhood and early adolescence, girls in the movie audience began to compare themselves with screen actresses. As the University of Chicago students recalled, girls became more conscious of their own changing bodies; they began to scrutinize the bodies of their favorite actresses and imitate their physical characteristics and mannerisms. At one point, they laboriously copied Mary Pickford's curls and spunk, and Theda Bara's "vamping" and man-killing stare, and at another, they adopted Clara Bow's hairstyle and coquettishness, and Greta Garbo's languid walk. Now, instead of exploring a variety of roles when playing "show" with neighborhood girlfriends, at adolescence, girls began to argue over playing the same part, the beautiful ingenue. A University of Chicago student recalled: "I always wanted to take the part of the heroine. How wonderful it must be to be loved by a handsome man and of course I was beautiful enough to be the heroine of any play. Alas! When I look upon myself now, how unfit I was to take the part of the beautiful lady of the film—I, the lanky and freckle-faced child."[29] For most of these young women, comparing themselves with movie stars was a painful process of self-discovery. They became doubtful and insecure about making their personal appearance fit the prevailing standards displayed in films, fan magazines, and advertisements. Almost inevitably, their self-images suffered in comparison with the unattainable beauty and seeming physical perfection of the silent screen stars.

Not only did young adolescent girls become more self-conscious about physical appearance; they also discovered sexual desire. One University of Chicago student recalled the movies' impact on the end of her free-spirited childhood at age fourteen or fifteen and her transformation into a young woman. "I had seen 'The Sheik' earlier and found only the desert warfare interesting. The next time I saw Rudolph Valentino, I was interested in his [love-making] technique." A second young woman remembered Valentino's seductive power in that 1921 film, which drew her into imagining herself in the film's ingenue role. "The more I saw the picture the more I fell in love with the handsome hero—I resented him for his abrupt and brutal manners but still I used to care for him despite his

cave man tactics." Not all young women succumbed to the lure of
Valentino, however, as a third student related. "The most disgusting display I have ever witnessed occurred one evening at the Trianon. A crowd
of my friends and I went to see Valentino in person with his wife, the former Miss Hudnut. When he appeared some of the girls simply went wild.
(Not any in our crowd, thank goodness!) Some threw diamond rings
from the boxes and others screamed, 'Oh Rudy! Just one kiss!' and
fainted."[30]

Movies such as *The Sheik* helped to open a new world of sexuality
for young people, but differences in the values and attitudes they held,
molded by class, religion, and gender, meant that teenage girls and boys
interpreted movies' sexual messages in different ways. Boys reached emotional and physical adolescence more slowly than girls, and most young
boys despised romantic films. But young men gradually became aware of
film performers other than Tom Mix, William S. Hart, and Charlie Chaplin. One University of Chicago student recalled the transformation of his
movie interests at age twelve or thirteen, as he began to notice actresses
as something more than objects of heroic rescues. "If I chanced upon a
movie in which the action was not very strong and I was not carried
away by the plot, I would console myself with an aesthetic appreciation
of the beauties of the heroine, but this appreciation never took in more
than the features of the face." At this stage of boys' emotional and physical development, the female sex was a very confusing issue. The young
man continued, "At this time also I occasionally saw pictures in company
with girls, but for the most part I was more conscious of the fact that
I was sitting next to a girl than I was as to what was taking place on
the screen."[31]

Maturing boys and girls became sensitive to movies' emphasis on the
stars. "The kids around school, both boys and girls, have their lockers
decorated with pictures [of stars]," commented a high-school student interviewed by Blumer. One thoughtful college student remembered, at age
sixteen, becoming greedily absorbed in the new images she encountered
in magazines and at the movies:

> A distinct change [came] in my attitude towards myself, often looking
> into the glass with newly opened eyes, and was surprised to see myself
> looking back with a level green-eyed stare. How ugly, I thought. But
> on Friday night I was beautiful, for I sat bolt upright at the show,
> watching the beautiful women of the picture, and I was drawn out of

the shell that was myself and became the equal of any of the heroines in loveliness. I always walked home with haughty mein, but when I arrived, I was confronted by the hall mirror which dispelled the pleasant illusion.[32]

Boys, too, extended their childhood experiments with movie role-models and moved from imitating dashing cowboys to trying on the attractive personae of movie characters in love stories, society dramas, and domestic comedies to help them negotiate new social situations involving the opposite sex. "As I got into high school and into my sixteenth and seventeenth year," one young man wrote, "I began to use the movies as a school of etiquette. I began to observe the table manners of the actors in the eating scenes. I watched for the proper way in which to conduct one's self at a night club, because I began to have ideas that way." The movies attractively repackaged and further built on messages put into the culture by manufacturers, magazine editors, fashion designers, cosmetic makers, and other arbiters of fashion and beauty, presenting adolescents an elegantly distorted mirror of the delights of consumer culture. If not the sole promoter of heightened longings for a new way of life, movies were one of consumption's most vivid outlets.[33]

Not only did the movies provide the standards by which moviegoing adolescents made personal judgments of their own bodies, mannerisms, and habits, but they also guided choices that adolescents made about social environment. Many students admitted selecting and evaluating their friends and dates by the new, external, movie-supplied models. One high-school girl interviewed by Blumer wrote: "I am rather particular as to the looks and general appearance of the boys and girls I go with and this I know is due to the movies. The fellows I am seen with often must be 'chalky.' That's silly I know but I can't get away from it. I have been in the habit of thinking of big good-looking boys so long that I'm sure I couldn't get along with a homely one."[34] Students' increasing emphasis on using movie star standards to evaluate their peers' outward appearance and popularity connected the movies' influence to other changes in the lives of American adolescents, such as the lengthening years they spent in high school and college in preparation for adulthood. Here, role models provided by the movies helped American teenagers to create a distinct youth culture within the broader framework of their parents' world.

As the student autobiography writers recalled, maturing adolescents still identified with the main characters as they watched movies, but the kinds of on-screen action in which young people wanted to participate, and the manner in which they wished to emulate the stars, changed as their favorite scenes shifted from sword fights and cattle roundups to more intimate, romantic encounters. Young men continued to want to take the place of the hero on the screen and conduct the character's action themselves. One student reported, "William Haines is one actor who, when he gets into very embarrassing situations, makes me feel as though I were experiencing the same, and I blush and get excited as he does; but still I like to see his pictures." Male viewers' experience of watching movies tended to be more active, the essay writers reported. Young women, on the other hand, increasingly wanted to become the object of the hero's desire. Alice Mitchell's survey of adolescent moviegoers found similar evidence. "The boys like to see acts of bravery because it makes them feel that they are participating in the brave deeds. The girls like to see scenes of love-making because it makes them wish that they could be so loved." Young women, Mitchell concluded, watched most films in a "longing phase." The autobiography writers provided evidence that maturing young women underwent a shift in the way they experienced films, moving from their childhood desires to take active roles and to emulate the serial queens to their adolescent choice of more passive roles as desirable objects. Being socialized at school and at home to be nonaggressive, and watching romantic films in which the female characters reinforced that passivity, these adolescent girls may have felt it wrong to say or do otherwise.[35]

While young men placed themselves inside the characters of the male actors in films, they also spent much of their time looking at the actresses. "More and more my whole attention focused on the women in the movie, not to the exclusion of the men, of course, but to a quite greater extent compared with my earlier days," wrote one young man. This student, who at age thirteen had chastely admired the beauty of actresses' faces, at sixteen and seventeen expanded his gaze and experienced more explicitly sexual longings at the movies. "I began to notice the swell of her bosom and watched it rise and fall as she breathed a little harder in passionate scenes. I had my eyes out for the shape of her legs, too, and the more I saw of them the better I liked it."[36]

The University of Chicago autobiography writers testified that much of the focus of teenage movie viewers, both male and female, was on the screen actress. Young women at the movies looked at the actresses more than they did at male film performers. Girls and boys alike obsessively concentrated on actresses' bodies, movements, and mannerisms. More often than in boys' relationships with male actors, young women remembered playing dual roles in the movie theater, both admiring the actresses and placing themselves in a woman's position in the film—a simultaneous detachment and involvement with on-screen role playing.[37]

Balking at Blumer's premise of the movies' powerful influence, several University of Chicago students were careful to note that motion pictures did not act as the sole agents awakening their sexual desires. The movies, they argued, were an outlet for wider trends in adolescent development. One writer remembered his initiation into sexual curiosity from the braggadocio of the older football players. "In the locker room after practice hot movies, necking, etc., were discussed. From then on I took more interest in the loves scenes of moving pictures." One male student wrote thoughtfully, "The movies went far to urge and develop an instinct which would have appeared sooner or later anyway. The movies merely made me sex conscious a little earlier than I would have become normally."[38]

Boys in their mid-teens discovered sexual desire both on the screen and in the dark intimacy of the theater auditorium. "The technique of making love to a girl received considerable of my attention," wrote the young man who had gazed at actresses' body parts so avidly. "[I]t was directly through the movies that I learned to kiss a girl on her ears, neck, and cheeks, as well as on the mouth, in a close huddle." Another male University of Chicago student wrote of the movies, "[I]t was a good place to go for a cheap date, and I thought that if the girl I took saw a real passionate scene it would make it easier for me to neck and kiss her after the show." Popular songs of the late 1910s and 1920s, such as "Take Your Girlie to the Movies (if You Can't Make Love at Home)," reinforced such ideas.[39]

For the majority of middle-class young men in the 1920s, however, the movies were a frustrating and unfulfillable sexual tease, promoting fanciful visions of willing young women anxious to receive young mens' sexual overtures. Socially conservative students such as these University of Chicago undergraduates were unable to translate movie promises into real-life experience with middle-class young women. Sighed one man, "[S]ometimes I live with the pictures and often leave a show with the desire to find a girl and engage in sexual intercourse. I have never satisfied this desire, however, as I never seem to have the courage that I have when I am watching the picture." Middle-class, college-age men were perplexed about the disparity between sexuality displayed in the movies and their real-life experiences. One student complained of the moral contradictions between movies and real life, wondering why he always desired the "bad women" in movies instead of the girlish and pure heroines. "This phenomenon occurred, I believe, not because the villainess in the movies is more beautiful, as a rule, than the heroine, but probably because sex desire and wickedness became associated in my mind through unfortunate conditioning in early childhood, which I have only partially outgrown."[40]

College-age women likewise found that relations between the sexes in movies made them ambivalent about what standards of morality and behavior they ought to hold. The increasing emphasis on female sexual display in the movies also provided new models with which students might experiment. Young women wrote about consciously following actresses' examples when trying to "vamp" or flirt with men. One high-school girl interviewed by Blumer commented, "No wonder girls of older days before the movies were so modest and bashful. They never saw Clara Bow and William Haines." She was sure that the movies had made an impact on her generation's "wildness" and sexual behavior. "If we didn't see such examples in the movies where would we get the idea for being 'hot'? We wouldn't."[41]

If movies encouraged late-adolescent sexual experimentation, it was a game with high emotional stakes for young women's self-perception as well as social reputation. A conservative University of Chicago sophomore criticized the pervasiveness of sexually titillating scenes in movies of the late 1920s, writing, "Personally I don't like them; it always worries me when a woman is losing her dress in a warm love scene." Nevertheless, she confessed, "Such scenes make me feel quite excited and tingly, emotions which people describe as 'animal sensations' and brand as unhealthy—since I am from this group I too must say such emotions should be kept under, although I wonder if I'm honest with myself; I'm afraid I'd like to be seductive, too."[42]

The ability of the new breed of movies to arouse teenagers' sexual longings was not universal. Still unsure of how to react to erotic movie love scenes, one college girl wrote: "I have been to the movies with other girls and had them grab my hand or tighten up at some of the more emotional love scenes. I used to pretend that I felt that way because it seemed the thing to do." Another college woman, who claimed to be untouched by the movies' suggestions, wrote, "The desperate love pictures I have seen have tended rather to disgust me or amuse me rather than arouse within me a desire to experience the same emotions."[43]

These University of Chicago students, attending a Baptist-affiliated school, probably expressed more conservative caution in their attitudes toward sexual matters than other members of their generation. Female high-school students surveyed by Blumer, who came from working-class urban backgrounds, openly expressed their enjoyment of the sexual stimulation offered by the movies, although it was unclear if they felt as comfortable acting on those desires as writing about them. Accounts such as these hint at the halting, uneven movement among women of various class and ethnic groups toward the more liberal sexual attitudes that social critics and educators claimed were pervasive on college campuses.[44]

The movies provided middle-class young people of the 1910s and 1920s, especially girls and young women, with a range of role models both empowering and limiting. Serial heroines showed how to be wily and strong in a world of constant danger. Most other movie images, in concert with fan magazines, advertisements, and other media, created new and almost impossible standards for women to attempt to meet. Movie characters vividly portrayed new behaviors and habits of sexuality that many young men and women felt pressured or desired to emulate—but kept sex and romance in a fantasy atmosphere that sexually regulated young people of the 1920s were mostly unable to achieve in real life.

Moviegoing in College

Most of the University of Chicago students reported severely curtailing their moviegoing habits once in college. They asserted to Blumer that they were serious students busy with their studies, and some others worked at after-school jobs. "The present claims my attention, a present which is almost devoid of moving picture experiences, which has no thoughts due to the reading of movie magazines, which finds its inspiration in other things," concluded one typically high-minded autobiography writer. Yet despite her brave front, she could not resist lamenting, "I wish I could see a show tonight."[45]

In many respects, confessing to being a movie fan was one of the most serious faux pas a University of Chicago undergraduate could commit. Announcing that you loved the movies and regularly wallowed in popular culture could cause embarrassment in front of the earnest young professor who disapproved of the movies and could undermine your standing among the campus intellectuals. Admitting that you had a regular moviegoing habit would mark you as déclassé to those wealthy and socially ambitious students on campus who looked down their noses on low commercial amusements and the hoi polloi who packed the movie theaters. And for a young man to propose taking a coed to even the finest movie palace on something so important as a date courted social disaster for the fellow and the ruin of the young woman's social reputation. "At present I don't go [to] the movies very often as I prefer dancing and anyway girls think that a movie date is too cheap," confessed one forlorn swain.[46]

Nevertheless, the students' denials had the same hollow ring of twenty years before when middle-class people who maintained they "did not need the movies" were discovered sneaking into nickelodeons. The students' professors exposed the truth. University of Chicago faculty, concerned that undergraduates were falling behind, conducted a survey of students' use of time. They calculated that students spent only between thirty-five and forty hours per week on their studies. All the rest went for social activities. More than two-thirds of undergraduate men and women attended every varsity football and basketball game and went to at least one dance, tea, or party weekly. The survey found that the average student frequented movie shows once or twice every week, alone or with a group of friends.

Familiarity with the latest film releases and knowledge of news and gossip of the movie stars was thus indeed part of the common cultural currency of college students. Blumer's own informal survey of the University of Chicago's fraternity houses found that Joan Crawford, with her shapely legs, her reputation as a "party girl" of loose morals, and her recent marriage to Douglas Fairbanks Jr., was the number one topic of conversation among male undergraduates.[47]

The young woman who questioned whether her "actions and ideas have been perfectly natural ones, hastened, possibly, by the inspiration of the movie," now was not so sure her armor of college sophistication and "adult discount" had been impervious to the movies' inroads on her sense of identity:

> I long for a figure of the willowy slimness of Greta Garbo, and I want my hair to grow to the length of hers, so I can curl my locks and wear

them as she does. I flirt when the proper occasion arises, and though I flatter myself that there is something of originality in my manner, I suspect that my actions are something akin to the wiles of Clara Bow, made over to correspond with my conception of what would suit me. I cannot force myself to believe that a kiss should almost never be, for though my theories about the matter are solid and somewhat old fashioned, they do not dominate the standards of this age, first shown to me in the moving pictures. And, of course, I would like to be a movie star, for a time, and I have the usual conception of my abilities, that is, I am sure I would be a great success—if only I were beautiful![48]

The student who had played cowboy in inner-city Chicago, riding a fish barrel, concluded that, overall, the movies had been very beneficial to him, providing him with a rich fantasy life and keeping him away from the influence of the neighborhood bullies, most of whom, he hastened to add, had become gangsters and convicts. But too many fantasies may perhaps have robbed him of some important real-life experiences. This "urban cowboy's" regret about growing up with the movies was that he was too shy to turn his adolescent fantasies into reality. "I never learned how to dance, for cowboys don't dance, in fact no he-man dances. Consequently, I never, even up to the present, had enough courage to ask a girl out on a date. My relations with the girls have always been restrained and formal and I hold the movies chiefly responsible for this."[49]

Finally, another undergraduate concluded his autobiography cynically, writing that he really was not certain why he kept going to the movies. "Maybe it is habit; maybe the chance to take my mind off the usual, personal things in my experience; maybe it's the companionship of my movie-going friends that I desire; or maybe it's the movie fan's eternal hope to see something exciting, stirring. Whatever the reason, I go." Despite the sophisticated and ambivalent attitudes toward motion pictures expressed in the present-day portions of their essays, most University of Chicago students, except the most cash strapped and the most elite, continued to attend movie shows. The movies were at best a well-deserved release of school-related tensions, at worst a frivolous distraction, but nevertheless a given part of their lives.[50]

Conclusion

In the early days of film, the relationship between audiences and film exhibition was characterized by tensions between novelty and continuity, between changing entertainment technologies and enduring patterns of audience desire. So it is not surprising that even as the University of Chicago undergraduates composed their moviegoing autobiographies in February 1929, momentous transformations were occurring in the film industry that would alter the moviegoing experience.

The "talkies," a sensational novelty a year and a half before, had become regularly featured attractions at major Chicago theaters. It appeared that the silent film era was over, but did anyone care? The reactions of these young, critical patrons to the new sound films were decidedly mixed. One student despaired that the elements of the movie show that meant the most to her would be lost. "Last year I used to go mainly to hear the organ music, but with the advent of the Vitaphone, this attraction is dispensed with." She claimed to prefer the simple movie shows of her small-town childhood to the elaborate song and dance presentations of Chicago's first-run movie theaters or the new and intrusive talkies. "I usually attend a movie for rest and relaxation, and a bellowing, hollow voice or a raucous vaudeville act does not add to my pleasure. I like my movies unadulterated."[1]

"The coming of the 'talkies' has to a certain extent lessened my interest in movies," grumbled another young man. "Until the actors accomplish the art of talking or until the Vitaphone is perfected so that the actors can be understood by the audience I will continue to dislike talking pictures." Despite the complaints of these undergraduates, the tremendous rise in box-office receipts in 1929 demonstrated that the majority of moviegoers across the country, young and old, enthusiastically embraced the talkies. One high-school senior interviewed by Herbert Blumer rapturously recalled her initial reactions to viewing *The Jazz Singer* (1927): "'Mammy,'—'Mammy'—who could forget the sensation of hearing Al Jolson singing 'Mammy' over the then newly-invented Vitaphone?"[2]

Film producers had originally considered the new sound technologies not a replacement for silent film but an addition or enhancement to the silent movie performance. Sound would bring professional-quality orchestral accompaniment, picture palace–style presentations, and vaudeville acts to even the most isolated backwater movie theaters, producers explained. Audiences in the hinterlands could finally "have the Strand" in their towns. But the studios' plans for offering audiences across the country a standardized moviegoing experience remained a dream for many film viewers. In 1929, only 800 theaters, mostly picture palaces in urban centers, were wired for sound, whereas 22,544 other theaters, small-town and older suburban movie houses, remained silent. Most of Metro-Goldwyn-Mayer's feature film releases in 1929 were offered to small-town exhibitors in either sound or silent formats.

The depression would further complicate small-town exhibitors' efforts to compete with big-city picture palaces, as rural entrepreneurs found it more difficult to obtain financing to wire their theaters for sound than did the major theater chains. Attendance at all movie theaters plummeted in 1933 and 1934, sending many exhibitors to the brink of bankruptcy. Thousands of older, tinier movie houses closed permanently as moviegoers either stayed home or traveled to more elegant theaters in the next-largest town. Exhibitors both large and small who survived the lean years slashed ticket prices, promoted "bank" and "dish" nights, and ran double features, but the larger theaters did better. The distribution and exhibition of the early talkies in this transitional period did not immediately bolster the consolidation of a nationwide movie audience. Instead, the unevenness of talkies' diffusion at least temporarily widened the gap between urban and small-town audiences' moviegoing experiences. Economic conditions compounded that difference until eventually the studios' distribution system reinforced an organized hierarchy of theaters.[3]

Film producers in the early 1930s had assumed that talkies would erase the final differences in regional exhibition and would further integrate thousands of local audiences into a national moviegoing public. Historians since then have argued that in the 1930s motion pictures moved to the center of American society, binding Americans of all walks of life in a common popular culture, acting akin to a "folklore of industrial society" and providing Americans with communal ways to release tension through laughter and escapist fantasy and to cope with the harsh realities of the depression.[4]

However, as this study has demonstrated, the central place the movies enjoyed across American popular culture in the 1930s could not have been reached without the solid foundations laid during a thirty-year relationship with the American public. The early itinerant exhibitors had quickly succeeded in reaching and shaping audiences for motion pictures in nearly every part of the country, in small towns and middle-class suburbs as well as the teeming city centers. Itinerant exhibitors like Bert and Fannie Cook created alternative practices of small-town moviegoing that departed from the dominant urban model in audience interaction, show performance, and sponsorship. The rapid spread of the movies was made possible by the availability of a standard film product to exhibitors in all regions of the country and by low technical and economic barriers to entry into the exhibition business, conditions similar to those that nurtured the wide distribution of mass-produced consumer goods in the United States at the turn of the century.

Class, gender, ethnic, and regional differences among film spectators, and the flexible conditions under which films could be shown, caused numerous variations in Americans' patterns of film attendance. Settlement patterns, the health of the local economy, and availability of reliable transportation played large roles in the location of movie theaters and their accessibility to patrons. While minorities were often discouraged from attending white theaters in all parts of the country, Hispanic, black, and Asian entrepreneurs in the North, South, and West opened ethnic movie theaters that brought mainstream white movie culture to disenfranchised groups.

Film exhibitors cemented the relationship between small-town audiences and motion pictures through the familiar novelties of the nick-elodeon show—the theater buildings, promotional strategies, and the mix of film genres they chose. Using techniques that combined traditions of the theatrical and amusement worlds with methods taken from the management and promotion of retail businesses, exhibitors constructed homey nickelodeon theaters, developed programs that would please the largest numbers of patrons, and formulated advertising strategies to build steady audiences that would return weekly. Fifteen years spent securing the loyalty of small-town and urban middle-class audiences began paying off for the movie industry in the late 1910s and 1920s. The urban middle-class family eventually provided the ideal model for its audience, and the big-city picture palaces arose to cement the attraction.

As the film industry grew and movie audiences' interests developed into increasingly meddlesome fans' pursuits, the opportunities for fan involvement through scriptwriting, performing in local movie theaters, and gaining personal acquaintance with actors became marginalized. What grew in place of viewer participation was a vibrant culture of movie stars and fan magazines that infused popular culture with references to film and performers in songs, comic strips, fashions, consumer products, souvenirs, and autographed photos.

Movie culture especially appealed to adult women and the young, the same groups being targeted by manufacturers and advertisers as key new customers in the expanding culture of consumption. Through the development of fan magazines such as *Photoplay*, film exhibitors, producers, and magazine editors exploited the interests of women, children, and teenagers in the cult of personality, in the construction of self-image, and in the fantasies of release, improvement, and well-being as promoted by advertising and consumption.

By involving itself so heartily in the creation of fan magazines, star personae, and movie culture, however, the film industry drew charges from critics that the movies had spawned a generation of gullible fans and uncontrollable, movie-made children who were unduly influenced by Hollywood's seductive attractions. The moviegoing autobiographies written by University of Chicago undergraduates for the Payne Fund Studies confirmed that the reach of motion picture influence from the nickelodeon era through the 1920s had touched even the most privileged middle-class and wealthy, intellectually elite young people. The students described their intimate relationships with film built over a lifetime of going to the movies, but even they were ambivalent about the long-term consequences.

Small-town and urban middle-class movie audiences had the free will to choose entertainments that pleased them, but only from among the options they were given. Film audiences across the country found movie shows of the silent film era entertaining, or they would not have supported them so wholeheartedly. Once they became moviegoers, it was not certain that small-town viewers would accept changes such as feature-length films or the introduction of sound, but their patronage continued to climb through the 1930s. Nevertheless, the mass media audiences' allegiance to motion pictures was never permanent. As Arthur Meloy, a theater architect, had warned back in 1916, "Pictures offer one of the best kinds of entertainment today, and will continue 'til someone can invent something better for the same admission fee." With the advent of competing entertainment forms such as radio and television, the post–Second World War baby boom, the middle class's migration from both city centers and small towns to the suburbs, and the decline of older urban shopping districts (where most movie theaters had been located), moviegoing changed from a nationwide communal activity to just one of many leisure-time pursuits.[5]

Film audiences continued to negotiate the construction of the moviegoing experience with exhibitors, filmmakers, and producers of movie-star culture. They never relinquished the ability and desire to enjoy the movie show on their own terms and to fabricate individual, sometimes oppositional meanings from films, performances, and movie culture they encountered and absorbed in thousands of small-town shadowlands.

Notes

Preface

1. Allan Bethel, "The Moving Picture," *Conestoga* 1:3 (May 1907), p. 17.

2. See, for example, Jane Addams, *The Spirit of Youth and the City Streets* (New York: Macmillan, 1909), and the classic studies of social life in Muncie, Indiana, by Robert S. Lynd and Helen Merrill Lynd, *Middletown: A Study in Modern American Culture* (New York: Harcourt, Brace, 1929) and *Middletown in Transition* (New York: Harcourt, Brace and World, 1937). The Payne Fund Studies, whose research program was undertaken between 1928 and 1932, was the largest, most comprehensive series of studies of the impact of films on young viewers. See Garth Jowett, Ian Jarvie, and Kathryn Fuller, *Children and the Movies: Media Influence and the Payne Fund Controversy* (New York: Cambridge University Press, 1996).

3. Mae Huettig, *Economic Control of the Motion Picture Industry: A Study in Industrial Organization* (Philadelphia: University of Pennsylvania Press, 1944), p. 33. See also Leo Handel, *Hollywood Looks at Its Audience* (Urbana: University of Illinois Press, 1950); Garth Jowett, "Giving Them What They Want: Audience Research before 1950," in *Current Research in Film: Audience, Economics, and Law,* ed. Bruce Austin, vol. 1 (Norwood, N.J.: Ablex, 1985), pp. 19–35; and Jowett, Jarvie, and Fuller, *Children and the Movies,* chap. 3.

4. Beginning with the two pathbreaking books, Garth Jowett, *Film: The Democratic Art* (Boston: Little, Brown, 1976), and Robert Sklar, *Movie-Made America: A Cultural History of American Movies,* rev. ed. (New York: Random House, 1995), excellent works with a focus on the social and cultural history of film audiences and exhibition include Mary Ryan, "The Projection of a New Womanhood: The Movie Moderns in the 1920s," in *Our American Sisters: Women in American Life and Thought,* ed. Jean E. Friedman and William G. Shade, 2d ed. (Boston: Allyn and Bacon, 1976); Lary May, *Screening Out the Past: The Birth of Mass Culture and the Motion Picture Industry* (New York: Oxford University Press, 1980); Roy Rosenzweig, *Eight Hours for What We Will: Workers and Leisure in an Industrial City, 1870–1920* (New York: Cambridge University Press, 1983); Francis Couvares, *The Remaking of Pittsburgh: Class and Culture in an Industrializing City, 1877–1919* (Albany: SUNY Press, 1984); Elizabeth Ewen, *Immigrant Women in the Land of Dollars* (New York: Monthly Review Press, 1985); Robert Allen and Douglas Gomery, *Film History: Theory and Practice* (New York: Knopf, 1985); Kathy Peiss, *Cheap Amusements: Working Women and Leisure in Turn-of-the-Century New York* (Philadelphia: Temple University Press, 1986); Bruce A. Austin, *Immediate Seating: A Look at Movie Audiences* (Belmont, Calif.: Wadsworth, 1989); Lizabeth Cohen, *Making a New Deal: Industrial Workers in Chicago, 1919–1939* (New York: Cambridge University Press, 1990); Eileen Bowser, *The Transformation of Cinema, 1907–1915* (New York: Charles Scribner's Sons, 1990); Charles Musser, *The Emergence of Cinema: The American Screen to 1907* (New York: Charles Scribner's Sons, 1990); Lawrence Levine, "The Folklore of Industrial Society: Popular Culture and Its Audiences," *American Historical Review* 97:5 (December 1992), pp. 1369–99; and Douglas Gomery, *Shared Pleasures: A History of Movie Presentation in the United States* (Madison: University of Wisconsin Press, 1992).

5. Beginning with Laura Mulvey's famous article "Visual Pleasure and Narrative Cinema," *Screen* 16:3 (autumn 1975), pp. 6–18, a rich literature on film spectatorship, particularly in the historical context of the era of Hollywood cinema, has grown up. It includes such excellent examples as Jeanne Allen, "The Film Viewer as Consumer," *Quarterly Review of Film Studies* 5:4 (fall 1980), pp. 481–99; Judith Mayne, "Immigrants and Spectators," *Wide Angle* 5:2 (1982), pp. 32–41; Janice Radway's related work on female novel readers, *Reading the Romance: Women, Patriarchy, and Popular Literature* (Chapel Hill: University of North Carolina Press, 1984); David Bordwell, Janet Staiger, and Kristen Thompson, *The Classical Hollywood Cinema: Film Style and Mode of Production to 1960* (New York: Columbia University Press, 1985); Tania Modleski, *The Women Who Knew Too Much: Hitchcock and Feminist Theory* (New York: Routledge, 1988); Mary Ann Doane, *The Desire to Desire: The Woman's Film of the 1940s* (Bloomington: Indiana University Press, 1987);

Miriam Hansen, *Babel and Babylon: Spectatorship in American Silent Film* (Cambridge: Harvard University Press, 1991); Janet Staiger, *Interpreting Films: Studies in the Historical Reception of American Cinema* (Princeton: Princeton University Press, 1992); Judith Mayne, *Cinema and Spectatorship* (New York: Routledge, 1993); and Jackie Stacey, *Star Gazing: Hollywood Cinema and Female Spectatorship* (New York: Routledge, 1994).

Related cultural studies literature on media fans and stars intersects spectatorship studies at many points. See Richard Dyer, *Stars* (London: BFI Publishing, 1979); Lisa A. Lewis, *Gender Politics and MTV: Voicing the Difference* (Philadelphia: Temple University Press, 1990); Christine Gledhill, ed., *Stardom: Industry of Desire* (New York; Routledge, 1991); Lisa A. Lewis, ed., *The Adoring Audience: Fan Culture and Popular Media* (New York: Routledge, 1992); and Henry Jenkins, *Textual Poachers: Television Fans and Participatory Culture* (New York: Routledge, 1992).

6. Two excellent discussions of ways to integrate divergent views of audience studies are found in Robert Allen, "From Exhibition to Reception: Reflections on the Audience in Film History," *Screen* 31:4 (winter 1990), pp. 347–56; and Jackie Stacey, "Textual Obsessions: Methodology, History, and Research in Female Spectatorship," *Screen* 34 (autumn 1993), pp. 260–74.

7. Some important works on the tumultuous changes the rise of mass media brought to American culture early in the twentieth century include Daniel Czitrom, *Media and the American Mind: From Morse to McLuhan* (Chapel Hill: University of North Carolina Press, 1982); Richard W. Fox and Jackson Lears, eds., *The Culture of Consumption: Critical Essays in American History, 1880–1980* (New York: Pantheon, 1983); Warren Susman, *Culture as History: The Transformation of American Society in the Twentieth Century* (New York: Pantheon, 1984); Roland Marchand, *Advertising the American Dream: Making Way for Modernity* (Berkeley and Los Angeles: University of California Press, 1985); Lawrence Levine, *Highbrow/Lowbrow: The Emergence of Cultural Hierarchy in America* (Cambridge: Harvard University Press, 1988); and Richard Butsch, ed., *For Fun and Profit: The Transformation of Leisure into Consumption* (Philadelphia: Temple University Press, 1990).

8. One widely referenced source of the "standard account" of early film audiences is Benjamin Hampton, *A History of the Movies* (1931; reprint, New York: Dover, 1970).

9. Several of the best examples are Robert Allen, "Contra the Chaser Theory," *Wide Angle* 3 (spring 1979), pp. 4–11; Robert Allen, *Vaudeville and Film, 1895–1915: A Study in Media Interaction* (New York: Arno, 1980); Charles Musser, "Another Look at the 'Chaser Theory,'" *Studies in Visual Communication* 10 (fall 1984), pp. 24–44, and Allen and Musser's further exchanges in that issue; Douglas Gomery, "Movie Audiences, Urban Geography, and the History of the American Film," *Velvet Light Trap* 19 (spring 1982), pp. 23–29; Calvin

Pryluck, "The Itinerant Movie Show and the Development of the Film Industry," *Journal of the University Film and Video Association* 25:4 (fall 1983), pp. 11–22; Charles Musser, in collaboration with Carol Nelson, *High-Class Moving Pictures: Lyman H. Howe and the Forgotten Era of Traveling Exhibition, 1880–1920* (Princeton: Princeton University Press, 1991); Daniel Czitrom, "The Politics of Performance: From Theater Licensing to Movie Censorship in Turn-of-the-Century New York," *American Quarterly* (December 1992), pp. 525–53; Gomery's discussion of the issues in chaps. 1–3 of *Shared Pleasures*.

    10. There is a growing literature on small-town exhibition and regional audiences. See, for example, Gregory A. Waller, *Main Street Amusements: Movies and Commercial Entertainment in a Southern City* (Washington, D.C.: Smithsonian Institution Press, 1995); Henry Jenkins, "'Shall We Make It for New York or for Distribution?': Eddie Cantor, Whoopee, and Regional Resistance to the Talkies," *Cinema Journal* 29:3 (September 1990), pp. 32–52.

Chapter 1: The Cook and Harris High Class Moving Picture Company

    1. Advertisements for Cook and Harris company performances, Columbia Center, New York, April 20, 1905; Carthage, New York, May 26–27, 1905; and Lestershire, New York, December 22–23, 1905, all in File—Advertisements, Cook and Harris Papers, New York State Historical Association, Cooperstown.

    2. Donald J. Bogue, *The Population of the United States: Historical Trends and Future Projections* (New York: Free Press, 1985), p. 113; Stuart Blumin, *The Emergence of the Middle Class: Social Experience in the American City, 1760–1900* (New York: Cambridge University Press, 1989), p. 298.

    3. Lewis E. Atherton, *Main Street on the Middle Border* (Bloomington: Indiana University Press, 1954); Richard Lingeman, *Small-Town America: A Narrative History, 1620–Present* (New York: Putnam, 1980).

    4. Edmund S. Morgan, "Puritan Hostility to the Theatre," *Proceedings of the American Philosophical Society* 110:5 (October 1966), pp. 340–47; Atherton, *Main Street on the Middle Border,* p. 136. See also Paul Johnson, *A Shopkeepers' Millennium* (New York: Hill and Wang, 1978), and Karen Halttunen, *Confidence Men and Painted Women: A Study of Middle-Class Culture in America, 1830–1870* (New Haven: Yale University Press, 1982). On opera houses, see Don B. Wilmuth, "American Small-Town and Provincial Operations," in *American and English Popular Entertainment: A Guide to Information Sources* (Detroit: Gale, 1980), pp. 343–55.

    5. Antrim History Committee, *Parades and Promenades: Antrim, New Hampshire . . . the Second Hundred Years* (Canaan, N.H.: Phoenix Publishing, 1977); James Turner, *Without God, without Creed: The Origins of Disbelief in America* (Baltimore: Johns Hopkins University Press, 1985).

6. Edmund S. Brunner, *Village Communities* (New York: George H. Doran, 1927), pp. 91–92.

7. Charles Musser, *The Emergence of Cinema: The American Screen to 1907* (New York: Scribner's, 1990), pp. 109–15; Douglas Gomery, *Shared Pleasures: A History of Movie Presentation in the United States* (Madison: University of Wisconsin Press, 1992), pp. 7–18; Calvin Pryluck, "The Itinerant Movie Show and the Development of the Film Industry," *Journal of the University Film and Video Association* 25:4 (fall 1983), pp. 11–22.

8. *Cooperstown (N.Y.) Freeman's Journal*, September 14, 1899, p. 4; ibid., October 26, 1899, p. 3; ibid., November 9, 1899, p. 4; "Lyman H. Howe's High Class Moving Pictures," handbill for performance, September 7, 1901, in File—Advertisements, Cook and Harris Papers; Charles Musser, in collaboration with Carol Nelson, *High-Class Moving Pictures: Lyman H. Howe and the Forgotten Era of Traveling Exhibition, 1880–1920* (Princeton: Princeton University Press, 1991). See also Edward Lowry, "Edwin J. Hadley, Traveling Film Exhibitor," in *Film before Griffith,* ed. John Fell (Berkeley and Los Angeles: University of California Press, 1983), pp. 135–37.

9. Sears, Roebuck and Company, *Catalog,* no. 107 (Chicago: Sears, 1898), p. 206.

10. Courtney T. Burns, "The Cook and Harris High Class Moving Picture Company" (master's thesis, State University of New York at Oneonta, Cooperstown Graduate Program, 1988), pp. 9–10; Sears, Roebuck and Company, *Catalog,* no. 107, p. 195.

11. Burns, "The Cook and Harris High Class Moving Picture Company," pp. 4, 7–8.

12. Ibid., pp. 8, 11; Larry Schoonover, "Letters: Fannie M. Shaw to B. Albert Cook: A Selection from the Cook-Harris Papers in the New York State Historical Association Archives," MS, in Cook and Harris Papers; Atherton, *Main Street on the Middle Border,* pp. 132–35; Sally McCloskey, telephone interview by the author, July 19, 1991.

13. Burns, "The Cook and Harris High Class Moving Picture Company," pp. 9–11, 15; Musser, in collaboration with Nelson, *High-Class Moving Pictures,* p. 128; Lyman H. Howe to B. A. Cook, January 16, 1903, in File 1903—Business Papers, Cook and Harris Papers.

14. Burns, "The Cook and Harris High Class Moving Picture Company," p. 18.

15. Ibid.

16. Fannie Cook to B. Albert Cook, September 4, 1905, in File Sept.–Oct. 1905, Cook and Harris Papers.

17. Sears, Roebuck and Company, *Catalog,* no. 107, p. 206. An article in *Moving Picture World* praised a St. Louis theater manager's "electrifying musical accompaniments which Howe wholly lacked." James S. McQuade, "Motion Picture Affairs in St. Louis," *Moving Picture World* 10:5 (November 4, 1911), p. 363.

18. *Albany (N.Y.) Journal,* October 27, 1904, quoted in advertisement for Cook and Harris show at M.P. Church, Columbia Center, [New York?], April 20, 1905, in File—Advertisements, Cook and Harris Papers; Musser, in collaboration with Nelson, *High-Class Moving Pictures,* pp. 104–9.

19. On the vaudeville format, see Henry Jenkins, *What Made Pistachio Nuts? Early Sound Comedy and the Vaudeville Aesthetic* (New York: Columbia University Press, 1992).

20. Calvin Pryluck to the author, January 12, 1994.

21. *Cooperstown (N.Y.) Freeman's Journal,* August 28 and September 11, 1902; Serge Duigou and Germain Lacasse, *Marie de Kerstrat: L'Aristocrate du cinematographe* (Quimper, France: Ressac, 1987).

22. Data tabulated from Burns, "The Cook and Harris High-Class Moving Picture Company," app. A; U.S. Bureau of the Census, *Thirteenth Census of the United States, 1910,* vol. 3, *Population* (Washington, D.C.: Government Printing Office, 1913), pp. 100–101, 207–9, 896–98.

23. Brunner, *Village Communities,* p. 86; Lingeman, *Small-Town America,* p. 409.

24. "Centennial Programme," *Cooperstown (N.Y.) Freeman's Journal,* August 1, 1907, p. 1; "The Centennial Opens," ibid., August 8, 1907, p. 1, and August 15, 1907, p. 5; Walter R. Littell, *History of Cooperstown* (Cooperstown, N.Y.: Freeman's Journal, 1929), p. 163.

25. Advertisement for Cook and Harris show, January 11, 1908, in File—Miscellaneous; receipt from Lubin Company, dated September 6, 1907, in File Sept. 1907—both in Cook and Harris Papers.

26. Charles A. Francis (Board of Trustees) to B. Albert Cook, August 26 and September 14, 1907; Roswell J. Spickerman (Sidney, New York) to B. Albert Cook, September 16, 1907—all in File Sept. 1907, ibid.

27. Musser, *The Emergence of Cinema,* p. 366; *Cooperstown (N.Y.) Freeman's Journal,* September 1, 1904, p. 2; September 15, 1904, p. 3; October 20, 1904, p. 3; October 27, 1904, p. 3.

28. Hugh D. Fryer to B. Albert Cook, n.d., in File Oct. 18–Dec. 1905, Cook and Harris Papers.

29. Hugh D. Fryer to B. Albert Cook,, October 24, October 29, and October 26, 1905, ibid.

30. Hugh D. Fryer to B. Albert Cook, October 24, 1905, in File Oct. 18–Dec. 1905; Rev. J. H. Migneron to B. Albert Cook, July 30, 1906, in File July–Aug. 1906—both ibid.

31. Fannie Cook to B. Albert Cook, September 6, 1906, in File Sept. 1–20, 1906; F. J. Mitchell to B. Albert Cook, October 22, 1906, in File Oct. 1906; advertisement for Cook and Harris performance, Delphi Opera House, Lestershire, New York, December 22 and 23 [1905], and advertisement for Cook and Harris performance, Cropsey's Opera House, Avoca, New York, January 22, 1906, both in File—Advertisements—all ibid.

32. F. J. Morgan to B. Albert Cook, September 26, 1906, in File Sept. 1906; and October 30, 1906, in File Oct. 1906—both ibid.

33. Musser, in collaboration with Nelson, *High-Class Moving Pictures*, pp. 180–82.

34. Copy for advertising notice, in File 1906, Cook and Harris Papers. A review of their September 6 performance noted: "A large audience was present, including many of our summer population, who pronounced it the best show of moving pictures they had seen. Especially interesting were the scenes of the San Francisco fire." *Cooperstown (N.Y.) Freeman's Journal*, September 5, 1906, p. 5. Biograph released its fire film May 16, 1906. See the advertisement, reprinted in Q. David Bowers, *Nickelodeon Theaters and Their Music* (Vestal, N.Y.: Vestal Press, 1986), p. 14.

35. J. H. Shepard to E. A. Richardson, November 21, 1906; E. A. Richardson to B. Albert Cook, November 23, 1906—both in File Nov. 21–30, 1906, Cook and Harris Papers.

36. E. A. Richardson to B. A. Cook, December 17, 1906, in File Dec. 1–17, 1906, ibid.

37. Burns, "The Cook and Harris High Class Moving Picture Company," p. 31; receipts to B. A. Cook from the Pathé company, dated March 26 and March 28, 1907, in File Feb. 15–Mar. 1907; programs, Cook and Harris show, April 20, 1905, M.P. Church, Columbia Center, [New York?], and December 22 and 23, 1905, Delphi Opera House, Lestershire, New York, in File—Advertisements—all in Cook and Harris Papers.

38. Program, Cook and Harris show, May 22, 1908, Opera House, Fillmore, New York, in File—Advertisements, ibid.

39. E. A. Richardson to B. Albert Cook, December 21, 1906, in File Dec. 18–30, 1906, ibid.

40. Burns, "The Cook and Harris High Class Moving Picture Company," app. A; contract between Cook and Harris company and Felix Blei circuit, performance, March 1–7, 1907, Bennington, Vermont, in File Feb. 1–14, 1907; J. O. Lawson to B. Albert Cook, December 8, 1907, in File Dec. 1907—both in Cook and Harris Papers.

41. Fred Waterbury to B. Albert Cook, January 28 and February 4, 1908—both in File Jan.–Feb. 1908, ibid.

42. Fred Waterbury to B. Albert Cook, February 25, 1907, in File Feb. 15–Mar. 1907, ibid.

43. Addie Hamilton to Fannie Cook, February 9, 1907, in File Feb. 1–14, 1907, ibid.

44. Sears, Roebuck and Company, *Catalog*, no. 117 (Chicago: Sears, 1908), p. 535.

45. *Cooperstown (N.Y.) Freeman's Journal*, September 19, 1907, p. 5; July 9, 1908, p. 5.

46. Ibid., August 6, 1908, p. 5.

47. Ibid., September 11, 1909, p. 1; September 18, 1909, p. 5; December 11, 1909, p. 1; February 5, 1910, p. 1; May 3, 1911, p. 4.

48. Advertisement for Cook and Harris performance at the M. E. Church, Unadilla, New York, March 11, 1910, in File—Advertisements; H. E. Jackson to B. Albert Cook, November 16, 1911, in File July–Dec. 1911—both in Cook and Harris Papers.

49. The itinerant movie-show person's role lasted longer in less compact areas of the country that were not as well linked by railroads as the northeast and mid-Atlantic states. In the more remote areas of the Plains states, the Northwest, and the South, where settlements were far apart and the communities too small or too poor to support a full-time or even weekly movie show, itinerant exhibitors continued to operate into the 1920s; and in west Texas and the Virginia mountains, and on the Oregon-Idaho border, a few were still traveling into the 1940s and 1950s. Pryluck, "The Itinerant Movie Show and the Development of the Film Industry," pp. 18–19; Mark E. Swartz, "Motion Pictures on the Move," *Journal of American Culture* 9 (1986), pp. 1–8.

Chapter 2: The Regional Diversity of Moviegoing Practices

1. On the coming of movies to various American small towns, see the bibliography in Douglas Gomery, *Shared Pleasures: A History of Movie Presentation in the United States* (Madison: University of Wisconsin Press, 1992), and Dan Strieble, coordinator, "The Literature of Film Exhibition: A Bibliography on Motion Picture Exhibition and Related Topics," *Velvet Light Trap* 25 (spring 1990), pp. 80–119. For examinations of the urban working-class movie audience in the silent film era, see Roy Rosenzweig, *Eight Hours for What We Will: Workers and Leisure in an Industrial City, 1870–1920* (New York: Cambridge University Press, 1983); Kathy Peiss, *Cheap Amusements: Working Women and Leisure in Turn-of-the-Century New York* (Philadelphia: Temple University Press, 1986); Elizabeth Ewen, *Immigrant Women in the Land of Dollars* (New York: Monthly Review Press, 1985); Lizabeth Cohen, *Making a New Deal: Industrial Workers in Chicago, 1919–1939* (New York: Cambridge University Press, 1990).

2. Edmund S. Brunner, *Village Communities* (New York: George H. Doran, 1927), p. 15; Katherine Jellison, "Women and Technology on the Great Plains, 1910–1940," *Great Plains Quarterly* 8 (summer 1988), p. 150.

3. Lary May and Stephen Lassonde, "Making the American Way: Moderne Theatres, Audiences, and the Film Industry, 1929–1945," *Prospects* 12 (1987), p. 112.

4. "Map 5—Indices to the National Market: Persons per Auto," in *National Markets and National Advertising* (New York: Crowell Publishing,

1923); Ella Gardner, *Leisure-Time Activities of Rural Children in Selected Areas of West Virginia,* U.S. Children's Bureau Publication 208 (Washington, D.C.: Government Printing Office, 1931), p. 74.

5. "New Empire Theatre in Montgomery, Ala., First Run Fox House, Classed among the Most Beautiful Edifices of the South," *Exhibitor's Trade Review* 6:1 (June 7, 1919), p. 69; Raymond Arsenault, "The End of the Long Hot Summer: The Air Conditioner and Southern Culture," *Journal of Southern History* 50:4 (November 1984), pp. 603–4; Gomery, *Shared Pleasures,* pp. 75–76.

6. Albert Bushnell Hart, *The Southern South* (New York: Appleton, 1910), pp. 116–17.

7. W. Stephen Bush, "Trade Review Editor Surveys Motion Picture Conditions in the South after Successful Tour of Several States," *Exhibitor's Trade Review* 1:18 (April 7, 1917), pp. 1220, 1262, discusses distributors' racial-blind rental charges. See also the excellent account of early moviegoing in Kentucky, in Gregory Waller, "Situating the Motion Picture in the Pre-Nickelodeon Period: Lexington, Kentucky, 1897–1906," *Velvet Light Trap* 25 (spring 1990), pp. 13–28; and Waller, "Another Audience: Black Movie-Going, 1907–1916," *Cinema Journal* 31:2 (winter 1992), pp. 3–25.

8. "Negro Is Important to Development of Exhibitor Prosperity in South, Is Assertion of E. V. Richards of First National Circuit," *Exhibitor's Trade Review* 5:7 (January 18, 1919), p. 562.

9. Thomas Cripps, "The Myth of the Southern Box Office: A Factor in Racial Stereotyping in American Movies, 1920–1940," in *The Black Experience in America: Selected Essays,* ed. James C. Curtis and Lewis L. Gould (Austin: University of Texas Press, 1970), pp. 116–44.

10. "Moving Pictures Crowding Traveling Shows Out of Small Town Theatres All over U.S.," *Exhibitor's Trade Review* 7:17 (March 27, 1920), p. 1871; Paul K. Edwards, *The Southern Urban Negro as Consumer* (Englewood Cliffs, N.J.: Prentice-Hall, 1932), p. 184.

11. William H. Jones, *Recreation and Amusement among Negroes in Washington, D.C.* (Washington, D.C.: Howard University Press, 1927; reprint, Westport, Conn.: Greenwood Press, 1970), pp. 112–18; film producer in Chicago, *Moving Picture World* (October 25, 1913), p. 363, quoted in Eileen Bowser, *The Transformation of Cinema, 1907–1915* (New York; Charles Scribner's Sons, 1990), pp. 10, 278n; Edwards, *The Southern Urban Negro as Consumer,* p. 184; *Film Daily Yearbook* (1931), p. 847.

12. Jones, *Recreation and Amusement among Negroes,* pp. 107–20; Thomas Cripps, "Making Movies Black," in *Split Image: African-Americans in the Mass Media,* ed. Jannette L. Dates and William Barlow (Washington, D.C.: Howard University Press, 1990), pp. 132–44. See also Thomas Cripps, *Slow Fade to Black: The Negro in American Film, 1900–1940* (New York: Oxford University Press, 1977).

13. Edwards, *The Southern Urban Negro as Consumer,* p. 184.

14. James Borchert, *Alley Life in Washington: Family, Community, Religion, and Folklife in the City, 1850–1920* (Urbana: University of Illinois Press, 1980), p. 239; Jones, *Recreation and Amusement among Negroes,* p. 112; James R. Grossman, *Land of Hope: Chicago, Black Southerners, and the Great Migration* (Chicago: University of Chicago Press, 1989), pp. 262, 86; Waller, "Situating Motion Pictures in the Pre-Nickelodeon Period," p. 18.

15. Harriet L. Herring, "The Industrial Worker," in *Culture in the South,* ed. W. T. Couch (Chapel Hill: University of North Carolina Press, 1934), p. 355; Edmund S. Brunner, *Industrial Village Churches* (New York: Institute of Social and Religious Research, 1930), p. 59. Brunner surveyed 69 industrial villages across the nation. Of 10 villages in the South, 8 had movie shows, 4 of which were company sponsored, matching the 48 percent of community activities funded by industry in surveyed southern towns. Overall, Brunner found 32 of 69 villages had movie shows, 10 sponsored by the company.

16. Hunter Dickinson Farish, *The Circuit Rider Dismounts: A History of Southern Methodism, 1865–1900* (Richmond, Va.: Dietz Press, 1938), p. 342.

17. John K. Morland, *Millways of Kent* (Chapel Hill: University of North Carolina Press, 1958); Ted Ownby, *Subduing Satan: Religion, Recreation, and Manhood in the Rural South, 1865–1920* (Chapel Hill: University of North Carolina Press, 1990).

18. Edward Ayers, *The Promise of the New South: Life after Reconstruction* (New York: Oxford University Press, 1992); Frances Sage Bradley and Margaret A. Williamson, *Rural Children in Selected Counties of North Carolina,* U.S. Children's Bureau Publication 33 (Washington, D.C.: Government Printing Office, 1918), pp. 52–55.

19. Morland, *Millways of Kent,* p. 137; "'Producers Should Quit Making Vulgar Films,' Say Tennesseans," *Exhibitor's Trade Review* 1:7 (January 20, 1917), p. 469.

20. Ownby, *Subduing Satan,* pp. 191–93.

21. Brunner, *Village Communities,* p. 16; "The Movies and I," p. 1 (MS p. 55), in Motion Picture Research Council Papers, box 4, Blumer File, Hoover Institution on War, Revolution, and Peace, Stanford University, Stanford, Calif.

22. Albert Blumenthal, *Small Town Stuff* (Chicago: University of Chicago Press, 1932); George Pratt, "The Jack-Rabbits of the Movie Business," *Image* 10:3 (1961), p. 10.

23. William T. Foster, *Vaudeville and Motion Picture Shows: A Study of Theatres in Portland, Oregon* (Portland, Ore.: Reed College, 1914).

24. Western states like California, Colorado, and Washington were more urban than the national average, with 40 percent of those westerners living in cities in the 1930s versus 29 percent for the nation as a whole. Lawrence H.

Larsen, *The Urban West at the End of the Frontier* (Lawrence, Kans.: Regents Press of Kansas, 1978), pp. 119–20.

25. "A Tribute to Moving Picture Shows," *Galveston (Tex.) Tribune,* n.d., reprinted in *Moving Picture World* 2:13 (March 28, 1908), p. 265.

26. Mario T. Garcia, *Desert Immigrants: The Mexicans of El Paso, 1880–1920* (New Haven: Yale University Press, 1981), pp. 211–12. The exhibitor trade press occasionally noted cases in the West of black patrons suing theater owners for discrimination; see "Colored Patrons Sue Pasadena Theatre," *Exhibitor's Trade Review* 17:10 (March 14, 1925), p. 22.

27. Junko Ogihara, "The Exhibition of Films for Japanese Americans in Los Angeles during the Silent Film Era," *Film History* 4:2 (summer 1990), pp. 81–87.

28. "Favors Picture Machines," *Springfield (Ohio) Sun,* n.d., reprinted in *Moving Picture World* 1:24 (August 17, 1907), p. 376. Muncie, Indiana, the Lynds' Middletown, had numerous movie theaters—eight in 1907, eleven in 1916, and nine in 1924. Some of those theaters showed films only one or two nights per week. In the 1930s, Muncie had seven theaters, the part-time movie houses having closed.

29. "Al Lichtman Outlines the Distribution Methods of Famous Players–Lasky Corp.," *Exhibitor's Trade Review* 6:4 (June 28, 1919), p. 287; Edgar A. Schuler and Carl C. Taylor, "Rural Recreation and Art," in *Rural Life in the United States,* by Carl C. Taylor et al. (New York: Alfred A. Knopf, 1949), p. 201.

30. Joseph Interrante, "You Can't Go to Town in a Bathtub: Automobile Movement and the Reorganization of Rural American Space, 1900–1930," *Radical History Review* 21 (fall 1979), pp. 158–60.

31. "The Methodist Amusement Ban," *Literary Digest* 44 (June 15, 1912), p. 1260; "'What Would You Do?' Wolfburg Asks Help in Solving Problem," *Exhibitor's Trade Review* 7:7 (January 17, 1920), p. 702.

32. Jellison, "Women and Technology on the Great Plains," pp. 145–57.

33. Grossman, *Land of Hope,* p. 262; Ira De A. Reid, *The Social Conditions of the Negro in the Hill District of Pittsburgh* (Pittsburgh: General Committee on the Hill Survey, 1930), pp. 79–81; "Kansas Theatres Face Negro Problem: Colored Folk Object to Segregation and Ask to Be Granted the Privileges of White People," *Moving Picture World* 33:9 (March 8, 1919), p. 1342; Mary Carbine, "'The Finest Outside the Loop': Motion Picture Exhibition in Chicago's Black Metropolis, 1905–1928," *Camera Obscura* 23 (May 1990), pp. 9–41; Lizabeth Cohen, "Encountering Mass Culture at the Grassroots: The Experience of Chicago Workers in the 1920s," *American Quarterly* 41:1 (March 1989), pp. 6–33.

34. Esther Alice Peck, "A Conservative Generation's Amusement: A Phase of Connecticut's Social History," *Maine Bulletin* 40:12 (April 1938), pp. x–xi, 5.

35. Clippings, Local History File, Amherst Public Library, Amherst, Mass.

36. Valerie F. McClead, "A History of the Strand Theatre in East Corinth, Maine, 1916–1932" (master's thesis, University of Maine, 1975); Beverly Smith and Carlisle Smith, Mattawamkeag, Maine, telephone interview by the author, June 26, 1990.

37. Alicia Boisnier, "Movie-Going Experiences of People of French-Canadian Descent Who Went to the Movies in the Burlington Area between 1920 and 1950: Synthesizing a Unique Movie-Going Experience," Division I project, February 1994, Department of Communication, Hampshire College, Amherst, Mass.

38. *Juvenile Delinquency in Maine,* U.S. Children's Bureau Publication 201 (Washington, D.C.: Government Printing Office, 1930), pp. 18–20, 54.

39. Brunner, *Village Communities,* p. 15.

Chapter 3: "Let's Go in to a Picture Show"

1. Farm Service Administration photographs of the late 1930s and 1940s documented a number of still-operating small theaters with the telltale nickelodeon fronts festooned with arches, lightbulb sockets, and plaster and tin cherubs and mermaids. Hidden behind layers of paint and neon-lit marquees, a few remnants of the nickelodeon era can still be found on Main Streets to this day.

2. Douglas Gomery, *Shared Pleasures: A History of Movie Presentation in the United States* (Madison: University of Wisconsin Press, 1992), pp. 20–32; Q. David Bowers, *Nickelodeon Theaters and Their Music* (Vestal, N.Y.: Vestal Press, 1986), pp. 6–10; Eugene LeMoyne Connelly, "The First Motion Picture Theater," *Western Pennsylvania Historical Magazine* 23 (March 1940), pp. 1–12; George Pratt, "The Jack-Rabbits of the Movie Business," *Image* 10:3 (1961), p. 10.

3. Ben Singer, "Manhattan Nickelodeons: New Data on Audiences and Exhibitors," *Cinema Journal* 3 (spring 1995), p. 5; Gomery, *Shared Pleasures,* pp. 18–33.

4. Singer, "Manhattan Nickelodeons," p. 9; Russell Merritt, "Nickelodeon Theaters, 1905–1914: Building an Audience for the Movies," in *The American Film Industry,* ed. Tino Balio, rev. ed. (Madison: University of Wisconsin Press, 1985), p. 91; Robert C. Allen, "From Exhibition to Reception: Reflections on the Audience in Film History," *Screen* 31:4 (1990), p. 350.

5. Bowers, *Nickelodeon Theaters and Their Music,* p. vii. The term *movies* was also initially considered to be a denigratory, slangy epithet applied to people in the film industry.

6. "A Novel Competition," *Moving Picture World* 7:4 (July 23, 1910), p. 194; "Concerning That $100 Essanay Word Competition," *Moving Picture*

World 7:6 (August 6, 1910), p. 292; "'Photoplay': Winning Name in the Essanay New Name Contest," *Moving Picture World* 7:16 (October 15, 1910), p. 858.

7. "The Name of the House," *Moving Picture World* 7:17 (October 22, 1910), pp. 918–19.

8. Further discussion of nickelodeon theaters and examples of their names may be found in Charlotte Herzog, "The Motion Picture Theater and Film Exhibition, 1896–1932" (Ph.D. diss., Northwestern University, 1980); Bowers, *Nickelodeon Theaters and Their Music*; Robert Kirk Headley Jr., *Exit: A History of Movies in Baltimore* (College Park, Md.: Robert K. Headley, 1974); Gomery, *Shared Pleasures*; and the exhibitor trade journals *Nickelodeon, Exhibitor's Trade Review,* and *Moving Picture World.*

9. Headley, *Exit,* p. 10; James Jones, "When Movies Showed the Commercials," *Baltimore Sun Magazine,* November 25, 1973, p. 2.

10. *Moving Picture World* 5:13 (September 25, 1909), p. 412; Edward Ayers, *The Promise of the New South: Life after Reconstruction* (New York: Oxford University Press, 1992), pp. 95, 99.

11. Headley, *Exit,* p. 10; Miriam Hansen, "Adventures of Goldilocks: Spectatorship, Consumerism, and Public Life," *Camera Obscura* 22 (January 1990), pp. 51–71. Baltimore's Teddy Bear Picture Parlor operated from 1909 until 1920. Bowers, *Nickelodeon Theaters and Their Music,* p. viii.

12. Helen Delpar, *The Enormous Vogue of Things Mexican: Cultural Relations between the United States and Mexico, 1920–1935* (Tuscaloosa: University of Alabama Press, 1992), pp. 130, 198–99.

13. Herzog, "The Motion Picture Theater," pp. 32–43; Gomery, *Shared Pleasures,* p. 28. Baltimore had theaters called the Wizard and the Great Wizard, named in honor of Thomas A. Edison, the "Wizard of Menlo Park." Headley, *Exit,* p. 136.

14. Brother Andrew C. Fowler, "Hippodromes," *Marquee* 25:4 (1993), pp. 4–18. Hippodrome was the name given by the Greeks and later Romans to arenas for chariot races. The London Hippodrome and the New York Hippodrome could house indoor circuses and were equipped with huge water tanks for aquatic shows.

15. The Nickeldome was located in Des Moines. Gomery, *Shared Pleasures,* p. 27.

16. Baltimore's Bunny Picture Theater operated from 1913 to 1922. Headley, *Exit,* p. 54, and Baltimore city directories, 1913 to 1924. Bunny Theaters have also been located in Brooklyn and Manhattan. The Gertrude McCoy Theater was still operating in 1926. There appear to have been no theaters named to commemorate other early film stars such as Chaplin or Pickford, although a Will Rogers Theater in Chicago opened in the mid 1930s. Theaters may have limited themselves to using only the names of popular movie

stars who died in midcareer. Howard McLellan, in "Away from Beaten Paths," *Exhibitor's Trade Review* 12:17 (September 23, 1922), p. 1099, wrote that "it is so seldom that a theatre is named after its owner nowadays that it is an eye-opener to see one."

17. Hazen Conklin, "What the People Want," *Moving Picture World* 27:10 (March 11, 1916), p. 1640. Terms like *movieland, filmland,* and *shadowland* were also widely used in the 1910s and 1920s to describe the film production industry and the sites of the movie studios (which were in the process of relocating to Los Angeles).

18. James K. Meade, "Advertising the Show," *Nickelodeon* 1:2 (February 1909), p. 43.

19. David Nye, *Electrifying America: The Social Meaning of a New Technology, 1880–1940* (Cambridge: Massachusetts Institute of Technology Press, 1990), pp. 4–29; John Kasson, *Amusing the Million: Coney Island at the Turn of the Century* (New York: Hill and Wang, 1978).

20. "Five-Cent Show Easily Started," *Chicago Tribune,* n.d., reprinted in *Moving Picture World* 1:24 (August 17, 1907), p. 376; F. H. Richardson, "Plain Talks to Theater Managers and Operators: Chapter 25, Decoration," *Moving Picture World* 5:21 (November 20, 1909), p. 713.

21. Victor Appleton [Edward Stratemeyer Syndicate pseud.], *The Motion Picture Chums' First Venture, or Opening a Photo Playhouse in Fairlands* (New York: Grosset and Dunlap, 1913), p. 119.

22. William Leach, "Transformations in a Culture of Consumption: Women and Department Stores, 1890–1925," *Journal of American History* 71:2 (September 1984), p. 324. Movie theaters did not have neon-lit marquees until the early 1930s.

23. Ibid., p. 327; P. A. Parsons, "A History of Motion Picture Advertising," *Moving Picture World* 40:11 (March 26, 1927), p. 308.

24. G. R. Scherman, "Days of the Nickel Movie," *Baltimore Sun Magazine,* November 25, 1956, in Clippings Files, Maryland Historical Society, Baltimore; Parsons, "History of Motion Picture Advertising."

25. Lucius H. Cannon, *Motion Pictures: Laws, Ordinances, and Regulations on Censorship, Minors, and Other Related Subjects* (St. Louis: St. Louis Public Library, 1920), p. 154; Frederick J. Haskin, "The Popular Nickelodeon," *Moving Picture World* 2:3 (January 18, 1908), p. 36.

26. J. Hartnett, "Theater Managers, Wake Up!," *Moving Picture World* 2:25 (June 20, 1908), p. 525.

27. Lucy France Pierce, "The Nickelodeon," *World Today* 15 (October 1908), p. 1054.

28. "Let's Go in to a Picture Show," words by Junie McCree, music by Albert Von Tilzer, copyright 1909, York Music Company, New York; Charles Hamm, *Yesterdays: Popular Song in America* (New York: Norton, 1983), p. 325.

29. Ben M. Hall, *The Best Remaining Seats* (New York: Bramhall House, 1961; reprint, New York: DaCapo, 1988), pp. 162–69; Eileen Bowser, *The Transformation of Cinema, 1907–1915* (New York: Charles Scribner's Sons, 1990).

30. Harold Edel, "Curtailing Expenses without Injuring Quality of Show," *Exhibitor's Trade Review* 4 (August 3, 1918), p. 739.

31. Ella Lott Goodman, "I Remember . . . Open Air Movies Forty Years Ago," *Baltimore Sun Magazine,* October 27, 1957, n.p., in Clippings Files, Maryland Historical Society. On air-conditioning, see Douglas Gomery, "The Movies Become Big Business: Publix Theaters and the Chain Store Strategy," *Cinema Journal* 18:2 (spring 1979), p. 29.

32. Among the many fine recent books on the nickelodeon era are Charles Musser, *Before the Nickelodeon: Edwin S. Potter and the Edison Manufacturing Company* (Berkeley and Los Angeles: University of California Press, 1991); William Uricchio and Roberta Pearson, *Reframing Culture: The Case of the Vitagraph Quality Films* (Princeton: Princeton University Press, 1993); Q. David Bowers, *Thanhouser Films: An Encyclopedia and History* (Vestal, N.Y.: Emprise Publications, forthcoming); Tom Gunning, *D. W. Griffith and the Origins of American Narrative Film: The Early Years at Biograph* (Urbana: University of Illinois Press, 1991); Roberta Pearson, *Eloquent Gestures: The Transformation of Performance Style in the Griffith Biograph Films* (Berkeley and Los Angeles: University of California Press, 1992); Scott Simon, *The Films of D. W. Griffith* (New York: Cambridge University Press, 1993); Charles Musser, *The Emergence of Cinema: The American Screen to 1907* (New York: Charles Scribner's Sons, 1990); Anthony Slide, *Early American Cinema,* rev. ed. (Metuchen, N.J.: Scarecrow Press, 1994).

33. File Oct. 11–Nov. 1911 and File Jan.–Feb., 1914, Cook and Harris Papers, New York State Historical Association, Cooperstown; *Cooperstown (N.Y.) Freeman's Journal,* January 10, 1912, p. 5; January 1, 1913, p. 5; January 7, 1914, p. 5; January 6, 1915, p. 8; January 12, 1916, p. 8; January 3, 1917, p. 8.

34. *Biograph* 1:38 (May 22, 1915), in Motion Picture Files, Warshaw Collection of Business Americana, National Museum of American History, Smithsonian Institution, Washington, D.C.

35. "The Tremendous Demand for Song Slides," *Moving Picture World* 1:30 (September 28, 1907), p. 467; John W. Ripley, "Song-Slides Helped to Unify U.S. Communities and Sell Sheet Music," *Films in Review* (March 1971), pp. 147–52.

36. S. M. Berg, "Community Chorus Singing in the Motion Picture Theater," *Exhibitor's Trade Review* 4:11 (August 17, 1918) p. 930.

37. "Music in Picture Theaters," *Nickelodeon* 2:1 (July 1909), p. 4; "Appropriate Music Creates Atmosphere for Pictures," *Exhibitor's Trade Review* 17:6 (November 11, 1924), p. 76; "Music That Fits Story Theme Enhances

Picture, Otherwise Worse Than Useless," *Exhibitor's Trade Review* 7:6 (January 10, 1920), p. 626; Clarence E. Sinn, "Music for the Picture," *Moving Picture World* 7:22 (November 26, 1910), p. 1227.

38. Walter Prichard Eaton, "The Canned Drama," *American Magazine* 68 (September 1909), p. 499.

39. "Moving and Talking Pictures Attract Many," *Moving Picture World* 2:26 (June 27, 1908), p. 541; "The Successful Exhibitor," *Moving Picture World* 2:20 (May 16, 1908), p. 431.

40. Charles E. Nolte, "I Remember . . . the Palace on South Broadway," *Baltimore Sun Magazine*, October 7, 1951, and Harry Lewy, "I Remember . . . Baltimore's First Movie Theater," *Baltimore Sun Magazine*, November 21, 1954, both found in Clippings Files, Maryland Historical Society; Headley, *Exit*, p. 12.

41. "The Value of a Lecture with the Show," *Moving Picture World* 2:8 (February 22, 1908), p. 143.

42. Herzog, "The Motion Picture Theater," pp. 38, 43, 51–70.

43. Jane Gaines, "From Elephants to Lux Soap: The Programming and 'Flow' of Early Motion Picture Exploitation," *Velvet Light Trap* 25 (spring 1990), p. 32; Gomery, *Shared Pleasures*, pp. 34–82. Movie theater chains became an issue as early as 1909, when a trade journal columnist commented on a number of chains that had formed in the previous few months, representing "scores of circuits of motion picture theaters, some of them embracing as many as 50 or 60 locations. These circuits will be operated on a basis similar to that upon which chains of stores in the commercial line are conducted. No one place will be expected to make large returns on the individual investment, but the combined surplus of all the places will afford a good dividend on the outlay." "Observations by Our Man about Town," *Moving Picture World* 5:8 (August 21, 1909), p. 251.

Chapter 4: Small-Town Alternatives

1. "Desirable Film Subjects," *Moving Picture World* 2:22 (May 30, 1908), p. 471.

2. David Grimsted, *Melodrama Unveiled: American Theater and Culture, 1800–1850* (Chicago: University of Chicago Press, 1968); Michael Denning, *Mechanic Accents: Dime Novels and Working-Class Culture in America* (London: Verso, 1987).

3. Margaret Thorp, *America at the Movies* (1939; reprint, New York: Arno Press, 1970), pp. 10, 12–13; Benjamin de Casseres, "Movies That People Want," *New York Times*, September 3, 1922, reprinted in Gene Brown, ed., *New York Times Encyclopedia of Film*, vol. 1 (New York: Times Books, 1984), September 1922 section.

4. Henry Jenkins, "'Shall We Make It for New York or for Distribution?': Eddie Cantor, Whoopee, and Regional Resistance to the Talkies," *Cinema Journal* 29:3 (September 1990), pp. 32–52.

5. H. F. Hoffman, "What People Want," *Moving Picture World* 7:2 (July 9, 1910), pp. 77–78.

6. Entrepreneurial advertiser James Collins in 1910 attempted to assure both consumer-product manufacturers and film exhibitors of the growing acceptance of industrial and educational varieties of advertising film by movie audiences. To the manufacturer he stressed the potent appeal of promotional films to the audience's subconscious. To interest the exhibitor, Collins claimed audiences would pay to see industrial films because they appealed to genteel middle-class audience members' fascination with films with educational topics and exotic locales. Indeed, Collins could state with confidence that, whereas obvious advertising was distasteful to "high-class" audiences, industrial films were popular with small-town, middle-class movie patrons and were widely acceptable to educators as learning tools for children. James H. Collins, "Advertising via the Moving Picture," *Printer's Ink*, n.d., reprinted in *Moving Picture World* 6:11 (March 19, 1910), p. 422. See also Charles F. Kear, "What Is the Most Popular Film?" *Moving Picture World* 6:10 (March 12, 1910), p. 373.

Perhaps the similar interest of adults and children in the educational aspects of nature programs and other instructive fare has spurred the contemporary success of cable stations like the Discovery Channel.

7. "About Moving Pictures," *Knoxville (Tenn.) Sentinel*, n.d., reprinted in *Moving Picture World* 1:36 (November 9, 1907), pp. 578–79; "Boosting the Show through the Pictures," 7:25 (December 17, 1910), p. 1425; "Selecting a Show," 6:16 (April 23, 1910), p. 652; Melvin G. Urnstock, "Educational Films Appreciated in the West," 6:16 (April 23, 1910), p. 653—all in *Moving Picture World*.

8. Wilson Mayer, "The Film-Lectures System of Advertising," 2:3 (September 1909), p. 83, and Mayer, "A Great Concern's Use of Moving Pictures," 2:4 (October 1909), pp. 111–12, both in *Nickelodeon*.

9. Collins, "Advertising via the Moving Picture," pp. 422–23; Sears, Roebuck and Company, *Catalog*, no. 107 (Chicago: Sears, 1898), p. 208. On the history of industrial and advertising films, see Kemp Niver, "Paper Prints of Early Motion Pictures," in *Film before Griffith*, ed. John Fell (Berkeley and Los Angeles: University of California Press, 1983), p. 260; Terry Ramsaye, *A Million and One Nights: A History of the Motion Picture through 1926* (1926; reprint, New York: Simon and Schuster, 1964), p. 345; Daniel J. Perkins, "The American Archives of the Factual Film," *Historical Journal of Film, Radio, and Television* 10:1 (1990), pp. 71–80. On the evolution of early advertising films, see Kathryn Helgesen Fuller, "Shadowland: American Audiences and the Movie-Going Experience in the Silent Film Era" (Ph.D. diss., Johns Hopkins University, 1992), chap. 5.

10. "Industrial Films: Their Uses and Popularity," *Moving Picture World* 6:17 (April 30, 1910), p. 688; Kay Sloan, *The Loud Silents: Origins of the Social Problem Film* (Urbana: University of Illinois Press, 1988); Kevin Brownlow, *Behind the Mask of Innocence: Sex, Violence, Prejudice, Crime; Films of Social Conscious in the Silent Era* (New York: Knopf, 1990). Additionally, Kristin Thompson has commented on the international scope of screen advertising in this period, noting that many American industrial films were shown abroad, in Africa, Asia, and South America, with great impact. Kristin Thompson, *Exporting Entertainment: America in the World Film Market, 1907–1934* (London: British Film Institute Books, 1985).

11. "Motion Pictures as an Advertising Proposition," *Moving Picture World* 3:3 (July 18, 1908), p. 43.

12. Kenneth S. Clark, "Children and 'The Movies,'" *Motion Picture Story Magazine* (August 1911), pp. 97–98. Some children expressed great interest in educational films of exotic places, animals, and people. See schoolchildren's debate, in "A Little Child Shall Lead Them," *Moving Picture World* 6:22 (June 4, 1910), p. 936.

13. David L. Lewis, *The Public Image of Henry Ford: An American Folk Hero and His Company* (Detroit: Wayne State University Press, 1976), pp. 114–15, 126; Lewis, "Pioneering the Business Film," *Public Relations Journal* 25 (June 1971), pp. 14–17; Mayfield Bray, *Guide to the Ford Film Collection in the National Archives* (Washington, D.C.: National Archives, 1970), p. 7. Ford's other film series, *The Ford Educational Library,* contained segments of the *Animated Weekly* and *Educational Weekly* repackaged as educational documentaries and sold to schools and libraries, which would then circulate the films. The program was a financial failure and was discontinued in 1925.

14. Michael Berger, *The Devil Wagon in God's Country: The Automobile and Social Change in Rural America, 1893–1929* (Hamden, Conn.: Archon Books, 1979), p. 49.

15. Watterson R. Rothacker, "Moving Pictures in Advertising: No Longer an Experiment—Used by Largest Advertisers in America—Value of the Descriptive Style—Inexpensive and Easily Transported," *Moving Picture World* 8:13 (April 1, 1911), p. 698.

16. Bray, *Guide to the Ford Film Collection,* pp. 5–19; *Wid's Year Book, 1920–1921* (New York: Wid's Films and Film Folk, 1921), p. 169; *Ford Animated Weekly* and *Ford Educational Weekly* films, in Film Archives, National Archives, Washington, D.C.

17. D. L. Lewis, *The Public Image of Henry Ford,* p. 115.

18. King Vidor, *A Tree Is a Tree* (1953; reprint, Hollywood: Samuel French, 1981), pp. 47–48, 50–51; Rothacker, "Moving Pictures in Advertising," p. 698.

19. Roy L. Smith, *Moving Pictures in the Church* (New York: Abingdon Press, 1921), p. 17.

20. E. Boudinot Stockton, "The Pictures in the Pulpit," *Moving Picture World* 14:13 (December 28, 1912), p. 1284.

21. Edward M. McConoughey, *Motion Pictures in Religious and Educational Work, with Practical Suggestions for Their Use* (Boston: Methodist Federation for Social Service, 1916), p. 12, in Motion Pictures Files, Warshaw Collection of Business Americana, National Museum of American History, Smithsonian Institution, Washington, D.C.

22. W. Stephen Bush, "Pictures for Churches," *Moving Picture World* 10:9 (December 2, 1911), pp. 701–2. One *Moving Picture World* correspondent complained of the lack of suitable religious-themed films available from commercial distributors; he reported that some church showings ceased abruptly when they were shipped violent melodramas or sex comedies. "Pictures for Church Work," *Moving Picture World* 6:4 (January 29, 1910), p. 121.

23. Gladys Bollman and Henry Bollman, *Motion Pictures for Community Needs* (New York: Henry Holt, 1922), p. 63. Ministers and community groups needing advice on movie show operation and film rentals could turn in the mid-1910s to new special-interest publications like *Moving Picture Age*, founded to promote the religious, educational, and industrial film market.

24. Gregory Waller, "Another Audience: Black Movie-Going, 1907–1916," *Cinema Journal* 31 (winter 1992), pp. 3–25; *Wid's Year Book, 1921–1922* (New York: Wid's Films and Film Folk, 1922), p. 115. The 1940 Preston Sturges film *Sullivan's Travels* contains a powerful scene in which movies are shown in a poor black church in Louisiana to parishioners and convict laborers. "Thousands of Catholic Parish Houses to Operate Movie Shows," *Educational Film Magazine* (September 1919), pp. 12–13.

25. Howard McLellan, "Away from Beaten Paths," *Exhibitor's Trade Review* 12:17 (September 23, 1922), p. 1099; "The Picture in Montclair," *Moving Picture World* 10:6 (November 11, 1911), p. 459.

26. McConoughey, *Motion Pictures in Religious and Educational Work* pp. 13–14.

27. Ibid., pp. 12–13. McConoughey played up a church show's supposed need for first-run theatrical films. "If a church wishes to compete for the motion picture goers it must handle new material as well as educational films. A good program always costs money," he chided. "Too much stress cannot be laid upon the importance of first-class films. It is a mistake to show in churches films that have already been discarded by photo-play houses. For everybody will recognize the pictures except the few who refuse to go see the 'movies.'" A better option than the old, worn-out theatrical trash, in his opinion, were industrial films from private companies. "An ever-increasing number of corporations (too many to be listed here) are loaning films illustrating the manufacture and use of their special products; for example, the International Harvester Co., the Barber Asphalt Paving Co., and the American Telegraph and Telephone Co" (pp. 14, 30–31).

28. Ibid., p. 15.

29. "Educational Pictures in Schools Are Making Fans and Fanettes, Says Perkins," *Exhibitor's Trade Review* 7:6 (January 10, 1920), p. 614; *Wid's Year Book, 1921–1922,* p. 113. Money to defray the cost of the Bay City Western High School movie program was collected from students' parents.

30. George J. Anderson, "The Case for Motion Pictures," *Nickelodeon* 4:4 (August 15, 1910), p. 98; "This Parson/Exhibitor Is Some Hypocritical Censor," *Moving Picture World* 33:10 (March 15, 1919), p. 1449.

31. "W. D. Foster Dies, Movie Innovator," *New York Times,* September 23, 1961, p. 19:1.

32. Index cards for Pickford, Chaplin, Gish, Griffith, and industrial films, in Warren Dunham Foster Files (microfilm), Motion Picture, Television, and Recorded Sound Division, Library of Congress. The hundreds of index card boxes that constitute the Foster Files were found in a barn and were donated by Foster's family to the American Film Institute in the early 1960s. In the 1980s, the files were transferred to the Motion Picture, Television, and Recorded Sound Division of the Library of Congress; the AFI staff used them to help compile its *Guide to American Feature Films, 1911–1920.*

33. "Community Motion Picture Bureau Growing," *Moving Picture World* 27:9 (March 4, 1916), p. 1508; "Exhibitors Should Fight Community Motion Picture Bureau by Adopting Its Own Methods, Says an Iowa Theatre Man," *Exhibitor's Trade Review,* 2:15 (September 15, 1917), p. 1153; Smith, *Moving Pictures in the Church,* p. 62.

34. "Millions of Feet of Movie Films for Soldiers: How a Woman Directs the Complex Task of Selecting Subjects, Censoring, and Shipping Motion Picture Equipment to All American Camps," *New York Times,* May 5, 1918, reprinted in Brown, ed., *New York Times Encyclopedia of Film,* vol. 1, May 1918 section; James W. Evans, *Entertaining the American Army: The American Stage and Lyceum in the World War* (New York: Association Press, 1921).

35. "Republic to Distribute Non-theatrical Films for the Community Motion Picture Bureau," *Exhibitor's Trade Review* 7:8 (January 24, 1920), p. 792.

36. "Neilan Asks Producers and Directors to End 'Sniping'; Rembusch Wires Ford, 'Pay Exhibitors to Show Weekly,'" *Exhibitor's Trade Review* 7:1 (January 31, 1920), p. 883; D. L. Lewis, *The Public Image of Henry Ford,* pp. 115–16.

37. "Hays and Exhibitor Groups Near Final Agreement on Standard Contract Clauses; Code of Ethics Drafted," *Exhibitor's Trade Review* 12:6 (July 8, 1922), p. 315. Historian Charles Eckert outlined the many connections between the film industry and consumer-product manufacturers in this transitional period of new technology. Charles Eckert, "The Carole Lombard in Macy's Window," *Quarterly Review of Film Studies* 3:1 (winter 1978), reprinted in *Fabrications: Costume and the Female Body,* ed. Jane Gaines and Charlotte Herzog (New York: Routledge, 1990), pp. 100–21.

38. "Resolutions Adopted by Cleveland Convention [of Motion Picture Theatre Owners of America]," *Exhibitor's Trade Review* 8:4 (June 26, 1920), p. 372; "Annual Report of National President M. J. O'Toole, Delivered on May 12, 1925, at Sixth Annual Convention of Motion Picture Theatre Owners of America," *Exhibitor's Trade Review* 18:1 (May 30, 1925), p. 11; Address by Will Hays to Women's City Club of Philadelphia, April 25, 1925, quoted ibid., p. 11.

39. Robert S. Lynd and Helen Merrill Lynd, *Middletown: A Study in Modern American Culture* (New York: Harcourt Brace, 1929), p. 359.

40. Ibid., 216, 342–43.

41. Ibid., 359, 359n, 398.

42. Ibid., 361, 363, 380–81.

43. Ibid., p. 292.

Chapter 5: "You Can Have the Strand in Your Own Town"

1. "Facts and Comments," *Moving Picture World* 10:5 (November 4, 1911), p. 356.

2. W. Stephen Bush, "Trade Review Editor Surveys Motion Picture Conditions in the South after Successful Tour of Several States," *Exhibitor's Trade Review* 1:18 (April 7, 1917), p. 1220.

3. "The East Side Standard," *Moving Picture World* 7:13 (September 24, 1910), p. 698. Important questions and new evidence on the composition of New York film audiences are presented in Ben Singer, "Manhattan Nickelodeons: New Data on Audiences and Exhibitors," *Cinema Journal* 3 (spring 1995), pp. 5–35.

4. Mary Heaton Vorse, "Some Picture Show Audiences," *Outlook* 98 (June 24, 1911), p. 442.

5. "New Strand Opens, Bigger of Movies," April 12, 1914; "'Society' Movie Playhouse," February 16, 1914; and "Hammerstein Wins Injunction," March 7, 1914—all in *New York Times* and reprinted in Gene Brown, ed., *New York Times Encyclopedia of Film,* vol. 1 (New York: Times Books, 1984), April 1914.

6. Ben M. Hall, *The Best Remaining Seats* (New York: Bramhall House, 1961; reprint, New York: DaCapo, 1988).

7. Russell Merritt, "Nickelodeon Theaters, 1905–1914: Building an Audience for the Movies," in *The American Film Industry,* ed. Tino Balio, rev. ed. (Madison: University of Wisconsin Press, 1985); Douglas Gomery, "Movie Audiences, Urban Geography, and the History of the American Film," *Velvet Light Trap* 19 (spring 1982), pp. 23–29.

8. Eileen Bowser, *The Transformation of Cinema, 1907–1915* (New York: Charles Scribner's Sons, 1990), pp. 255–56; Lary May, *Screening Out the Past:*

The Birth of Mass Culture and the Motion Picture Industry (New York: Oxford University Press, 1980); Robert Allen, *Vaudeville and Film, 1895–1915: A Study in Media Interaction* (New York: Arno Press, 1980).

9. On urban middle-class amusements in the early twentieth century, see Lewis Erenberg, *Steppin' Out: New York Nightlife and the Transformation of American Culture, 1890–1930* (Westport, Conn.: Greenwood Press, 1981); Lois Banner, *American Beauty* (New York: Knopf, 1983); Lawrence Levine, *Highbrow/Lowbrow: The Emergence of Cultural Hierarchy in America* (Cambridge: Harvard University Press, 1988).

10. F. H. Richardson, "Plain Talks to Theatre Managers and Operators, Chapter 24: Selecting a Theater Location," *Moving Picture World* 5:20 (November 13, 1909), p. 676; "The Educated Classes and the Moving Picture," ibid., 6:14 (April 9, 1910), p. 545.

11. Michael M. Davis, *The Exploitation of Pleasure: A Study of Commercial Recreation in New York City* (New York: Russell Sage Foundation, 1911), pp. 30, 35.

12. Ibid., pp. 30, 35.

13. Erenberg, *Steppin' Out*.

14. "The Cinematograph Man," words by Joseph W. Herbert, music by Reginald de Koven, copyright 1909 by Joseph W. Stern and Company, New York; "At the Picture Show," words and music by Irving Berlin, copyright 1912 by Watson, Berlin, and Snyder, New York (from a musical review called *The Sun Dodgers*, words by E. Ray Goetz, starring Eva Tanguay, produced by Lew Fields); "The Moving Picture Glide," words by Harold R. Atteridge, music by Harry Carroll, copyright 1914 by Shapiro, Bernstein and Co., New York—all in box 699, DeVincent Sheet Music Collection, National Museum of American History, Smithsonian Institution, Washington, D.C. *The Beauty Spot* was a hit, running 137 performances.

15. Gomery, "Movie Audiences, Urban Geography, and the History of American Film," pp. 23–29; Russell Merritt, "Nickelodeon Theaters: Building an Audience for the Movies," *American Film Institute Reports* (May 1973), pp. 4–8.

16. "Picture Shows Popular in the 'Hub,'" *Boston Journal,* n.d., reprinted in *Moving Picture World* 2:20 (May 16, 1908), p. 433.

17. W. W. Winters, "With the Picture Fans," *Nickelodeon* 4:5 (September 1, 1910), p. 123.

18. Gomery, "U.S. Film Exhibition: The Formation of a Big Business," in *The American Film Industry,* p. 219.

19. "Advertising for You," *Exhibitor's Trade Review* 2:13 (September 1, 1917), pp. 64–65.

20. "There Are No More Nine O'Clock Towns," *Saturday Evening Post,* April 10, 1920, p. 37.

21. "And They Both Show the Same Pictures!," ibid., September 20, 1919, p. 39.

22. Charles W. Kohl, "A Few Suggestions," *Moving Picture World* 1:38 (November 28, 1907), p. 610; Bertram Adler, "How to Run a Moving Picture Show," *Nickelodeon* 2:3 (September 1909), p. 85; Thornton Parker, "Florida Exhibitor Enters Protest vs. Exchange Method of Palming Off Worn-Out Films on Small Audiences 'Out in the Sticks,'" *Exhibitor's Trade Review* 5:8 (January 25, 1919), p. 638.

23. Edward T. Heald, "Movies, 1926–1957," in *The Stark County Story*, vol. 4 (Canton, Ohio: Stark County Historical Society, 1958), pp. 506–8; James Ink, interview by Edward Heald, n.d., in Motion Pictures Files, Stark County Historical Society, Canton, Ohio. See also Marianne Triponi, "The New Ironwood Theater in Context: Movie Palace as Symbol," *Journal of American Culture* 13:4 (1990), pp. 1–7.

24. Lary May and Stephen Lassonde, "Making the American Way: Moderne Theaters, Audiences, and the Film Industry, 1929–1945," *Prospects* 12 (1987), pp. 89–124.

25. Gomery, "U.S. Film Exhibition: The Formation of a Big Business," in *The American Film Industry*, pp. 220–21.

26. "Adams Circuit Owner Says Small-Town People Demand City Presentation Standard," *Exhibitor's Trade Review* 7:17 (March 27, 1920), p. 1894.

27. W. H. Bridge, "The 'Movie' and the Small Town," *Drama* 11 (July 1921), pp. 363–64. On film themes of the 1920s, see Richard Koszarski, *An Evening's Entertainment: The Age of the Silent Feature Picture, 1915–1928* (New York: Charles Scribner's Sons, 1990); David Bordwell, Janet Staiger, and Kristin Thompson, *The Classical Hollywood Cinema: Film Style and Mode of Production to 1960* (New York: Columbia University Press, 1985); Mary P. Ryan, "The Projection of a New Womanhood: The Movie Moderns in the 1920s," in *Our American Sisters: Women in American Life and Thought,* ed. Jean Friedman and William G. Shade, 2d ed. (Boston: Allyn and Bacon, 1976), pp. 366–84.

28. Robert S. Lynd and Helen Merrill Lynd, *Middletown: A Study in Modern American Culture* (New York: Harcourt Brace, 1929), pp. 263–69.

Chapter 6: The Rise of the Movie Fan

1. Janice Radway, *Reading the Romance: Women, Patriarchy, and Popular Literature* (Chapel Hill: University of North Carolina Press, 1984); Lisa A. Lewis, *Gender Politics and MTV: Voicing the Difference* (Philadelphia: Temple University Press, 1990); Henry Jenkins, *Textual Poachers: Television Fans and Participatory Culture* (New York: Routledge, 1992); Lisa A. Lewis, ed., *The*

Adoring Audience: Fan Culture and Popular Media (New York: Routledge, 1992); Jackie Stacey, *Star Gazing: Hollywood Cinema and Female Spectatorship* (New York: Routledge, 1994).

2. Susan J. Douglas, *Inventing American Broadcasting, 1899–1922* (Baltimore: Johns Hopkins University Press, 1987).

3. Leo Braudy, *The Frenzy of Renown: Fame and Its History* (New York: Oxford University Press, 1986), p. 380; Paul Dickson, ed. and comp., *The Baseball Dictionary* (New York: Facts on File, 1989), p. 153; *Oxford English Dictionary*, 2d ed., vol. 5 (Oxford: Clarendon Press, 1989), p. 711.

4. See Ken Burns, *Baseball* (Alexandria, Va.: PBS Home Video, 1994), video documentary.

5. See Benjamin McArthur, *Actors and American Culture, 1880–1920* (Philadelphia: Temple University Press, 1984), pp. 208–11; Lois Banner, *American Beauty* (New York: Alfred A. Knopf, 1983); Karen Halttunen, *Confidence Men and Painted Women: A Study of Middle Class Culture in America, 1830–1870* (New Haven: Yale University Press, 1982); Warren Susman, *Culture as History: The Transformation of American Society in the Twentieth Century* (New York: Pantheon, 1985), pp. 271–85.

6. Braudy, *The Frenzy of Renown*, p. 508; Richard Schickel, *Intimate Strangers: The Culture of Celebrity* (New York: Doubleday, 1985), p. 25.

7. "Photograph of Moving Picture Actors," 6:2 (January 5, 1910), p. 50; "From a Member of the Public," 7:21 (November 19, 1910), p. 1184; "On the Screen," 6:5 (February 5, 1910), p. 167—all in *Moving Picture World*.

8. See Richard deCordova, *Picture Personalities: The Emergence of the Star System in American Film, 1907–1920* (Urbana: University of Illinois Press, 1990) for examples of fan letters written by men to Florence Lawrence. Extremely few of these letters survive.

9. Robert Jay, *The Trade Card in Nineteenth-Century America* (Columbia: University of Missouri Press, 1987); Q. David Bowers, *Muriel Ostriche: Princess of Silent Films* (Vestal, N.Y.: Vestal Press, 1987); John Ripley, "Song Slides Helped to Unify U.S. Communities and Sell Sheet Music," *Films in Review* (March 1971), pp. 147–52.

10. "On the Screen," *Moving Picture World* 6:5 (February 5, 1910), p. 167.

11. "The Actor—Likewise the Actress," *Moving Picture World* 7:20 (November 12, 1910), p. 1099.

12. W. W. Winters, "With the Picture Fans," *Nickelodeon* 4:5 (September 1, 1910), pp. 123–24.

13. See Carolyn Marvin, *When Old Technologies Were New: Thinking about Communication Technologies in the Late Nineteenth Century* (New York: Oxford University Press, 1988); Daniel Czitrom, *Media and the American Mind: From Morse to McLuhan* (Chapel Hill: University of North Carolina Press, 1982).

14. Victor Appleton [Edward Stratemeyer Syndicate pseud.], *The Motion Picture Chums' First Venture, or Opening a Photo Playhouse in Fairlands* (New York: Grosset and Dunlap, 1913).

15. Patricia Zimmerman, *Reel Families: A Social History of Amateur Film* (Bloomington: Indiana University Press, 1995); *Nickelodeon* 1:6 (June 1909), p. 157; "The Young Idea," *Moving Picture World* 6:2 (January 5, 1910), p. 48.

16. Lux Graphicus [pseud.], "On the Screen," *Moving Picture World* 7:15 (October 8, 1910), p. 807. See also "From a Member of the Public," 7:21 (November 19, 1910), p. 1184; "On the Screen," 6:5 (February 5, 1910), p. 167; "The Stories of the Films," 6:13 (April 2, 1910), p. 502; "A 'Crank Turner' Wants to Know," 10:9 (December 2, 1911), p. 739—all in *Moving Picture World.*

17. Roy L. McCardell, "Writing for the Movies Is NOT a Gold Mine for . . . , Who Predicts a Great Battle . . ." *Moving Picture World,* n.d. [probably October or November 1913], in scrapbook 11,800, Epes Winthrop Sargent Papers, New York Public Library, New York City.

18. Herman A. Blackman to E. W. Sargent, September 19, 1916, in box 794, Sargent Papers; Walter Prichard Eaton, "Wanted—Moving Picture Authors," *American Magazine* 81 (March 1916), pp. 34, 67–70, 73.

19. Epes Winthrop Sargent, "Fifty Years on Broadway," MS, 1938, chap. 10, p. 17, in Sargent Papers.

20. Edward Wagenknecht to the author, November 29, 1990.

21. Giles Warren, "Scenarios," *Moving Picture World* 7:25 (December 17, 1910), pp. 1424–25.

22. McCardell, "Writing for the Movies"; Q. David Bowers, *Thanhouser Films: An Encyclopedia and History* (Vestal, N.Y.: Emprise Publications, forthcoming); "Working Girl Receives $10,000 for Ideas She Thought Worthless," handbill, in Motion Pictures File, Warshaw Collection of Business Americana, National Museum of American History, Smithsonian Institution, Washington, D.C.

23. Walter Prichard Eaton, "The Canned Drama," *American Magazine* 68 (September 1909), p. 499.

24. "Scouts in Moving Pictures: The Vitagraph Actors Will Arrive This Week," July 12, 1911, p. 4; "Vitagraph Visitors: Who They Are and What They Are Doing in Cooperstown," July 19, 1911, p. 1—both in *Cooperstown (N.Y.) Freeman's Journal.*

25. Bowers, *Thanhouser Films.*

26. "Since Sarah Saw Theda Bara," words by Alex Gerber, music by Harry Jentes, copyright 1916 by Leo Feist, New York; "I Want to Be Loved Like the Girls on the Film," words and music by Hank Hancock and Tom McNamara, copyright 1915 by Werblow-Fisher Company, New York; "Come Out of the Kitchen, Mary Ann," words and music by James Kendis and Charles Bayha,

copyright 1917 by Kendis-Brockman Music Company, New York; "She's Back among the Pots and Pans," words by William Jerome and Bert Hanlon, music by Seymour Furth, copyright 1917 by William Jerome Publishing, New York— all in DeVincent Sheet Music Collection, National Museum of American History, Smithsonian Institution, Washington, D.C.

27. "A Novel Idea!" [1914], handbill, in Motion Pictures File, Warshaw Collection of Business Americana; Beverly Smith (town clerk), Carlisle Smith, and Glenda Mason, all of Mattawamkeag, Maine, telephone interview by the author, June 26, 1990.

28. "A Song Novelty for Licensed Exhibitors," *Moving Picture World* 10:4 (October 28, 1911), p. 300; Anthony Slide, *The Big V: The Story of Vitagraph* (Metuchen, N.J.: Scarecrow Press, 1985), pp. 38–39.

29. Lux Graphicus [pseud.], "On the Screen," *Moving Picture World* 7:15 (October 8, 1910), p. 807.

Chapter 7: *Motion Picture Story Magazine* and the Gendered Construction of the Movie Fan

1. On fans, readers, and movie fan culture, see Henry Jenkins, *Textual Poachers: Television Fans and Participatory Culture* (New York: Routledge, 1992); Lisa A. Lewis, *Gender Politics and MTV: Voicing the Difference* (Philadelphia: Temple University Press, 1990); Janice Radway, *Reading the Romance: Women, Patriarchy, and Popular Literature* (Chapel Hill: University of North Carolina Press, 1984); Lisa A. Lewis, ed., *The Adoring Audience: Fan Culture and Popular Media* (New York: Routledge, 1992); Jackie Stacey, *Star Gazing: Hollywood Cinema and Female Spectatorship* (New York: Routledge, 1994).

2. "Eugene V. Brewster," *Who Was Who in America*, vol. 1, *1897–1942* (Chicago: A. N. Marquis Co., 1943), p. 136. Later, Brewster was also editor of *Motion Picture Classic, Movie Monthly,* and *Shadowland.* He left those positions about 1927 and died in 1939.

3. "The Stories of the Films," *Moving Picture World* 6:13 (April 2, 1910), p. 502; "A 'Crank Turner' Wants to Know," *Moving Picture World* 10:9 (December 2, 1911), p. 739.

4. "Popular Magazine for Film Fans," *Nickelodeon* 4:12 (December 15, 1910), p. 339.

5. "Increase Your Attendance," *Moving Picture World* 10:10 (December 9, 1911), p. 829.

6. "The Motion Picture Story Magazine," *Moving Picture World* 8:5

(February 4, 1911), p. 228. The Motion Picture Patents Company was involved in the magazine's founding, contributing one hundred thousand dollars for initial start-up costs and requiring that coverage be limited to Motion Picture Patents Company films and that a two-hundred-dollar fee be paid by each studio wishing to have a scenario and accompanying photographs published each month. After this initial involvement, it is unclear whether the patents company had a powerful role in the month-to-month operation of the magazine. After the trust disbanded, *Motion Picture Story Magazine* continued to thrive for many years. Anthony Slide, *Early American Cinema,* rev. ed. (Metuchen, N.J.: Scarecrow Press, 1994), pp. 40–41, 141.

7. Kay Sloan, *The Loud Silents: Origins of the Social Problem Film* (Urbana: University of Illinois, 1988); Kevin Brownlow, *Behind the Mask of Innocence: Sex, Violence, Prejudice, Crime; Films of Social Conscience in the Silent Era* (New York: Knopf, 1990).

8. "Musings of the Photoplay Philosopher," *Motion Picture Story Magazine* (October 1912), p. 140. Anthony Slide notes that the Selig company was not convinced of the benefits of association with a publicity and fan publication and ended its participation. Slide, *Early American Cinema,* p. 141.

9. "The Actor—Likewise the Actress," *Moving Picture World* 7:20 (November 12, 1910), p. 1099; *Motion Picture Story Magazine* (February and April 1911) and "Letters to the Editor" (August 1911), p. 139.

10. "Appreciations and Criticisms of Popular Plays and Players by our Readers," *Motion Picture Story Magazine* (December 1912), p. 131. Blackton's role in *Motion Picture Story Magazine* appeared much reduced after the publication was underway.

11. *Motion Picture Story Magazine* (January 1913), p. 123.

12. "The Cash Prize Contest," *Motion Picture Story Magazine* (September 1911), p. 141.

13. *Motion Picture Story Magazine* (March 1912)

14. Edward Wagenknecht to the author, October 29, 1990.

15. *Motion Picture Story Magazine* (March 1912). On complaints about Biograph's no-name policy, see *Motion Picture Story Magazine* (August 1912), p. 170, where the Answer Man loses his temper about readers' persistent interest in finding out who Biograph players were. Slide, *Early American Cinema,* pp. 140–43.

16. *Motion Picture Story Magazine* (August 1912), p. 170. On the faking of Florence Lawrence's streetcar accident in St. Louis, see Jane Gaines, "From Elephants to Lux Soap: The Programming and 'Flow' of Motion Picture Exploitation," *Velvet Light Trap* 25 (spring 1990), pp. 29–43, and Richard deCordova, *Picture Personalities: The Emergence of the Star System in American Film, 1907–1920* (Urbana: University of Illinois Press, 1990).

17. The August 1913 issue of *Motion Picture Story Magazine* contained 613 letters from readers in the "Answer Man" column; the August 1915 issue had 344 letters.

18. See discussion of the 1902 film *Uncle Josh at the Moving Picture Show,* in Miriam Hansen, *Babel and Babylon: Spectatorship in American Silent Film* (Cambridge: Harvard University Press, 1991), pp. 25–28. See also an *Uncle Josh*-inspired cover of the *Saturday Evening Post* (May 17, 1913), reproduced in Q. David Bowers, *Nickelodeon Theaters and Their Music* (Vestal, N.Y.: Vestal Press, 1989), p. xii.

19. La Touche Hancock, "The Motion Picture Fan," *Motion Picture Story Magazine* (August 1911), p. 93.

20. Susan J. Douglas, *Inventing American Broadcasting, 1899–1922* (Baltimore: Johns Hopkins University Press, 1987).

21. *Motion Picture Supplement* (September 1915), p. 63; "Dream of a Movie Fan" (November 1915), p. 147, and "The Adventures of Flim Flam, the Film Fan" (March 1916), p. 159—both in *Motion Picture Magazine.*

22. *Motion Picture Magazine* (February 1916). "Beauty Hints" first appeared in September 1916 issue.

23. Ernest A. Dench, "Cupid, Movie, and Company, a Popular Firm," *Motion Picture Classic* (April 1916), pp. 33–35. *Motion Picture Classic* was first published as the *Motion Picture Supplement* in September 1915. Although overshadowed by *Photoplay* in the 1920s, *Motion Picture Classic* and *Motion Picture Magazine* remained high quality, popular publications throughout the decade.

24. "Letters to the Editor," *Motion Picture Magazine* (November 1916), pp. 168, 170.

25. See Paula Fass, *The Damned and the Beautiful: American Youth in the 1920s* (New York: Oxford University Press, 1977).

26. Roberta Courtlandt, "Feminine Fads and Fancies," *Motion Picture Magazine* (January 1917), pp. 36–37.

27. "Question and Answer Column," *Photoplay* (December 1917), p. 108.

28. "Thoughts at Random," *Exhibitor's Trade Review* 2:17 (September 27, 1917), p. 1322.

29. Anthony Slide, "Early Film Magazines: An Overview," in *Aspects of Film History Prior to 1920* (Metuchen, N.J.: Scarecrow Press, 1978), p. 102; Slide, ed., *International Film, Radio, and Television Journals* (Westport, Conn.: Greenwood Press, 1985); Robert S. Lynd and Helen Merrill Lynd, *Middletown: A Study in Modern American Culture* (New York: Harcourt Brace, 1929). On fan magazine readers in the 1920s, see Gaylyn Studlar, "The Perils of Pleasure: Fan Magazine Discourse as Women's Commodified Culture in the 1920s," *Wide Angle* 13:1 (1991), pp. 6–33.

30. Douglas, *Inventing American Broadcasting.* One volume of the series

is: Allen Chapman [Edward Stratemeyer Syndicate pseud.], *The Radio Boys Trailing a Voice* (New York: Grosset and Dunlap, 1922).

Chapter 8: *Photoplay* Magazine, Movie Fans, and the Marketplace

1. Anthony Slide, "Early Film Magazines: An Overview," in *Aspects of Film History Prior to 1920* (Metuchen, N.J.: Scarecrow, 1978), p. 102. See also Slide, ed., *International Film, Radio, and Television Journals* (Westport, Conn.: Greenwood Press, 1985). Also Q. David Bowers to the author, April 15, 1992.

2. "James R. Quirk," *Who Was Who in America,* vol. 1, *1897–1942* (Chicago: A. N. Marquis Co., 1943), p. 1005. Quirk edited *Photoplay* until his death in 1932.

3. Ibid.

4. Slide, "Early Film Magazines: An Overview," in *Aspects of Film History Prior to 1920,* p. 102.

5. Gaylyn Studlar, "The Perils of Pleasure: Fan Magazine Discourse as Women's Commodified Culture in the 1920s," *Wide Angle* 13:1 (1991), pp. 6–33.

6. "*Photoplay* Magazine Medal of Honor," *Photoplay* (September 1924), p. 64. The earliest awards honored *Humoresque* in 1920, *Tolable David* in 1921, and *Robin Hood* in 1922.

7. Contributing authors included Adela Rogers St. John, F. Scott Fitzgerald, and Joseph Hergesheimer.

8. "What's in the Book?," *Printer's Ink* (February 28, 1918), pp. 22–23.

9. Robert S. Lynd and Helen Merrill Lynd, *Middletown: A Study in Modern American Culture* (New York: Harcourt, Brace, 1929).

10. "The Movie Maniac," *Motion Picture Magazine* (September 1916), p. 172.

11. Scott Eyeman, *Mary Pickford: America's Sweetheart* (New York: Donald Fine, 1990), p. 76.

12. Mary Pickford, *Sunshine and Shadow* (New York: Doubleday, 1955), p. 101.

13. "Announcement," advertisement for Pompeian Manufacturing Company, Cleveland, Ohio, in *Motion Picture Story Magazine* (September 1916), p. 159. The May 1915 issue of *McClure's* magazine featured an article about Pickford entitled "This Little Girl Earns $100,000 a Year." After the Pompeian endorsement contract, she seems to have taken few others. "Despite my concern over money and my fears for the future," Pickford later wrote, "I was persuaded to reject a contract with an advertising firm offering me as much as Mr. Zukor was now paying me—$1000 a week, for the commercial use of my name" (Pickford, *Sunshine and Shadow*). Although the Pompeian contract

offered her additional fringe benefits such as dresses and cars, it is probable that Pickford, a wily negotiator, persuaded Zukor to deal generously with her.

14. In the 1920s, Coca-Cola returned to anonymous models, only to return to Hollywood star endorsements in the 1930s. See Allen Petretti, *Petretti's Coca-Cola Collectibles Price Guide,* 8th ed. (Hackensack, N.J.: Nostalgia Publications, 1992), pp. 359-78. See also Kathy Peiss, "Making Faces: The Cosmetics Industry and the Cultural Construction of Gender, 1890–1930," *Genders* 7 (spring 1990), pp. 143–69.

15. L. F. Guimond, "The Good and Bad Methods of Exploiting Stars," *Exhibitor's Trade Review* 15:12 (February 16, 1924), p. 34.

16. "Sincerely, John Smith," *Photoplay* (August 1924), p. 17, is a typical example of Quirk's educational campaign.

17. "Everybody's Other Business," *Printer's Ink* (February 14, 1918), pp. 22–23. Concern about women's vulnerability to the inducements of consumer culture had been evident since the latter half of the nineteenth century, when the image of middle-class women emphasized their "frailty and vulnerability, physical as well as mental, their irresponsibility and their paradoxical moral sensibility," historian Elaine Abelson argues, noting that the "female 'shopping habit' or 'mania' . . . was thought to originate in the inherent weakness of women and to rest upon the 'savage passions'—vanity and self-indulgence." Elaine Abelson, *When Ladies Go A-Thieving: Middle-Class Shoppers in the Victorian Department Store* (New York: Oxford University Press, 1989), pp. 30, 37; "Shopping," *New York Times,* 1881, quoted in Abelson, p. 30.

18. "Yesterday and Today," *Printer's Ink* (November 11, 1920), pp. 130–31.

19. "Here's Your Audience!" (August 11, 1921), p. 161, and (December 8, 1921), p. 177—both in *Printer's Ink.*

20. "The Moving Picture—Master Salesman" (February 9, 1922), p. 181; "Consider the Spending Suggestiveness of the Moving Picture" (February 2, 1922), p. 121—both in *Printer's Ink.*

21. "When You Are the Hero," *Printer's Ink* (May 11, 1922), p. 193.

22. Ibid.; "Are You Closing Your Screen-Made Prospects?" *Printer's Ink* (March 9, 1922), p. 185; F. Scott Fitzgerald, "The Popular Girl," *Saturday Evening Post* (February 18, 1922), pp. 3–5, 82–89, quoted in *Photoplay* advertisement, ibid.

23. "Introducing the Age Factor in Selling and Advertising" (January 25, 1923), pp. 137–40; "Photoplay Is Predominant with the Eighteen-to-Thirty Age Group" ((November 15, 1923), pp. 102–3—both in *Printer's Ink.* See also Stuart Ewen, *Captains of Consciousness: Advertising and the Social Roots of the Consumer Culture* (New York: McGraw Hill, 1976), especially pp. 139–49.

24. "Introducing the Age Factor in Selling and Advertising" (January 25, 1923), pp. 136–38; "Least Sales Resistance between the Ages of Eighteen and

Thirty, Says Mr. Platt" (April 26, 1923), pp. 192–93; "We Know That Young People Make Up Our Best Prospects" (October 11, 1923), pp. 94–95; "Youth Is the Dictator of Style and Fashion" (December 6, 1923), pp. 114–15; "From 18 to 26 They Buy Freely" (June 7, 1923), p. 94–95—all in *Printer's Ink.*

25. "Youth Is the Dictator of Style and Fashion," p. 114.

26. "Photoplay Is Predominant with the Eighteen-to-Thirty Age Group," p. 103.

27. "Photoplay Adds Versatility to Your Selling Plan" (February 7, 1924), pp. 102–3; "Even the Best Advertisement Is Ineffective without . . . " (July 9, 1923), p. 171; "Photoplay Offers Special Predominance with the Eighteen-to-Thirty Age Group" (March 27, 1924), pp. 70–71; "That Fine Precious Thing—Enthusiasm" (April 17, 1924), pp. 94–95; "Which Group Will You Sell? The Sneering Section—or the Cheering Section?" (May 22, 1924), pp. 74–75—all in *Printer's Ink.*

28. "The Message of the Dressing Table," *Printer's Ink* (August 13, 1925), p. 171, notes that toiletries ads were still only 20 percent of total ads in *Photoplay.* See also Roland Marchand, *Advertising the American Dream: Making Way for Modernity* (Berkeley and Los Angeles: University of California Press, 1985), p. 56.

29. "One of the Reasons Why Oneida Community Ltd. Uses *Photoplay*" (February 25, 1926), pp. 174–75; "Selling Influences Enjoyed by the Selby Shoe Company through *Photoplay*" (March 25, 1926), pp. 154–55—both in *Printer's Ink.*

30. Paul K. Edwards, *The Southern Urban Negro as Consumer* (Englewood Cliffs, N.J.: Prentice-Hall, 1932), pp. 203–9.

31. Average monthly circulation figures for 1928 were: *Photoplay,* 542,874; *Motion Picture Magazine,* 340,883; *Motion Picture Classic,* 198,541; *Screenland,* 200,000; *Picture Play,* 145,140; *Film Fun,* 96,769. The total was 1,524,207 for the top six magazines. Meanwhile, comparable numbers for other popular magazines were: *True Story* 2,016,923, and *Ladies' Home Journal,* 2,514,092. *Critchfield Digest of Merchandising and Advertising Information* (Chicago: Critchfield and Company, 1928).

32. *Charm* was absorbed into *Glamour* in 1959.

Chapter 9: Coming of Age at the Picture Show

1. Herbert Blumer, *Movies and Conduct* (New York: Macmillan, 1933), p. 213.

2. Ibid.

3. "Autobiography of My Moving Picture Experiences," p. 1, in Motion Picture Research Council Papers, box 4, Herbert Blumer File, Archives of the

Hoover Institution on War, Revolution, and Peace, Stanford University, Palo Alto, Calif., hereinafter cited as MPRC Papers.

4. For more about the Payne Fund Studies and Blumer's role in them, see Garth Jowett, Ian Jarvie, and Kathryn Fuller, *Children and the Movies: Media Influence and the Payne Fund Controversy* (New York: Cambridge University Press, 1996).

5. Ibid., 237–41.

6. Blumer, *Movies and Conduct*, 203–7.

7. Ibid.

8. Jowett, Jarvie, and Fuller, *Children and the Movies*, pp. 57–91.

9. Paula Fass, *The Damned and the Beautiful: American Youth of the 1920s* (New York: Oxford University Press, 1977), p. 8; Clarence Perry, *The Attitudes of High-School Students Towards Motion Pictures* (New York: National Board of Review of Motion Pictures, 1923); Alice Miller Mitchell, *Children and Movies* (Chicago: University of Chicago Press, 1929).

10. Untitled essay, p. 2, in MPRC Papers; Perry, *The Attitude of High-School Students*, pp. 10–14. One female student recalled growing up in "a small [Baptist] town whose only picture palace was a small, dark, ill-ventilated hole, frequented by every type of person," and called the Critic theater. Blumer, *Movies and Conduct*, p. 213.

11. "My Movie Experiences," p. 1; "Autobiography Concerning the Effect of Moving Pictures on My Life," p. 1; untitled essay, p. 2—all in MPRC Papers.

12. "The Effects the Movies Have Had on Me," p. 1, ibid.

13. Mitchell, *Children and Movies*, p. 119; "The Effect of Movies upon Me," p. 1, in MPRC Papers.

14. "My Moving Picture Autobiography," p. 1; "Autobiography of My Motion Picture Experiences," p. 1; "My Moving Picture Experiences," p. 1—all in MPRC Papers.

15. "Autobiography of My Motion Picture Experiences," p. 1, ibid. One of the most well-known studies of the influence of movies on children's racial prejudice is one of the Payne Fund Studies: Ruth C. Peterson and Louis Leon Thurstone, *Motion Pictures and the Social Attitudes of Children* (New York: Macmillan, 1933).

16. "The Effect of Movies upon Me," p. 1, in MPRC Papers.

17. "The Influence of the Movies," p. 1; "My Movie Experiences," p. 1—both ibid.

18. "My Movie Experiences," p. 1, ibid.

19. See Laura Mulvey, "Visual Pleasure and Narrative Cinema," *Screen* 16:3 (1975), pp. 6–18; Mary Ann Doane, *The Desire to Desire: The Women's Film of the 1940s* (Bloomington: Indiana University Press, 1987).

20. Ben Singer, "Female Power in the Serial Queen Melodrama: The Etiology of an Anomaly," *Camera Obscura* 22 (January 1990), pp. 91–129; untitled

essay, p. 2, in MPRC Papers. Alberta Vaughn was one of the later serial queens, appearing in films through the 1920s.

21. Leonard D. White, foreword to Mitchell, *Children and Movies,* p. xii; "Autobiography Concerning the Effect of Moving Pictures on My Life," p. 1, in MPRC Papers.

22. Untitled essay, pp. 1–4, in MPRC Papers; Perry, *The Attitudes of High School Students,* pp. 32, 38.

23. "The Movies and I," p. 1; "My Movie Autobiography," p. 1—both in MPRC Papers.

24. "Autobiography Concerning the Effect of Moving Pictures on My Life," p. 2; "The Effects the Movies Have Had on Me," p. 3; "My Movie Experiences," p. 2; "Autobiography of Number 30," p. 1; "My Movie Autobiography," p. 1—all ibid.

25. "My Moving Picture Experiences," p. 2; "The Movies and I," p. 1—both ibid.

26. "The Effect of the Movies upon Me," p. 1; "The Effects the Movies Have Had on Me," p. 2—both ibid.; Kenneth S. Clark, "Children and 'The Movies,'" *Motion Picture Story Magazine* (August 1911), p. 98.

27. Perry, *The Attitudes of High School Students.*

28. "My Movie Autobiography," p. 2, in MPRC Papers; Perry, *The Attitudes of High School Students,* p. 14.

29. "The Influence of the Movies," p. 2; "Autobiography of Motion Pictures," p. 1—both in MPRC Papers.

30. "Autobiography of Motion Pictures," p. 1; untitled essay, p. 2; "The Influence of Movies on My Life," p. 3—all ibid. "Miss Hudnut" was better known as actress Natasha Rambova.

31. "My Movie Experiences," p. 2; untitled essay, p. 2—both ibid.

32. "My Movie Autobiography," pp. 1–2, ibid.

33. "My Movie Experiences," p. 2, ibid.

34. "My Life as Affected by the Screen," p. 1, ibid.

35. "Movies, and Their Effect Upon Me," p. 7, ibid.; Mitchell, *Children and Movies,* p. 124.

36. "My Movie Experiences," p. 2, in MPRC Papers.

37. Mulvey, "Visual Pleasure and Narrative Cinema"; Doane, *The Desire to Desire.*

38. Herbert Blumer, "Movies and Sex," [1929], MS, p. 9; "Movies, and Their Effect Upon Me," p. 4—both in MPRC Papers. Another student wrote: "The temptations furnished by this type of movie have been to get drunk and to engage in sexual intercourse. However, these temptations are experienced only while watching the picture and do not exist after leaving the theatre." Quoted in Blumer, "Movies and Sex," p. 11. Most autobiography authors were too embarrassed to discuss their film-influenced sexual fantasies in detail. "Because I

have spoken frankly I hope that you will not regard me as one of moron mentality or actions—as you know I speak merely of the effect of motion pictures," one chagrined student appended to his paper. "Autobiography Concerning the Effect of Moving Pictures on My Life," p. 3, in MPRC Papers.

39. "My Movie Experiences," p. 2; "Autobiography Concerning the Effect of Moving Pictures on My Life," p. 2—both in MPRC Papers; "Take Your Girlie to the Movies (if You Can't Make Love at Home)," words by Edgar Leslie and Bert Kalmar, music by Pete Wendling, copyright 1919 by Waterson, Berlin, and Snyder, New York.

40. Blumer, "Movies and Sex," p. 5; "Autobiography Concerning the Effect of Moving Pictures on My Life," pp. 2–3; Blumer, "Movies and Sex," p. 10.

41. "My Life as Affected by the Screen," p. 2.

42. Blumer, "Movies and Sex," p. 5.

43. Ibid., p. 2; "The Movies and I," p. 4, in MPRC Papers.

44. Blumer, "Movies and Sex," p. 12.

45. "My Movie Autobiography," p. 4.

46. "Autobiography Concerning the Effect of Moving Pictures on My Life," p. 3; Helen Lefkowitz Horowitz, *Campus Life: Undergraduate Cultures from the End of the Eighteenth Century to the Present* (New York: Knopf, 1987), pp. 211–12.

47. "My Moving Picture Autobiography," p. 1; Blumer, "Movies and Sex," pp. 23–25; *Report of the Faculty-Student Committee on the Distribution of Students' Time* (Chicago: University of Chicago Press, 1925), pp. 9, 22–23, 45, 68–69. Of surveyed men and women, 17.8 percent of men and as many as 26.3 percent of women claimed never to attend movies or sporting events, whereas 23.4 percent of men and only 11.8 percent of women said they spent no time at parties and dances.

48. "My Movie Autobiography," p. 4.

49. Untitled essay, p. 7, in MPRC Papers.

50. "My Moving Picture Autobiography," p. 1. University of Michigan students surveyed in 1929 and 1930 figured moviegoing as a regular expense into their personal budgets. The first year of the depression saw student patronage of movie theaters, pool halls, and bowling alleys drop off by 35 to 40 percent in Ann Arbor. Robert C. Angell, "The Influence of the Economic Depression on Student Life at the University of Michigan," *School and Society* 34:881 (November 14, 1931), p. 654.

Conclusion

1. Herbert Blumer, *Movies and Conduct* (New York: Macmillan, 1933), app. C, p. 217.

2. "Autobiography Concerning the Effects of Motion Pictures on My Life," p. 3, Motion Picture Research Council Papers, Archives of the Hoover Institution on War, Revolution, and Peace, Stanford University, Palo Alto, Calif.; Blumer, *Movies and Conduct,* app. C, p. 241.

3. *Film Daily Yearbook, 1929* (New York: Film Daily, 1929), p. 250; *Film Daily Yearbook, 1941* (New York: Film Daily, 1941), p. 43; Lary May and Stephen Lassonde, "Making the American Way: Moderne Theaters, Audiences, and the Film Industry, 1929–1945" *Prospects* 12 (1987), pp. 89–124.

4. Lawrence Levine, "The Folklore of Industrial Society: Popular Culture and Its Audiences," *American Historical Review* 97:5 (December 1992), pp. 1369–1399.

5. Arthur S. Meloy, *Theatres and Motion Picture Houses* (New York: Architects Supply and Publishing Company, 1916), p. 1. Today a myriad of cable television channels and highly segmented audiences allow the coexistence of many alternative programming strategies, from travelogues and documentaries to religious programs to boxing matches to pornographic films.

Bibliography

Manuscript Collections

Maryland Historical Society. Baltimore.

Cook and Harris Papers. New York State Historical Association. Cooperstown, N.Y.

DeVincent Sheet Music Collection. National Museum of American History. Smithsonian Institution. Washington, D.C.

Motion Picture, Television, and Recorded Sound Division. Library of Congress. Washington, D.C.

Motion Picture Research Council Papers. Hoover Institution on War, Revolution, and Peace. Stanford University. Palo Alto, Calif.

Sargent, Epes Winthrop, Papers. New York Public Library. New York City.

Warshaw Collection of Business Americana. National Museum of American History. Smithsonian Institution. Washington, D.C.

Sheet Music

"The Cinematograph Man." Words by Joseph W. Herbert. Music by Reginald de Koven. Copyright 1909 by Joseph Stern and Company, New York.

"Come Out of the Kitchen, Mary Ann." Words and music by James Kendis and Charles Bayha. Copyright 1917 by Kendis-Brockman Music Company, New York.

"I Want to Be Loved Like the Girls on the Film." Words and music by Hank Hancock and Tom McNamara. Copyright 1915 by Werblow-Fisher Company, New York.

"If That's Your Idea of a Wonderful Time, Take Me Home." Words and music by Irving Berlin. Copyright 1914 by Waterson, Berlin, and Snyder, New York.

"Let's Go in to a Picture Show." Words by Junie McCree. Music by Albert Von Tilzer. Copyright 1909 by York Music Company, New York.

"The Moving Picture Glide." Words by Harold R. Atteridge. Music by Harry Carroll. Copyright 1914 by Shapiro and Bernstein, New York.

"She's Back among the Pots and Pans." Words by William Jerome and Bert Hanlon. Music by Seymour Furth. Copyright 1917 by William Jerome Publishing, New York.

"Since Mother Goes to Movie Shows." Words by Charles McCarron. Music by Albert Von Tilzer. Copyright 1916 by Broadway Music Corporation, New York.

"Since Sarah Saw Theda Bara." Words by Alex Gerber. Music by Harry Jentes. Copyright 1916 by Leo Feist, New York.

"Take Me Out to the Ball Game." Words by Jack Norworth. Music by Albert Von Tilzer. Copyright 1908 by York Music Company, New York.

"Take Your Girlie to the Movies (if You Can't Make Love at Home)." Words by Edgar Leslie and Bert Kalmer. Music by Pete Wendling. Copyright 1919 by Waterson, Berlin, and Snyder, New York.

"They're All Going in to the Movies." Words and music by Thomas S. Allen. Copyright 1915 by Daly Music Publishers, Boston.

"The Vitagraph Girl." Words by J. A. Leggett. Music by Henry Frantzen. Copyright 1910 by F. B. Haviland, New York.

Articles

"About Moving Pictures." *Knoxville (Tenn.) Sentinel,* n.d. Reprinted in *Moving Picture World* 1:36 (November 9, 1907), pp. 578–79.

"Advertising Slides." *Nickelodeon* 2:1 (July 1909), p. 3.

"Al Lichtman Outlines the Distribution Methods of Famous Players–Lasky Corporation." *Exhibitor's Trade Review* 6:4 (June 28, 1919), p. 287.

Anderson, George J. "The Case for Motion Pictures." *Nickelodeon* 4:4 (August 15, 1910), p. 98.

"Appropriate Music Creates Atmosphere for Pictures." *Exhibitor's Trade Review* 17:6 (November 11, 1924), p. 76.

Berg, S. M. "Community Chorus Singing in the Motion Picture Theater." *Exhibitor's Trade Review* 4:11 (August 17, 1918), p. 930.

Bethel, Alan. "The Moving Picture." *Conestoga* 1:3 (May 1907), pp. 17–22.

Bush, W. Stephen. "Pictures for Churches." *Moving Picture World* 10:9 (December 2, 1911), pp. 701–2.

———. "Trade Review Editor Surveys Motion Picture Conditions in the South after Successful Tour of Several States." *Exhibitor's Trade Review* 1:18 (April 7, 1917), p. 1220.

Collins, James H. "Advertising via the Moving Picture." *Printer's Ink*, n.d. Reprinted in *Moving Picture World* 6:11 (March 19, 1910), pp. 422–23.

"Community Motion Picture Bureau Growing." *Moving Picture World* 27:9 (March 4, 1916), p. 1508.

"Concerning That $100 Essanay Word Competition." *Moving Picture World* 7:6 (August 6, 1910), p. 292.

Conklin, Hazen. "What the People Want." *Moving Picture World* 27:10 (March 11, 1916), p. 1640.

Cook, Lawrence F. "Advertising the Picture Show." *Nickelodeon* 4:4 (August 15, 1910), p. 91.

"The East Side Standard." *Moving Picture World* 7:13 (September 24, 1910), p. 698.

Eaton, Walter Prichard. "The Canned Drama." *American Magazine* 68 (September 1909), pp. 499–500.

"Educational Pictures in Schools Are Making Fans and Fanettes, Says Perkins." *Exhibitor's Trade Review* 7:6 (January 10, 1920), p. 614.

"Exhibitors Demand Share in Profit from Advertising Hidden in Films." *Exhibitor's Trade Review* 6:10 (August 9, 1919), p. 788.

"Favors Picture Machines." *Springfield (Ohio) Sun*, n.d. Reprinted in *Moving Picture World* 1:24 (August 17, 1907), p. 376.

"Five-Cent Show Easily Started." *Chicago Tribune*, n.d. Reprinted in *Moving Picture World* 1:24 (August 17, 1907), p. 376.

"Free Industrial Shows in Amusement Parks." *Nickelodeon* 4:11 (December 1, 1910), p. 302.

"From a Member of the Public." *Moving Picture World* 7:21 (November 19, 1910), p. 1184.

Hancock, LaTouche. "The Motion Picture Fan." *Motion Picture Story Magazine* (August 1911), p. 93.

Hartnett, J. "Theater Managers Wake Up!" *Moving Picture World* 2:25 (June 20, 1908), p. 525.

Haskin, Frederick J. "The Popular Nickelodeon." *Moving Picture World* 2:3 (January 18, 1908), p. 36.

Hoffman, H. F. "What People Want." *Moving Picture World* 7:2 (July 9, 1910), pp. 77–78.

Linz, Clarence L. "No Ad Films Wanted." *Moving Picture World* 25:8 (August 21, 1915), p. 1347.

McGuirk, Charles J. "Chaplinitis." *Motion Picture Story Magazine* (July and August 1915), pp. 121–24, 85–89.

McLellan, Howard. "Away from Beaten Paths." *Exhibitor's Trade Review* 12:17 (September 23, 1922), p. 1099.

Mayer, Wilson. "Factory Inspection by Motography." *Nickelodeon* 2:1 (July 1909), p. 9.

———. "The Film-Lecture System of Advertising." *Nickelodeon* 2:3 (September 1909), pp. 83–84.

———. "A Great Concern's Use of Motion Pictures." *Nickelodeon* 2:4 (October 1909), p. 112.

———. "Moving Pictures as Salesmen." *Nickelodeon* 1:3 (March 1909), pp. 71–72.

Meade, James K. "Advertising the Show." *Nickelodeon* 1:2 (February 1909), p. 43.

"Methodist Amusement Ban." *Literary Digest* 44 (June 15, 1922), p. 1260.

"The Motion Picture Story Magazine." *Moving Picture World* 8:5 (February 4, 1911), p. 228.

"Motion Pictures as an Advertising Proposition." *Moving Picture World* 3:3 (July 18, 1908), p. 43.

"The Movie Maniac." *Motion Picture Magazine* (September 1916), p. 172.

"Moving and Talking Pictures Attract Many." *Moving Picture World* 2:26 (June 27, 1908), p. 541.

"Moving Pictures Crowding Traveling Shows Out of Small-Town Theaters All over U.S." *Exhibitor's Trade Review* 7:17 (March 27, 1920), p. 1871.

"Music in Picture Theaters." *Nickelodeon* 2:1 (July 1909), p. 4.

"Music That Fits Story Theme Enhances Picture, Otherwise Worse Than Useless." *Exhibitor's Trade Review* 7:6 (January 10, 1920), p. 636.

"The Name of the House." *Moving Picture World* 7:17 (October 22, 1910), pp. 918–19.

"Negro Is Important to Development of Exhibitor Prosperity in South, Is Assertion of E. V. Richards of First National Circuit." *Exhibitor's Trade Review* 5:7 (January 18, 1919), p. 562.

"Neilan Asks Producers and Directors to End 'Sniping'; Rembusch Wires Ford, 'Pay Exhibitors to Show Weekly.'" *Exhibitor's Trade Review* 7:1 (January 31, 1920), p. 883.

"A Novel Competition." *Moving Picture World* 7:4 (July 23, 1910), p. 194.

"Observations by Our Man about Town: Local Pictures." *Moving Picture World* 5:9 (August 28, 1909), pp. 277–78.

Parsons, P. A. "A History of Motion Picture Advertising." *Moving Picture World* 40:11 (March 26, 1927), pp. 301, 304–5, 308–9.

"'Photoplay': Winning Name in the Essanay New Name Contest." *Moving Picture World* 7:16 (October 15, 1910), p. 858.

"Picture Shows Popular in the 'Hub.'" *Boston Journal,* n.d. Reprinted in *Moving Picture World* 2:20 (May 16, 1908), p. 433.

"Picture Theater Advertising." *Nickelodeon* 4:4 (August 15, 1910), p. 89.

Pierce, Lucy France. "The Nickelodeon." *World Today* 15 (October 1908), pp. 1052–57.

"Popular Magazine for Film Fans." *Nickelodeon* 4:12 (December 15, 1910), p. 339.

"'Producers Should Quit Making Vulgar Films,' Say Tennesseans." *Exhibitor's Trade Review* 1:7 (January 20, 1917), p. 469.

Rhodes, Harrison. "The Majestic Movies." *Harper's Monthly* 138 (January 1919), pp. 183–94.

Richardson, F. H. "Plain Talks to Theater Managers and Operators, Chapter 24: Selecting a Theater Location." *Moving Picture World* 5:20 (November 13, 1909), p. 676.

———. "Plain Talks to Theatre Managers and Operators; Chapter 25: Decoration." *Moving Picture World* 5:21 (November 20, 1909), p. 713.

Rittelmeyer, George M. "Slide Advertising: What the Public Thinks about It and What Effect It Will Have on Patronage." *Moving Picture World* 17:11 (September 13, 1913), p. 1178.

Rothacker, Watterson R. "Moving Pictures in Advertising: No Longer an Experiment—Used by Largest Advertisers in America—Value of the Descriptive Style—Inexpensive and Easily Transported." *Moving Picture World* 8:13 (April 1, 1911), p. 698.

Simmons, Michael. "Say It with Players." *Exhibitor's Trade Review* 15:10 (February 16, 1924), p. 5.

Sinn, Clarence E. "Music for the Picture." *Moving Picture World* 7:22 (November 26, 1910), p. 1227.

"A Song Novelty for Licensed Exhibitors." *Moving Picture World* 10:4 (October 28, 1911), p. 300.

Stockton, E. Boudinot. "The Pictures in the Pulpit." *Moving Picture World* 14:13 (December 28, 1912), p. 1284.

Stoll, Horatio. "Value of the Moving Pictures for Advertising." *Moving Picture World* 8:10 (March 11, 1911), pp. 519–21.

"The Stories of the Films." *Moving Picture World* 6:13 (April 2, 1910), p. 502.

"The Tremendous Demand for Song Slides." *Moving Picture World* 1:30 (September 28, 1907), p. 467.

"Tribute to Moving Picture Shows." *Galveston (Tex.) Tribune,* n.d. Reprinted in *Moving Picture World* 2:13 (March 28, 1908), p. 265.

Urnstock, Melvin G. "Educational Films Appreciated in the West." *Moving Picture World* 6:16 (April 23, 1910), p. 653.

"The Value of a Lecture with the Show." *Moving Picture World* 2:8 (February 22, 1908), p. 143.

Vorse, Mary Heaton. "Some Picture Show Audiences." *Outlook* 98 (June 24, 1911), pp. 441–47.

Winters, W. W. "With the Picture Fans." *Nickelodeon* 4:5 (September 1, 1910), pp. 123–24.

Books

Addams, Jane. *The Spirit of Youth and the City Streets.* New York: Macmillan, 1909.

Appleton, Victor [Edward Stratemeyer Syndicate pseud.]. *The Motion Picture Chums' First Venture, or Opening a Photo Playhouse in Fairlands.* New York: Grosset and Dunlap, 1913.

Blumenthal, Albert. *Small-Town Stuff.* Chicago: University of Chicago Press, 1932.

Blumer, Herbert. *Movies and Conduct.* New York: Macmillan, 1933.

Bollman, Gladys, and Henry Bollman. *Motion Pictures for Community Needs.* New York: Henry Holt, 1922.

Bradley, Frances Sage, and Margaret A. Williamson. *Rural Children in Selected Counties of North Carolina.* U.S. Children's Bureau Publication 33. Washington, D.C.: Government Printing Office, 1918.

Brunner, Edmund S. *Industrial Village Churches.* New York: Institute of Social and Religious Research, 1930.

———. *Village Communities.* New York: George H. Doran, 1927.

Cannon, Lucius H. *Motion Pictures: Laws, Ordinances, and Regulations on Censorship, Minors, and Other Related Subjects.* St. Louis: St. Louis Public Library, 1920.

Davis, Michael M. *The Exploitation of Pleasure: A Study of Commercial Recreation in New York City.* New York: Russell Sage Foundation, 1911.

Edwards, Paul K. *The Southern Urban Negro as Consumer.* Englewood Cliffs, N.J.: Prentice-Hall, 1932.

Farish, Hunter Dickinson. *The Circuit Rider Dismounts: A History of Southern Methodism, 1865–1900.* Richmond, Va.: Dietz Press, 1938.

Foster, William T. *Vaudeville and Motion Picture Shows: A Study of Theaters in Portland, Oregon.* Portland, Ore.: Reed College, 1914.

Gardner, Ella. *Leisure-Time Activities of Rural Children in Selected Areas of West Virginia.* U.S. Children's Bureau Publication 208. Washington, D.C.: Government Printing Office, 1931.

Handel, Leo. *Hollywood Looks at Its Audience.* Urbana: University of Illinois Press, 1950.

Hart, Albert Bushnell. *The Southern South*. New York: Appleton, 1910.

Huettig, Mae. *Economic Control of the Motion Picture Industry: A Study in Industrial Organization*. Philadelphia: University of Pennsylvania Press, 1944.

Jones, William H. *Recreation and Amusement among Negroes in Washington, D.C.* Washington, D.C.: Howard University Press, 1927.

Juvenile Delinquency in Maine. U.S. Children's Bureau Publication 201. Washington, D.C.: Government Printing Office, 1930.

Littell, Walter R. *History of Cooperstown*. Cooperstown, N.Y.: Freeman's Journal, 1929.

Lynd, Robert S., and Helen Merrill Lynd. *Middletown: A Study in Modern American Culture*. New York: Harcourt Brace, 1929.

———. *Middletown in Transition*. New York: Harcourt Brace, 1937.

McConoughey, Edward M. *Motion Pictures in Religious and Educational Work, with Practical Suggestions for Their Use*. Boston: Methodist Federation for Social Service, 1916.

Mitchell, Alice Miller. *Children and Movies*. Chicago: University of Chicago Press, 1929.

Perry, Clarence. *The Attitudes of High-School Students towards Motion Pictures*. New York: National Board of Review of Motion Pictures, 1923.

Ramsaye, Terry. *A Million and One Nights: A History of the Motion Picture through 1926*. 1926; reprint, New York: Simon and Schuster, 1964.

Report of the Faculty-Student Committee on the Distribution of Students' Time. Chicago: University of Chicago Press, 1925.

Sears, Roebuck and Company. *Catalog*. No. 107 (Chicago: 1898) and No. 117 (Chicago: 1908).

Short, William H. *A Generation of Movies: A Review of Social Values in Recreational Films*. New York: National Committee for the Study of Social Values in Motion Pictures, 1928.

Smith, Roy L. *Moving Pictures in the Church*. New York: Abingdon Press, 1921.

Thorp, Margaret. *America at the Movies*. New Haven: Yale University Press, 1939; reprint, New York: Arno Press, 1970.

U.S. Bureau of the Census. Thirteenth Census of the United States, 1910. Vol. 3, *Population*. Washington, D.C.: Government Printing Office, 1913.

Index